JEWISH ENCOUNTERS

Jonathan Rosen, General Editor

Jewish Encounters is a collaboration between Schocken and Nextbook, a project devoted to the promotion of Jewish literature, culture, and ideas.

>nextbook

PUBLISHED

FORTHCOMING

Menachem Begin

DANIEL GORDIS

MENACHEM BEGIN

The Battle for Israel's Soul

NEXTBOOK · SCHOCKEN · NEW YORK

Copyright © 2014 by Daniel Gordis
All rights reserved. Published in the United States by
Schocken Books, a division of Random House LLC, New York,
and in Canada by Random House of Canada Limited, Toronto,
Penguin Random House Companies.

Schocken Books and colophon are registered trademarks of
Random House LLC.

Graph on page 243 by Erica Halivni.

Library of Congress Cataloging-in-Publication Data
Gordis, Daniel, author.
Menachem Begin: the battle for Israel's soul / Daniel
Gordis.
    pages   cm
Includes bibliographical references and index.
ISBN 978-0-8052-4312-3 (hardcover)
ISBN 978-0-8052-4313-0 (eBook)
    1. Begin, Menachem, 1913–1992. 2. Revisionist Zionists—
Israel—Biography. 3. Prime ministers—Israel—Biography.
4. Israel—Politics and government—20th century. I. Title.
    DS126.6.B33G67 2014   956.9405'4092—dc23   [B] 2013023333

www.schocken.com

Jacket photograph of Menachem Begin, May 21, 1977,
Tel Aviv-Yafo, Israel. Bettmann / Corbis
Jacket design by Pablo Delcán

Printed in the United States of America
First Edition
2 4 6 8 9 7 5 3 1

For my parents,
with gratitude, with admiration, and with love

בני שמונים לגבורה
(ע"פ אבות ה:כא)

And in memory of Sami Rohr,
who, like Menachem Begin,
loved Jewish books and the Jewish people

לא בזכות הכח שבנו לארץ אבותינו, שבנו אליה בכח הזכות

We returned to the land of our ancestors not by virtue of might but by the virtue of right. —MENACHEM BEGIN

CONTENTS

INTRODUCTION

Who Was That Man?

"I observed all the oppression that goes on under the sun;
the tears of the oppressed, with none to comfort them;
and the power of their oppressors—with none to comfort them."
—*Ecclesiastes 4:1*

One of my most vivid college memories is of Menachem Begin. It was November 1977, the first semester of my freshman year. The radio was on, and I heard the news that President Anwar Sadat of Egypt had accepted Prime Minister Begin's invitation to come to Jerusalem.

I can still picture the moment. The doorway in front of me, my roommate's desk to the left. The cinder-block walls we'd painted soon after we'd moved in. I leaned my head against the door frame, closed my eyes, and prayed that Begin would stay alive long enough to see the process through.

I knew virtually nothing about Begin then. I'd lived in Israel for a couple of years as a young child but had been all too happy to depart, and subsequently ignored Israeli politics almost entirely. I still cared enough about Israel, though, that the newscast stopped me in my tracks. The prospect of peace in Israel was so stunning that, for the first time in my life, I found myself begging some power out there to take care of Menachem Begin.

It may have been the first time that I truly prayed.

Four years later, on my honeymoon in Hawaii, I was walking back from the beach with my new wife when we stopped to peer into a local newspaper vending machine. "Israel Bombs Iraqi Nuclear Reactor," the headline said, and we both laughed out loud. People in Hawaii, it seemed, would believe anything.

Back at the hotel, we absentmindedly turned on a brand-new cable network called CNN. Israel, it reported, had destroyed Iraq's Osirak nuclear reactor. The attack had been ordered by Menachem Begin. We asked ourselves and each other questions people had been asking about Begin for decades: Had he just made the world safer, or had he recklessly endangered it? Was the attack reprehensibly irresponsible, as the United States would soon claim, or was it the courageous step of someone who knew better than anyone else how to safeguard the future of the Jewish people?

I never met Begin, never even saw him in person. But he is an indelible part of my freshman year, my honeymoon, and many other subsequent moments I will never forget. When my wife and I eventually moved our family to Israel many years later, countless taxi drivers, listening to the news of whatever calamity was unfolding at the moment, would turn around to tell me, "You know what this country needs? We need Menachem Begin."

It was not only the taxi drivers. Even Israel's left-leaning newspaper, *Haaretz*, which had regularly railed against his policies, sometimes wondered wistfully when the next Begin would appear. In 2012, twenty years after Begin died, *Haaretz* published a long retrospective on his life entitled "Menachem Begin—the Man Who Transformed Israel." And several months later, when Israel was caught up in yet another international crisis, a *Haaretz* column noted that "in 1977, it was Menachem Begin who began to extricate Israel from its isolation. It is unclear if there is anyone willing and able to do so in 2013."[1]

Everyone, it seems, misses Menachem Begin.

I wrote this book to find out why. I wanted to understand how someone so polarizing, so controversial, in his own country and abroad, can appear today as the soul not only of Israel's best self but as a living fusion of Jewish consciousness and national aspiration.

A ll of Israel's founders made extraordinary journeys, but it is hard to imagine any of them enduring an odyssey anything like Begin's. He fled the Nazis, lost his parents and brother, was imprisoned by the Soviets and hunted by the British. Condemned by Albert Einstein and Hannah Arendt in the pages of *The New York Times*, scorned by Israel's political elites, portrayed by many as a demagogue, and relegated to the political opposition for twenty-eight years, he served as prime minister for six years, and in that time made peace with Egypt, received the Nobel Peace Prize, and destroyed Iraq's nuclear reactor. He also led Israel into its most unpopular war, resigned as a result of the war's dark course before his term was completed, and went into seclusion for almost a decade. An orator who thrived on crowds, he was almost never seen or heard from again.

When he died, though, tens of thousands of people choked the streets of Jerusalem, desperate to make their way to the Mount of Olives, where he was buried. They hadn't forgotten him. They wanted to say good-bye. And they wanted to thank him.

To thank him for what? What was it that Menachem Begin evoked in Israelis and in Jews worldwide? Loved by many, reviled by others, his life and the principles to which he was committed touched something profound in Jews almost everywhere. The key to Begin's abiding grip on the memory and fascination of Israelis and Jews around the world was bound up with his unabashed, utter devotion to the Jewish people. Committed to Israel though he was, Menachem Begin's life was a story of commitment first and foremost to the Jewish people. Many of Israel's founders Hebraized their names (Ben-Gurion actually required diplomatic personnel and civil servants above a certain rank to do so[2]). David Ben-Gurion was born David Grün. Ariel Sharon's original last name was Scheiner-mann. Golda Meir had been Golda Meyerson. But Menachem Begin did not change his name. His Jewish roots were the only roots that he needed or wanted; when called upon to testify before a commission of the Knes-set toward the end of his life, and asked to state his name, he answered, simply, "Menachem ben Dov ve-Chasia Begin." It was not an Israeli name, but a Jewish one. It was a reminder that Israel mattered only if the Jews mattered. He never became the toned and bronzed Israeli in the new tradition of Dayan, Sharon, or Yitzhak Rabin, nor a self-invented member of the old guard like Ben-Gurion. He had no need for that. His devotion to Israel was an irrepressible facet of the European Jew he had always been, and unlike many of Israel's founders, he saw no reason to leave that tradition or legacy behind.

In the age of the "new Jew," Begin carried with him a fierce pride in what he had inherited. The love that Israelis and Jews around the world felt for him, regardless of what they may have thought of his policies, derived in large measure from his having reminded them who they were and would always be.

This book is the story of Menachem Begin's life, but it is also the story of what he evoked in Jews, of what he said to the world about Jewish history and the Jewish people, and of the legacy he bequeathed to the state he was instrumental in creating.

G iven how fascinating, perplexing, controversial, and beloved he was, it should come as no surprise that Menachem Begin's life has been thoroughly researched. He is the subject of several biographies, including the recent comprehensive treatment by Avi Shilon, *Menachem Begin: A Life* (recently translated from the Hebrew). Other biographies have been written by a longtime friend and advisor (Harry Hurwitz), by foreign journalists (Eric Silver and Ned Temko), by an Israeli journalist (Eitan Haber), by those who served with Begin in the Jewish underground or worked with him in government (Aryeh Naor, among others). Other writers composed biographies even when he was still in office (Aviezer Golan and Shlomo Nakdimon), and another wrote a volume with a psychological bent (Ofer Grosbard), seeking to get to the core of what animated him. Memoirs, such as Hart Hasten's *I Shall Not Die*, include lengthy personal recollections of Begin. Yehuda Avner (Begin's colleague, friend, and English speechwriter, who subsequently served as Israel's ambassador to Australia and the United Kingdom) is the author of *The Prime Ministers*, which has done more than any other book to bring Menachem Begin to the attention of an English-reading generation that knew little of him. All of these books have contributed immensely to this volume.

In addition to these and other biographies, Begin was covered widely in the press, both in Israel and abroad. There are voluminous archives at the Menachem Begin Heritage Center, the Jabotinsky Institute in Israel, and Israel's National Archives. And, because Begin lived not long ago, there are still scores of people alive who had extensive interaction with him. Many of those people were kind enough to be interviewed and to contribute further insight to this study.

This book makes no attempt to offer itself as a definitive biography of Menachem Begin. It takes no stand on what Begin would have thought Israel ought to do today. Nor does it pretend to cover every dimension of Begin's fascinating, multifaceted public and private life. Many of the events in which Begin was involved are still shrouded in mystery or mired in controversy. I have adopted the positions that seem to me supported by the strongest evidence, but I am fully aware that on some key issues, deeply knowledgeable people disagree on key facts and interpretations.

In a book of this length, there are, of necessity, many dimensions of Begin's life that are either addressed far too briefly or left altogether untouched. Drawing on research already done and coupling it with new archival work and numerous new interviews, my goal was—a century after Begin's birth—to bring his extraordinary life to the attention of an even wider audience and to look at his life through the lens of the passion he still evokes. What was the "magic" of his draw? What was it about him that touched so deep a nerve in Jewish people, as well as in non-Jews, in

Israel and throughout the world? I hope that this book will help address those questions.

Perhaps most important, I hope that this book will lead us all to examine once again what it was about Menachem Begin's view of the world that led him to defend his people with such devotion, and what it is about rediscovering his legacy that might prompt us to do the same.

Menachem Begin

1

Between the Kaiser and the Czar

"I will lay your cities in ruin . . . And you I will scatter among the
nations . . . As for those of you who survive, I will cast fear into
their hearts in the land of their enemies. The sound of a driven
leaf shall put them to flight."   —*Leviticus 26:31–36*

On a summer Sabbath in 1913, in the Polish town of Brisk (otherwise
known as Brest-Litovsk, in Yiddish, as Brisk) a son was born to
Ze'ev Dov and Chasia Begin. It was four days after Tisha B'Av, the annual
fast day mourning the destruction of the Temples in Jerusalem and the
exiles that followed them, on the Sabbath known as *Shabbat Nachamu,*
the Sabbath of Comfort. So the Begins named their son Menachem, "The
Comforter."

He was born on August 16, 1913, on the eve of World War I. He would
later say that he was born *into* the war, that he spent his childhood years
in Brisk, lying "on the battlefield between the Czar's army and the Kaiser's army."[1] He was the youngest of three children; his sister, Rachel, had
been born in 1907 and his brother, Herzl, followed in 1910. "Menachem
was born into *Gone with the Wind*! The war tore everything apart," Rachel
would later recall. "He did not have a childhood like me or my other
brother, Herzl. He did not even remember his grandparents. He knew
nothing."[2]

What he learned quickly enough were the miseries of statelessness and
the lessons of powerlessness in an age of war. In 1915, Brest was taken from

Russia by the Germans. In 1918, it was made part of the short-lived Belarusian Democratic Republic. Poland grabbed it back in 1919. It changed hands twice more during the Polish-Soviet War.

World War I forced the Begins to flee Brisk. They lived in an abandoned country house; Chasia Begin took her young son Menachem with her once a month to chop wood—German soldiers periodically picked them up in a carriage and brought them to the village.[3] But Menachem's father, Ze'ev Dov, was determined that his children not grow up in the wild; he rented a room in Kobryn, the nearest town, yet could not find work there. The family became destitute. Nevertheless, Menachem's memories of these early years were warm:

> Our house was full of happiness, light and love. My parents had a wonderful sense of humor. There is something about that that us children inherited as well. We always had friends over, and our pleasant laughter filled the two rooms in which we lived. Even the leak in the harsh autumn days did not depress our spirits. We knew how to joke even at the expense of our suffering.[4]

It was training of a sort that would serve Begin well in his years in prison, in safe houses, and in hiding. In 1918, Ze'ev Dov returned to Brisk, and the family joined him in 1919. The city to which six-year-old Menachem returned was in ruins. Russian Jewry as a whole was shattered; somewhere between 500,000 and 1,000,000 Jewish civilians were forced from their homes and exiled, simply because they were Jewish.[5]

Unlike many of the Jewish communities that had been part of the Russian Empire and were now destroyed, the Jewish community of Brisk recovered after the war, to some extent. Brisk had a population of 50,000, about half of whom were Jewish. There were dozens of functioning synagogues. Numerous Jewish organizations were created to take care of the town's poor, sick, widows, and orphans. The Bikur Cholim distributed food and medicine at little cost to the needy; the Women's Society provided poor women with milk and food, and there was an orphanage where children were educated and eventually taught a trade. The "Righteous Fund" provided poorer businesspeople with interest-free loans.[6]

Ze'ev Dov Begin had studied in Rabbi Chaim Soloveitchik's yeshiva in Brisk when he was not helping his father with the family wood business.[7] The Brisk tradition was known for its emphasis on intellect over emotion and for a commitment to the punctilious observance of the details of Jewish law. His yeshiva years notwithstanding, Ze'ev Dov was not particularly inclined to punctiliousness; he carved out his own, unique way of religious life—reverence coupled with iconoclasm—an attitude that had a lasting influence on his youngest son. Ignoring the traditional Yom Kippur prohibition, for example, Ze'ev Dov instructed his children to brush their teeth before prayer because they were, after all, speaking to God. When Menachem's sister, Rachel, needed to sign a form at the university on Shabbat, she was loath to violate the prohibition against writing on the Sabbath. Ze'ev Dov told her, "Knowledge is like a matter of life and death. So sign."[8]

At first, the Begin parents sent Menachem to study in a *cheder*, a traditional Jewish "yeshiva" for young children, but after only a year, Ze'ev Dov transferred him to the more moderate religious school, a cross between the *cheder* and the local secular Hebrew school, where Begin remained until high school.[9] The Begin children's education was as much a product of their home as it was of their school. Menachem once recalled, "[My father] knew the Bible by heart, almost the entire thing. He and the three children . . . loved a sort of family Bible contest. One of the children would recite a verse from the Torah, the Prophets, or the Writings, and our father would complete the chapter from memory."[10]

For high school, Ze'ev Dov decided that his children would attend the state schools, since doing well there could secure the Begin children acceptance to university, and unlike the Jewish schools, the state schools were free.[11] Thus, at fourteen Menachem found himself enrolled at the Romuald Traugutt Memorial Gymnasium, one of seven state schools serving Brisk.[12] About a tenth of the students in the state schools were Jews.[13] Academically, it was an excellent school, but the Gymnasium taught him a great deal about other dimensions of life, as well. This was Poland, after all, and before long, Menachem Begin had learned the need for self-defense.

He was frail, short, and Jewish—a social outsider who did not have many friends and was frequently bullied.[14] At the same time, in what must have been a painful contrast, Menachem grew up with a father who prided himself on never having backed down in the face of anti-Semitism. When a wave of pogroms swept the city in 1905, some Jews—including Ze'ev Dov Begin—organized a Jewish self-defense force. In one legendary incident, Polish soldiers instigated a pogrom and Menachem's father went out to the street to investigate. Menachem later recalled that he and the rest of the family received the tragic news that a soldier had shot Ze'ev Dov. In fact, the soldier had missed, though the danger had been real enough. The mystique surrounding Ze'ev Dov as a result marked him as a new kind of Jewish leader. As Menachem later wrote, it turned his father into "a defender of his brethren against attacks, pogroms and oppression. As a defender on occasions of a mass slaughter or great danger, not always could he avert a tragedy, but he was always ready to act when someone was threatened, even at great danger to himself."[15]

Ze'ev Dov, who achieved a modicum of prominence in the Jewish community, had a bit of a reputation as a Jewish firebrand. He refused to speak Polish. Calling it an "anti-Semitic language," he encouraged his children not only to speak Hebrew but to list it as their native tongue.[16] As secretary of the community council, Ze'ev Dov organized a prayer minyan with complete disregard for the requirements that he obtain proper government licenses.[17] No one was going to tell him where he could and could not pray. In another incident, Ze'ev Dov attacked a Polish officer who was trying to cut off a rabbi's beard. This "proud Jew," as Menachem referred to his father, took his walking stick, on which was engraved a line from Emile Zola's defense of Alfred Dreyfus,[18] and clubbed the Pole over the head.[19]

Different though he was from Ze'ev Dov, Menachem clearly inherited some of his father's instincts. He once refused to take a Latin exam on Shabbat, to the amusement of his classmates. He said to the teacher, "This is my belief, and I won't write on the Sabbath under any circumstances." The teacher gave him an F; but when Begin refused to back down, the teacher relented and gave him his typically high grade.[20]

This insistence on Jewish pride would shape virtually everything about Menachem's life. He would later say of his revolt against the British that it, too, was about reinstilling pride in the Jewish people. Rachel Halperin, Menachem's sister, recalled that there were four values that her father drilled into his children: respect for others; a love for Zion above all else; pride in being a Jew; and confidence, hope, and faith in the future establishment of a Jewish state.[21]

Each year, the three Begin children—Herzl, Rachel, and Menachem— witnessed Ze'ev Dov weeping on Passover as he recited *vehi she'amda*, the quintessential prayer of Jewish trust in God to rescue the Jews from the clutches of the enemy.[22] But God, it seemed, was not doing much to rescue the Jews of Europe. While it remained Sabbath-observing and synagogue-going, the Begin household grafted nationalist longing onto traditional Jewish life. Given his father's distaste for all things Polish, it is ironic that the Zionism that came to shape Begin's entire life was in many ways enriched and formed by the renaissance of Polish national yearnings. In school, Begin's favorite teacher was an assimilated Jew who taught him the Polish national epic, *Pan Tadeusz*, written by Adam Mickiewicz nearly a century earlier. The poem, with its messianic nationalism and powerful imagery, coupled with Mickiewicz's personal story of waiting in Paris in exile for the reunification of his land, was a powerful influence in Begin's early years.[23] His school "encouraged in a largely poor, Polish student body a crusade to ensure that no one would humble Poland again."[24]

Like Zionism, Polish nationalism was fueled fundamentally by deep resentment of foreign occupation, mostly by Russia between 1764 and the twentieth century. Polish nationalism became so potent a force that, by the middle of the nineteenth century, Russia went to great lengths to try to extinguish it altogether. But Polish nationalism simply morphed; instead of laboring unrealistically for the establishment of a Polish sovereign state, it took on an almost mystical, messianic quality.

Ironically, Jewish nationalism was undergoing precisely the opposite transformation. Little more than a religious aspiration for two thousand years, Zionism had recently been reinvented as a political movement by Theodor Herzl, who had convened the First Zionist Congress in Basel in 1897. The Jews, like the Poles, wanted their land back. The Polish national anthem declared, "Poland is not yet lost while we live / We will fight (with swords) for all / That our enemies had taken from us . . . ," while "Hatikvah," the Zionists' anthem, ended with the words "Our hope is not yet lost, the hope of two millennia, to be a free people in our land."

At least in Begin's case, the Polish nationalist message did not fall on deaf ears, though it was not the liberation of Poland that moved him. Years later, as he labored for the liberation of Zion, he would quote Mickiewicz from memory in speeches and he liked to emphasize the man's (unlikely but possible) Jewish heritage, calling him a poet of "Jewish origin" who greatly influenced him.[25]

But more than anything else, it was his father's Zionism that proved dominant. In his memoir *The Revolt*, Begin recalled:

> From my early youth I had been taught by my father—who, as I was later told, went to his death at Nazi hands voicing the liturgic declaration of faith in God and singing the Hebrew national anthem, "Hatikvah"—that we Jews were to return to *Eretz Israel* [the Land of Israel]. Not to "go" or "travel" or "come"—but to return.[26]

Because the religious leadership in Brisk saw Zionism as a new movement, and thus a threat to long-hallowed ways of life, Ze'ev Dov's zeal for Zionism and his leadership of the Zionist community often put him at odds with the rabbis there.[27] Menachem was raised on the story that in 1904, Ze'ev Dov broke down the door of Rabbi Chaim Soloveitchik's synagogue to conduct a memorial service for the recently deceased Theodor Herzl, despite Reb Chaim's explicit insistence that no service be held.[28] Assisting Ze'ev Dov was his friend and neighbor Mordechai Scheinermann, whose grandson Ariel Sharon would play a powerful role in Menachem's own contentious career.

Ze'ev Dov, who had named his firstborn son Herzl, renewed the celebrations of Lag Ba-Omer, a holiday that, in the Zionist tradition, commemorated the ancient revolt of the Jews against Rome. When Hashomer Hatzair, the secular labor Zionist movement, opened a chapter in Brisk in 1923, Ze'ev Dov served as its chairman. Later that year, a ten-year-old Menachem gave his first public speech, celebrating the heroism of Bar Kokhba, the last Jewish military leader in ancient Palestine who rebelled against the Romans.[29]

Although his father was closer to Menachem's popular older brother, Herzl, Menachem was the child who would most fervently embrace their father's Zionism. When he joined the youth group affiliated with Hashomer Hatzair as a young boy, he sensed that he'd finally found a social and ideological home. He could have done without the outdoor hikes; but with his sister, Rachel, in a leadership role, he danced, sang Zionist songs, and even at a young age spoke excellent Hebrew during the meetings.[30]

He remained a member until the age of thirteen, when all the Begin children left the movement, again at Ze'ev Dov's insistence. Their father had decided that the group was overly committed to socialism, to the detriment of an explicitly Jewish, Zionist agenda. It was time for the children to join Betar, he felt, the movement being spearheaded by the powerful intellectual firebrand Ze'ev Jabotinsky.

2

A Pit of Decay and Dust

"Be strong and courageous; for you shall cause this people to
inherit the land which I swore to their fathers to give them."
                                                    —*Joshua 1:6*

Begin was only thirteen years old when he made the move to Betar,
but it was a step that would forever alter the course of his life. Joining
Betar hurled Begin into the orbit of Vladimir (Ze'ev) Jabotinsky, one of
the most dynamic and misunderstood—or, more likely, misrepresented—
figures of early Zionism. There is no understanding Begin without understanding Jabotinsky.

Born in Odessa in 1880, Vladimir (he later used the Hebrew name Ze'ev)
Jabotinsky spent his early years as a journalist and foreign correspondent
in Europe and in the Russian Empire. The young Jabotinsky was a largely
assimilated, certainly private, Jew; like many Jews of his period, he publicly blended into the larger Christian social and intellectual culture, at
least to the degree that it would allow, all while retaining a core commitment to his Jewish roots.[1] But as he reached his twenties, the gifted
writer and orator was deeply shaken by the pogroms that convulsed the
European Jewish world around the turn of the century. After the 1903
pogrom in Kishinev (about which Chaim Nachman Bialik, the Israeli
national poet, wrote his epic poem *The City of Slaughter*, which brought the
pogroms to the attention of a world Jewish audience but also implicated
the Jews for having knowingly embraced weakness), Jabotinsky became

an official member of the Zionist Organization. Not long thereafter, he was organizing Jewish self-defense units across the Russian Empire.

During World War I, Jabotinsky supported the British allied forces and created a "Jewish Legion" to fight in Palestine; he hoped that in return for this support, the British would allow the Jews to settle in Palestine once the Ottoman Empire collapsed, an eventuality he hoped was not far off.[2] Like Jabotinsky himself, many members of the Jewish Legion who had fought during the war remained in Palestine when the war ended. When Arab violence against Jews demonstrated a need for self-defense, Jabotinsky helped to organize hundreds of volunteers for the Haganah, an independent military unit in Palestine. He trained his volunteers and former Jewish Legionnaires to protect themselves against the Arab rioters; the attempt was only moderately successful, since the British enforced the Mandate's provision that they would control the flow of all weapons.

After the outbreak of Arab violence in the Old City of Jerusalem in 1920, Jabotinsky voluntarily handed himself over to the British authorities after they called for his arrest. Convicted of arms possession, he was sentenced to fifteen years in prison. He spent time in Acre Prison amid an outpouring of international support—London newspapers reminded the public that international Jews would likely rally in support of Jabotinsky, whom they considered their Garibaldi. The Jewish press, and even *The Times* of London, published favorable pieces about him. The British relented, and he was released in July.[3]

Jabotinsky was adamant that the entire affair be excised from the public record, and he traveled to London for a trial. But the Zionist powers-that-be were uninterested in assuming the costs and liabilities of defending Jabotinsky—a man who rejected their socialism and openly advocated the use of force to obtain a national homeland. Indeed, Zionist leaders (including Chaim Weizmann, the Russian-born chemist and president of the Zionist Organization, who would eventually become the first president of Israel) had been all but silent while Jabotinsky was jailed in Acre. Disgusted with the accommodating policies of the Zionist leadership of the time, Jabotinsky resigned from the Zionist Organization in

1922. With that, he moved into the opposition within the Zionist movement and became the perennial gadfly, a position he would retain for the
remainder of his life.

Jabotinsky became convinced that the current Zionist leadership was
too weak and far too passive. It was time, he insisted, to "revise" the
then-Zionist establishment's pragmatic and political Zionism, which supported a more gradual approach to acquiring land and building settlements where it was most practical. The mainstream Zionists, led by
Chaim Weizmann (and soon thereafter, by David Ben-Gurion), were
by no means territorial minimalists. They believed that the Jews had a
right to the entire Land of Israel as outlined in the Bible, but nonetheless
stressed the importance of ongoing cooperation with the British authorities, hoping that cooperation would eventually help them realize their
goal of establishing an independent Jewish state, even if on less of the land
than they truly deserved.

Jabotinsky and his fellow "Revisionists" believed that the sole purpose of Zionism should be the establishment of a Jewish state on both
sides of the Jordan River—the land promised by God to Abraham in the
Bible and where Jewish self-rule had existed for hundreds of years. While
there was no point in *seeking* conflict with the Arabs, force might have to
be used to make way for a Jewish majority in Palestine if there were no
alternative. In many respects, their ultimate goals were the same as those
of the Zionist establishment: both favored the establishment of Jewish
settlements in Palestine, the right to a Jewish armed force, and free Jewish immigration to Palestine, all accomplished through diplomacy with
the British. The Revisionists were not unique in *what* they advocated; it
was in *how* they planned to achieve their goals—by force if necessary—
that they differed from the Labor Zionists, who, the Revisionists felt,
harbored too sanguine a view of the Arab response to Jewish national
aspirations.[4]

The Revisionists had a youth movement; known as Betar, its name
referred to the last standing Jewish fortress in the Bar Kokhba rebellion against the Romans (in 135 CE). Betar was also an acronym for *Brit*

Trumpeldor ("the covenant of Trumpeldor"). Joseph Trumpeldor, a Russian Jew who had helped Jabotinsky establish the Jewish Legion in World War I, was the subject of a popular legend, according to which his last words as he lay dying after a 1920 clash in which he had helped defend Tel Hai (a Jewish settlement in the Upper Galilee) from local Arab raiders were "it is good to die for our country."[5] No short phrase could have better captured the Revisionists' commitment to Jewish military power, self-defense, and national pride—or struck the Zionist establishment as so dangerous.

As Jabotinsky explained in an essay entitled "The Idea of Betar," the organization's aim was

> very simple though difficult: to create that type of Jew which the nation needs in order to better and quicker build a Jewish state . . . The greatest difficulty is encountered because, as a nation, the Jews today are neither "normal" nor "healthy" and life in diaspora affects the intelligent upbringing of normal and healthy citizens.[6]

Jabotinsky fully appreciated the degree to which his worldview both irritated and frightened the establishment, and he understood that he and his organization were quickly becoming pariahs in many Zionist circles. But his defense of Betar's focus on fighting tactics and physical training placed the justification for it on the "our country" portion of Trumpeldor's possibly apocryphal words.

Jabotinsky, in the language of his day, claimed that the Jewish claim for an ancestral homeland was simply one more example of a native people's legitimate assertion of rights, strictly limited by what he considered ancient and legitimate borders:

> There are two sorts of nationalism: If a nation dwells in its country but also desires to annex the land of its neighbors—that is bad nationalism. On the other hand, when a nation is entirely homeless and demands for itself a portion of God's earth, it is a good nationalism about [which] there is nothing to be ashamed of. The same

applies to "Militarism." If a power, unharmed by anybody, begins to arm in order to attack its peaceful neighbors, it is a bad militarism. In, however, the case of Jews, who are being beaten everywhere, and even in Palestine are being threatened with destruction—it is certainly proof of good nationalism to arm for the defense of our lives, property and future. We may then well be proud of it.[7]

One fascinating window into the differences between the mainstream and Revisionist movements in Zionism is the difference between their two anthems. "Hatikvah," which was already the anthem of political Zionism and would eventually become the anthem of the Jewish state, was entirely nonmilitaristic:

> As long as in the heart, within
> A Jewish soul still yearns
> And beyond, toward the end of the east
> An eye gazes toward Zion
>
> Our hope is not yet lost,
> That hope of two thousand years,
> To be a free nation in our land,
> The land of Zion and Jerusalem.

"As long as a heart yearns," "Hatikvah" insisted, all was not lost. But that was not the worldview expressed in the Betar anthem (which Jabotinsky himself had written):

> From the pit of decay and dust
> Will arise to us a generation
> Proud, generous, and fierce
> Fallen Betar
> Yodfat and Masada
> Risen again in strength and dignity [*hadar*]
>
> Dignity [*Hadar*]
> A Jew, though in poverty, is of royal strain

Slave or refugee—the son of a king
Crowned with the diadem of David
In the open or in concealment
Remember the crown
Symbol of pride and fortitude [*tagar*]

Fortitude [*Tagar*]
In the face of every obstacle
In times of ascent, and of setbacks
A fire may still be lit
With the flame of revolt
For silence is dirt
Sacrifice blood and spirit
For the hidden glory

To die or to conquer the mountain
Yodfat, Masada, Betar.

The meaning of the anthem's historical references was lost on none of the Revisionists. At both Masada and Yodfat, Jews had opted to commit suicide rather than submit to the Roman forces. And "Betar," of course, had clear revolutionary resonance.

Jabotinsky's reimagination of the Jew centered largely on the notion of dignity, or *hadar*. One of the critical dimensions of the Betar anthem was the centrality of the word *hadar*, which became a defining concept for Jabotinsky, for Betar, and, in due course, for Begin as well. In an essay on Betar, Jabotinsky outlined its meaning, noting that in many ways, the Hebrew term was fundamentally untranslatable:

"Hadar" is a Hebrew word which hardly is at all translatable into another language: It combines various conceptions such as outward beauty, respect, self-esteem, politeness, faithfulness. The only suitable "translation" into the language of real life must be the Betari [member of Betar]—in his dealings, actions, speech and thought . . .
. . . we Jews are the most "aristocratic" people in the world . . .

[Jews] have seventy generations of men in the past; men who could read and write; men who studied and discussed God, history, ideas of justice, human problems and the future. In this sense, every Jew is a "prince" and the bitterest of all jokes that the Diaspora played upon us is, that the Jews are generally considered as hailing from God knows where.[8]

Jabotinsky, like many of the early Zionists, was a gifted and prolific writer. He wrote poetry and prose, translated important Russian works into Hebrew and great Hebrew poetry into Russian. Some of the most important Zionist essays came from his pen. He was not alone; the Zionist revolution was a highly literary one. Ben-Gurion, Weizmann, Jabotinsky—and later Begin—were all accomplished writers and lovers of literature. This was in part about leaving a written legacy—natural for the people of a word-loving culture. But it was also about *imagining* a new and renewed Jewish future. Ben-Gurion would wear his fez, Jabotinsky became known for his brown shirts, other young Israelis like Rabin had their distinct ways of dress. These were costumes, in a way, all part of imagining the renewed Jew in the renewed Jewish homeland.

In 1923, the same year that he officially launched Revisionist Zionism and Betar, Jabotinsky wrote his famous essay "The Iron Wall," his now classic statement on the conflict between the Zionists and the Arabs in Palestine. Jabotinsky recognized that just as Jewish nationalism was an impulse that could not be subdued, so, too, the Arabs would not give up their homeland, either. Though he was a romantic in many ways, Jabotinsky's practicality allowed him to acknowledge that though the Jews were metaphysical and in historical terms literal natives of the land of Israel, so were the Arabs, for whom the Jews would always be outsiders.

Every indigenous people will resist alien settlers as long as they see any hope of ridding themselves of the danger of foreign settlement. That is what the Arabs in Palestine are doing, and what they will persist in doing as long as there remains a solitary spark of hope that they will be able to prevent the transformation of "Palestine" into the "Land of Israel."

Thus, he understood, notions that the conflict could be settled were misguided and naïve:

> Zionist colonization, even the most restricted, must either be terminated or carried out in defiance of the will of the native population. This colonization can, therefore, continue and develop only under the protection of a force independent of the local population—an iron wall which the native population cannot break through. This is, *in toto*, our policy towards the Arabs . . . As long as there is a spark of hope that they can get rid of us, they will not sell these hopes, not for any kind of sweet words or tasty morsels, because they are not a rabble but a nation, perhaps somewhat tattered, but still living.

It is critical not to misunderstand Jabotinsky's unblinkered awareness of nascent Palestinian nationalism as a rejection of Jewish claims. In no way did he see the Jews as analogues to the British in India, for example. The Jews were "natives," returning to their ancestral homeland. This was not a conflict between native and conqueror as far as Jabotinsky was concerned; it was a battle between two competing indigenous groups.

The British, who wanted quiet in Palestine, had no use for Jabotinsky; when he departed Palestine for a lecture circuit in 1930, they informed him that he would not be allowed to reenter. He would spend the rest of his life exiled to the Diaspora.

It was then that Menachem Begin, around the time of his high school graduation, heard Jabotinsky speak for the first time. Squeezed into the orchestra pit of a sold-out auditorium, Begin was overwhelmed: "You sit there, down below, and begin to feel in every fiber of your body that you are being lifted up, borne aloft, up, up . . . Have you been won over? No, more than that. You have been consecrated to the ideal, forever."[9] As one childhood companion noted with a touch of the dramatic: "Jabotinsky became God for him."[10]

In 1929, Begin attended a lecture at the Jewish high school given by Moshe Steiner, a Revisionist Zionist. Begin peppered Steiner with questions: "How do you expect to become a majority?" he asked. Steiner was sufficiently intrigued by the young man's questions that he invited him to talk after the lecture.[11]

Begin had read Jabotinsky's articles and spoke to Steiner about his interest in Betar. The more he learned, the more Begin was fascinated by Betar; he used his already well-known oratory skills to draw his friends and classmates to the group after he joined. In a move that must have been seen as odd by some, the newly infatuated teenager wore his brown Betar uniform everywhere except to his Polish high school. He was often seen with Avraham Stavsky, who was not only a close friend but also a quasi-bodyguard. At sixteen, Begin was still beardless, slight, and walked with a slouch.[12] But in his uniform, he had found a cause; he had, in fact, found himself.

Begin rapidly rose in Betar's ranks and was soon appointed commander of the Brisk Betar and spoke in public weekly, encouraging poor and wealthy Jews alike to join in the cause. After each speech, more young people joined the movement, inspired by his ability to cast a spell over his audience, according to one listener. He often started a speech with German quotes from Goethe, but he always reverted to Yiddish, to ensure that the Jewish audience, most of whom came from impoverished families, could fully appreciate what he was saying. One Lithuanian Jew recalled that Begin's "great talent was to speak from the very soul of the *shtetl* [Jewish village], to make things simple—black and white—and to offer real salvation. Full salvation!"[13]

David Ben-Gurion, an increasingly powerful figure in the Jewish community in Palestine (and by 1935, as chair of the Jewish Agency, its titular head), despised Jabotinsky's Revisionism. Ben-Gurion was a committed socialist, while Jabotinsky—though committed to five elements of what he considered a decent society, including housing, food, and education—rejected socialism writ large. Ben-Gurion was less the pacifist than Weizmann, but as early as World War I, he had opposed the formation of the Jewish Legion, asserting that the Jews of Palestine should remain loyal to the Ottomans instead of the British. When the demise of the Ottoman Empire seemed imminent, however, Ben-Gurion shifted course and reluctantly supported Jabotinsky's plan.[14]

Jabotinsky, in turn, resented the monopoly of Ben-Gurion's Labor Zionism over the Keren Hayesod, the main organization for funds for Israel. At stake was not only an ideological divide between the capitalist Jabotinsky and the socialist Ben-Gurion, but also power. Ben-Gurion was firmly in control, and did all he could to ensure that Revisionism did not encroach on the hegemony that Labor enjoyed.[15]

The deep divisions between the Zionist factions intensified when, in June 1933, Chaim Arlosoroff, a prominent Labor Zionist leader, went to Germany in order to negotiate with the Third Reich. He proposed a deal in which the Nazis would permit Jews to emigrate to Palestine with some of their assets, while the rest of their net worth would be transferred to the Germans, who would in turn use the cash to purchase and ship raw materials to Palestine. Jews would be saved, the Germans would get a market for exports, and Palestine would receive the raw goods it so desperately needed. But negotiating with the Nazis, even in 1933, was highly controversial.

A few days after his return to Palestine, Arlosoroff was shot and killed on the Tel Aviv beach. Labor blamed the Revisionists for the Arlosoroff murder, and kept up the pressure on Betar in every way that it could. Abraham Stavsky, a Revisionist and (years earlier) Begin's close companion in high school, was charged with the murder and sentenced to death. But he appealed the sentence and was ultimately acquitted of the crime, though his reputation was marred.[16] Whether Arlosoroff was killed in a random act of violence or because he was negotiating with the Germans has never been determined.

The distrust and animosity between Jabotinsky and Ben-Gurion became toxic. Physical attacks on Betar members in Palestine were common, and Betar workers in Palestine were sent by Revisionists to break strikes organized by the Histadrut, the all-powerful Labor trade union. Ben-Gurion regularly insulted Jabotinsky in public; Jabotinsky never responded *ad hominem*[17] (his commitment to *hadar* precluded that), but their public and relentless feud was a festering wound in a Zionist movement that could scarcely afford it.

In 1934, the year after the Arlosoroff murder, Jabotinsky and Ben-Gurion held a series of unlikely meetings in London, where Jabotinsky lived following his exile from Palestine. Eventually, the two men agreed to "refrain from party warfare," stop libel and slander campaigns against the other party, and "eradicate all acts of terror or violence" among their members. Betar and the Revisionists were promised their own labor union, and immigration "certificates" to Palestine were to be restored for Betar members. The relationship was never fully trusting, but with time, the two influenced each other more than either might have admitted.[18]

The partial rapprochement did not mean that Jabotinsky's fundamental disagreements with Ben-Gurion had dissipated, however. Jabotinsky's popularity continued to soar, and he began to build his own institutional base. In 1935, the Revisionists seceded from the World Zionist Organization and formed the New Zionist Organization, with Jabotinsky as president. It was a move that would color the Zionist movement for decades. Revisionism was now officially an organized "opposition," a position it would occupy, under Begin's leadership, for decades even after Israel's independence.

After graduating from high school in 1931, Begin matriculated in the law program of the University of Warsaw. But law was not his passion; he had already found a calling. On his application, he wrote "Hebrew" for his native language precisely as his father had instructed him years earlier. During one four-hour train ride, he was seated next to the prettiest girl in Brisk, but all he talked about was his hero, Jabotinsky.

In Warsaw, Begin took an official position as the head of the Organizational Department of Betar and his reputation as a gifted public speaker spread. He had a way of "making you believe," recalled one audience member. Begin had learned from Jabotinsky what it meant to make his beleaguered listeners feel "borne aloft." His frail appearance led some organizers to book a second speaker, worried that Begin would not be able to last through an entire speech, but the second speaker was never necessary.[19] He went on lecture tours around Eastern Europe, during which he slept on park benches, because he did not feel comfortable sleeping in strangers' houses without charge; he skipped meals in order to pay for Betar posters and pamphlets. *Hadar* was a preeminent concern at every turn; he developed a reputation for ceremony and decorum, particularly after he instated a rule that Betar members must stand at attention for commanders.[20] The small, unassuming boy with thick glasses, who was overlooked on the guest lists of parties and who had never courted a girl in high school, was coming of age, emerging as a presence to be reckoned with.[21]

Not only was Begin growing up, but slowly, the student began to rival his master. By 1937, the twenty-four-year-old Begin was considered by some to be a better orator than Jabotinsky.[22] Begin's oratorical prowess would remain one of the defining characteristics of his public life; indeed, Minister Dan Meridor remarked years later that it was not only the members of the Knesset who knew that Begin was perhaps the best speaker they would ever hear—everyone working in the Knesset building did. When word spread that Begin was about to speak, Meridor recalled, the cafeteria would empty and the hallways would be silent—everyone who could headed into the chamber to listen.[23]

Ideological rifts between Begin and Jabotinsky began to surface, as well. Begin and his Betar comrades had been steeped in the Polish nationalism of revolutionaries such as Josef Pilsudski; Jabotinsky, in contrast, was more influenced by British and Italian writers and their commitment to democracy.[24] Just as Jabotinsky had been frustrated by Ben-Gurion's accommodationism, Begin was now frustrated by Jabotinsky, who, while advocating violent reprisals against the Arabs, endorsed only diplomacy when dealing with the British. The last thing the Jews needed, Jabotinsky thought, was for the Jews to be fighting the Arabs and the British at the same time.

Begin disagreed with Jabotinsky about the British, and was particularly critical of Jabotinsky's willingness to forgive Ben-Gurion's public dismissals of Jabotinsky. In January 1935, he had been openly derisive of Jabotinsky's agreement to use only "legitimate political channels"—that is, to refrain from violence—to fight the British. Later that year, at Betar's Second International Conference, Begin once again denounced Jabotinsky's London pact with Ben-Gurion, reminding the audience that "unlike my teacher, I have not forgotten that Ben-Gurion called him Vladimir Hitler."

Jabotinsky, surely no great friend of Ben-Gurion's, reprimanded Begin: "I will never forget that people like Ben-Gurion . . . wore the uniform of the battalions, fought together with me, and I am sure that if Zionism will require it, they will not hesitate to wear those uniforms again and fight." The public rebuke from his teacher actually furthered Begin's reputation. He was now someone to whom the master had to respond. He was a force Jabotinsky could not ignore.[25]

By the early 1930s, Jabotinsky was convinced that Jewish survival in Palestine would require a Jewish military presence there. Betar youth in Palestine created a military unit known as the Irgun Zva'i Leumi, meaning "National Military Organization"; it was commonly called the Etzel, an acronym derived from the organization's three word name.

The Etzel, though, was not the only Jewish military organization in Palestine. Ben-Gurion's Haganah (the same Haganah that grew out of Jabotinsky's Jewish Legion) was popular among the *yishuv* (literally, the "settlement," as the prestate Jewish community of Palestine was known). Relationships between the organizations were often contentious, both because of their different strategies and in no small measure due to the personal antipathies and distrust that reigned between the leaders of the movements that they represented.

The Etzel was embroiled in conflict not only with Ben-Gurion's Haganah, but with Jabotinsky's own Betar, as well. While the Etzel stressed the need for counterattacks against the Arabs, Betar remained ambivalent about such retaliation. In 1936 and 1937, Begin and Jabotinsky crossed swords over the military actions of the Etzel; Jabotinsky, steadfastly clinging to the original Revisionist credo, insisted on issuing warnings to civilians whenever the Etzel planned to attack, and to attack only in self-defense, while Begin argued that preemptive action was necessary (though he, too, was opposed to attacks on civilians).

In the Betar-Etzel tension, Jabotinsky, like Ben-Gurion, was unwittingly following a pattern common to "founding fathers" everywhere, creating organizations that he both fathered and then argued with. It was virtually inevitable that the Etzel, transplanting Jabotinsky's own military credo to Palestinian soil, would reshape its ideology in that much harsher landscape. Begin, after initial resistance, was persuaded by the Etzel's arguments; Jabotinsky was not.

Matters became so acrimonious that Begin left Poland for Galicia in 1937. Officially he asked for the leave of absence for a legal apprenticeship, but many believed he had left because he needed time apart from Jabotinsky and their increasingly bitter competition.[26] Others surmised that Jabotinsky had sent him packing.

Why did Begin not go to Palestine? He simply knew that he would not be granted permission to enter. The British were dispensing a meager number of "certificates," the coveted documents permitting immigration to Palestine, through the Jewish Agency, which was under the control of Ben-Gurion's minions, and it was commonly known that despite Ben-Gurion's and Jabotinsky's agreement the Jewish Agency was giving very few certificates to members of Betar. In 1937, Begin was actually arrested and jailed for a few weeks after a protest he led against the Jewish Agency's miserly policy on certificates became violent; that same year, Jabotinsky wrote a scathing poem after a young man with the last name of Ploshinsky committed suicide when the Jewish Agency would not give him a certificate due to his being a member of Betar. For petty political reasons, Jews were keeping other Jews penned in an increasingly hostile Europe, and Jabotinsky was appalled:[27]

> From the day I was called to the wonder
> of Betar and Zion and Sinai,
> It was my brothers' hand that jailed me
> and locked my motherland before me.

In 1938, at the Third International Betar Conference in Warsaw, Begin clashed with Jabotinsky once again, declaring that the era of political Zionism was over and that the Zionist movement should thus redirect its energies toward a military conquest of the land.[28] Jabotinsky unequivocally rejected Begin's argument as mere "creaks": "We endure the creaking of machines, carriages and so forth . . . . Speeches and applause are also creaking doors, which have no use or reason . . . . The things that have been said here by Mr. Begin are such creaks, and we must cruelly suppress such creaks."[29]

It was during this conference that Begin successfully proposed to amend the Betar pledge for new recruits. Originally, Jabotinsky's version of the pledge had read: "only in defense will I raise my hand." Begin proposed an amendment that would read: "I will prepare my hand for the defense of my people and for the conquest of my homeland."[30] The Etzel's argument for self-defense in Palestine was casting a long shadow, reaching all the way to Betar in Europe. It was adopted over Jabotinsky's objections.

Despite their ongoing and increasingly bitter clashes, Jabotinsky appointed Begin as the commander of Betar Poland in 1939. Begin was now in charge of all 70,000 members of the organization in the country, and one of his main activities was to coordinate with the Irgun's military efforts in Palestine.

The on-and-off feud between them notwithstanding, Begin would always refer to Jabotinsky as "my master and teacher."[31] In Jabotinsky, Begin had found a father figure, another man like Ze'ev Dov whose Zionism he had first inherited and then refashioned.

B egin took only one break from his now frenetic activities on behalf of Betar—for the purpose of marrying Aliza Arnold. He had met the dark-haired girl in Galicia in 1937, when he stayed with her family after a speech he delivered at the local Betar chapter. The day after he met her, he delivered a note to her: "I saw you, my lady, for the first time, but I feel as if I have known you all my life." He warned Aliza that life with him would be difficult, for he was committed to a lifelong battle for a Jewish state; but she was undeterred.[32]

They were married while wearing their Betar uniforms in May 1939, with Jabotinsky in attendance.[33] Begin returned to Warsaw the next day to continue Betar's preparation in anticipation of the war, running training camps and accelerating the efforts to enable Jews to emigrate from Poland to Palestine.

But by summer's end, Hitler and Stalin had signed their nonaggression pact, and Hitler invaded Poland on September 1, 1939. Then the Russians invaded two weeks later. The Red Army took Brisk, but in June 1941, the Germans attacked and the Russians withdrew. Brest-Litovsk was transferred to the Ukraine, which operated under the thumb of the Germans, and remained essentially under German control for three years. The Red Army retook the city on July 28, 1944, but by then it was too late for the city's Jews. By the time the Soviets regained control of the city, the Jewish community of Brisk—a symbol of Jewish religious, cultural, and educational glory for half a millennium—had been erased, almost as if it had never been.

For Begin, obliteration of Brisk was emblematic of the ease with which the sheer evil of the Jews' enemies could erase centuries of Jewish accomplishment, and therefore of the need for Jews to be able to protect themselves. But he and his bride did not witness the destruction themselves. They boarded one of the last trains out of Warsaw, fleeing toward Romania, and from there, they hoped, they would somehow find a ship bound for Palestine.

3

This Year We Are Slaves

Though I walk through a valley of deepest darkness, I fear no evil,
for You are with me.   —*Psalms 23:4*

One of the abiding mysteries of Begin's life is his decision to flee while
his parents and brother, and Aliza's twin sister, as well as some
90,000 members of Polish Betar under his leadership,[1] had nowhere to
run. It was a decision that would haunt him for the rest of his life, especially after most of Aliza's and his own family were murdered.

Leaving Poland was itself a perilous journey. The train that Menachem and Aliza took out of Warsaw was bombed repeatedly; dozens
died from the assault.[2] They were headed for Kovel, in Romania, but
the treacherous travel conditions and Aliza's asthma forced them to stop
in Lvov, where they acquired exit visas for Romania. The Begins then
headed north to Vilna, which was still a free city under Stalin's control,
accompanied by Betar comrades such as Nathan Friedman-Yellin. While
there, Begin received a letter from a Betar-Etzel organizer in Palestine
who accused Begin of having abandoned his Betar members. "When the
ship is sinking, the captain leaves *last*, not first!" it stated. Begin, stung
by the critique, suddenly changed his mind and sought to persuade his
entourage—though it is not clear how passionately—that the displaced
Betar group should go back to Poland. He was outvoted,[3] but the pain of
the rebuke would linger, and would color his actions for decades.

The free city of Vilna was hardly free for Jews. Soviet authorities tailed

Jews at every turn, arresting them without cause. Many of those arrested simply disappeared and were never heard from again. Everyone knew that the appearance of calm was an illusion; Menachem and Aliza had escaped the Nazis, but the city in which they now found themselves was not much less dangerous. They lived in a small house with a few friends and couples. Begin continued to lead Betar from his new refuge, setting up dormitories for displaced members, producing a newspaper, and giving political lectures, and he continued to pay salaries from Etzel funds. He organized a rally in July 1940 commemorating the eightieth anniversary of Theodor Herzl's birth, and acquired exit visas for fellow Betar members, insisting this time that he would not take his own until the rest of the group had left.[4]

On August 3, 1940, Jabotinsky, who had run himself ragged in the United States raising money and laboring tirelessly to save whatever was left of European Jewry, paid one of his regular visits to the Betar Camp in Hunter, New York. He had long been ailing, but had sworn his doctor (who had diagnosed angina pectoris) to secrecy. When Jabotinsky arrived at the camp, he barely had the strength to review the Betar Honor Guard that had been assembled in his honor, and slowly made his way to the room prepared for him. A doctor was summoned, but as a friend helped him undress, Jabotinsky whispered, "I am so tired, I am so tired."[5] Those were his last words.

The news deeply traumatized Begin. "I felt that the bearer of home was gone, never to return; and with him—perhaps never to return—hope itself," he later wrote.[6] Despite the dangers, just as his father, Ze'ev Dov, had helped organize a clandestine memorial service for Theodor Herzl in 1904, Menachem now held a secret memorial ceremony for the man who had been a father figure and childhood mentor, and who had provided the inspiration that would shape his life.[7]

Begin may have sensed that the Soviet noose was tightening. His rally commemorating the anniversary of Herzl's birth had been public, but the memorial ceremony for Jabotinsky was kept secret. The Municipality of Vilna had developed a peculiar way of arresting people; it issued them "invitations" to appear at the police station. Upon arriving at the station, the unsuspecting recipients of the invitations would promptly be sent off to jail, often never to be seen or heard from again. Begin knew that his invitation would eventually come; yet when it did, he simply ignored it. Detectives hovered around his house for weeks. Finally, in late September 1940, the NKVD, a precursor to the KGB, ran out of patience and arrested him for anti-Soviet and anti-Communist propaganda—that was how they portrayed his work for Betar.

When the detectives entered the house, he and Aliza offered them refreshment. Begin took time to polish his shoes, and to inform his wife that he had conceded his ongoing chess game with his friend Israel Scheib. He paused to grab some books to take with him to prison.[8]

Today, it is easy to forget that, despite his grace under pressure when he was arrested, Begin was well aware that most people arrested by the NKVD were never heard from again. He began his internment at Lukishki Prison, forced to sit on a chair in a corner for sixty hours, his knees pressed uncomfortably into the walls. Sleep became a treasured opportunity; more than once in prison he thought about the Talmudic dictum that a man who does not close an eye for three days will die.[9] His knowledge of Jewish texts continually provided him a framework for his suffering. When prisoners were given dirty spittoons instead of cups for their coffee, it was Ecclesiastes that came to his mind: "Man hath no preeminence above a beast."[10]

But prison, though a time of profound physical and emotional pain, was also a period of intellectual tempering and seemingly endless conversations. Begin spoke to his interrogator, his guards, his translators, and his cell mates. What he talked about more than anything was Zionism. Nearly half of *White Nights*—the book he wrote in 1951 looking back on his incarceration—recounts his sessions with Soviet interrogators, detailing "conversations" (more aptly, "interrogations") in which Begin vehemently denied the charge that Zionism constituted anti-Communist activity. He refused to deny that he was a Zionist, defending instead the Jewish national self-determination to which he had now committed his life. "In the course of these endless nights of interrogation I took part in wide-ranging debates on the Russian Revolution, on Britain and Zionism, on Herzl and Jabotinsky, on Weizmann's meetings with Mussolini," he later recalled.[11] "At times it was much more of a free discussion than an interrogation."

Despite his knowledge that he faced the possibility of a life sentence, Begin proved fearless in his interrogations. At one point, he even requested that the interrogator change the wording on his transcription of the meeting to erase "confess" and replace it with "admit." He *admitted* rather than *confessed* (which would imply guilt) for all four months of interrogations that he was the leader of Betar, but he insisted throughout that there was nothing at all criminal or anti-Soviet in the group's activities.

At the start of his imprisonment and interrogations, Begin asked for a translator. As luck would have it, Begin's translator proved to be a well-read, educated Jew deeply knowledgeable about Theodor Herzl and Zionism, who didn't balk at arguing with Begin. When the interpreter told Begin that "Zionism . . . is one big fraud," and its early leaders had no intention of creating a Jewish state, Begin was appalled. For the life of him, Begin could simply not fathom how a Jew could not be a Zionist, or how anyone might doubt Zionists' sincerity and their desire to create a state.[12] The interpreter, interrogator, and Begin had a three-way debate in which Begin defended Zionism and the two officers denounced it.[13] Begin did not budge from his position.

Indeed, he offered his interrogator what would become one of his best-known explanations and defenses of Zionism. As he recorded it in *White Nights*, he offered the "citizen-judge" the following analogy:

A fire breaks out in a house, and you happen to pass by. What do you do? Naturally, you hasten to telephone the fire brigade, but if you hear the voice of a woman or a child screaming in the flames, will you wait for the fire brigade to get there? Of course you won't.

You will try immediately to save the woman or child from the burn-
ing house. That was exactly our situation. Do you know what anti-
Semitism did to us? Our house was on fire, and in it our brothers
and our children were about to be burnt to death. Could we wait?
Let us suppose that the Revolution was a sort of fire brigade for the
Jews who were being persecuted by anti-Semitism in Poland or in
Germany, or in any other place; but we could not wait for it to come.
What if it came too late, as often happened with fire brigades? We
had to try and save them, and that is what Herzl did, that is what
Jabotinsky did, that is what we all did.[14]

His interrogator could not have known it, but the metaphor of a man
fleeing a burning house was a classic Talmudic sort of analogy. For Begin,
the manifest morality of the rabbinic tradition was no less obvious than
the legitimacy of the Zionist movement. He had no doubt of either the
justice of his cause or of its fundamental Jewish roots.

Begin also butted heads with a fellow prisoner, a Communist Jew named
Garin, formerly the assistant editor of *Pravda*, the Communist Party
newspaper. Garin, who was accused of Trotskyism,[15] argued that Zionism was actually not a form of anti-Communism, but of anti-Semitism.
Anti-Semitism and Zionism, he insisted, were both embodiments of a
"racialist, nationalistic prejudice."[16] Begin actually seemed to enjoy the
conversations with Garin; his new interlocutor at least knew something,
and there was nothing Begin liked to do more than to argue. More important, his conversations with Garin were a precursor to a lifelong claim
that nothing about passionate Jewish particularism or devotion to Jewish
nationalism was in any way in conflict with commitments to humanity
at large. He rejected absolutely the notion that these were incompatible
convictions.

Likewise, Begin never saw his Zionism as a substitute for Jewish faith;
it was, rather, an application of his faith. At one point, his interrogator insisted that an educated man cannot believe in God. Begin replied,
"Faith does not stand in contradiction to intelligence; but man, in his

intelligence, understands that there are things he cannot fathom by rationality, and so he believes in a Higher Power."[17] He was, and remained, a man of rock-solid faith. Like Zionism and humanism, his Zionism and his religiosity were inseparable; as far as he was concerned, neither made sense without the other.

Though he'd never been religiously punctilious, Begin made efforts to commemorate Jewish holidays while in prison. Despite the overwhelming hunger that ravaged all the prisoners, he surprised his two cell mates in October 1940 when he refused his daily portion of soup. It was Yom Kippur, the Day of Atonement, he explained to the confused prison guard, and he was fasting. His ravenous cell mates ate his portion.

The following spring, Begin and his friend Meir Sheskin held a makeshift Passover Seder in which they drank four cups of coffee, carefully rationed and saved, rather than the traditional four cups of wine. Begin would later recall: " 'This is the bread of affliction,' we intoned. And what affliction it was! . . . We lifted our voices in prayer, in supplication: 'This year we are slaves, next year may we be free men. This year we are here, may we next year be in Jerusalem.' "[18]

The Jewishness that made up his very core was made manifest not only in his conversations about God and his observance of holidays, but through his instinctive connection to other Jews, as well. Though he referred in *White Nights* to a certain sense of unity among all of the Polish and Soviet prisoners, especially while in the communal prison cells, he clearly felt a particular affinity to other Jews, even those, like Garin, who disagreed with him. Indeed, although he became friendly with non-Jewish prisoners, he did not refer to them by name in *White Nights;* those whom he named in the book were the Jewish prisoners.

Garin, a Communist, had been physically weak even before his imprisonment, and eventually turned to Begin, and through Begin to Judaism. He and Begin were aboard the *Etap*, a miserable ship with eight hundred prisoners but only two toilets, where lice covered everyone's bodies and stealing from other inmates was part of the fabric of life.[19] One day, Garin asked Begin to sing him the song "Loshuv" ("To Return"), by which he meant an early version of "Hativkah." Begin knew that Garin was ignorant about the anthem's history, but was struck that "nevertheless, embedded in his memory for more than thirty years were the first words of the line: 'To return to the land of our forefathers.' "[20]

For Begin, Garin's request spoke volumes about a deep-seated Jewish yearning that could not be extinguished. When the criminal prisoners witnessed their singing and asked what they were doing, someone responded, "They're praying." Begin recalled, "the *Urki* [criminal prisoners] were right. It was a prayer, not a song."[21]

"When the time comes," mused Begin years later, "after infinite trials and tribulations, what does the assistant editor of *Pravda*, General Secretary of the Ukrainian Communist Party, remind himself of? He reminds himself of *Loshuv* [return]. 'To return to the land of the fathers.' That is his consolation."[22] That, of course, was Begin's consolation, too. He could not then have possibly imagined the central role he would eventually play in making the dream of return a reality.

Even in the depths of the Soviet prison system, Begin was not entirely cut off from the outside world. Shortly after he was informed that he had been sentenced to eight years in a labor camp (which there was no reason to assume he would survive), Begin received packages from friends (ostensibly Betar members) with warm winter clothes.

He apparently knew that he could get documents out, as well. At one point during his incarceration, when he realized that he might well not survive his ordeal, he considered writing a traditional Jewish divorce document that would stipulate that should he fail to return in a specified number of years, Aliza would then be divorced and free to marry someone else. His prison companion Matvei Bernsztejn (whose daughter, Masha Leon, went on to become a well-known columnist for the *Forward*), persuaded him to abandon the idea. Once Aliza got the document, he convinced Begin, she would lose all hope. She deserved better.

Aliza, in fact, lost neither her hope nor the daring that it had taken to marry Begin or to flee with him. A few months later, Menachem received a handkerchief in prison, with "OLA" embroidered on it. At first, he had no idea what the letters meant, assuming that they might have been a reference to Aliza's nickname, Ala. It was Bernsztejn who ultimately solved the riddle for him. "OLA" was not a set of initials, he explained to Begin, but the Hebrew word *olah*, which means "immigrating to Israel."[23] Aliza was headed to Palestine to await her husband's return.

While he waited to be taken to a labor camp from prison, Begin was granted a visitor. He had requested to see Aliza, but in her place came a similar-looking Betar girl named Paula. Paula had posed as Aliza in order to give him a message. In carefully worded conversation, Paula let Begin know that Aliza and their friends had successfully arrived in Palestine. Paula also gave Begin a bar of soap. The prison guards cut it in half to inspect it for messages, but found nothing. Begin, more thorough, found a note. It was from a friend, informing him that officials in the United States and the Jewish community of Palestine were working to secure his release.

Paula later died while fighting the Nazis in Vilna, and the plan to advance Begin's freedom came to naught. But when Germany invaded the USSR in June 1941, the Soviet Union and Poland reestablished an alliance that included the liberation of Polish prisoners kept in the Soviet Union. Begin was set free from his labor camp in September 1941,[24] and spent months wandering through south Russia and Central Asia. He eventually found his way to his sister, Rachel Halperin, and her husband near the Afghan border and stayed with them for several months.

It was Yochanan Bader, later to become a member of the Knesset in Israel's first eight governments, who suggested to Begin that he join the Free Polish Army. "I doubt whether in all his judicial and public career he ever gave anyone a better piece of advice," Begin later commented.[25] With General Wladyslaw Anders's Army, which was dedicated to fighting the Germans, Begin traveled through Central Asia, moving south through Persia into Iraq, hoping all the while to make it to Palestine to serve under David Raziel, commander of the Etzel (who died west of Baghdad on assignment for the British).[26] But Begin did reach the Land of Israel, at least.

The military convoy stopped. We rested. I left the automobile, waded a little into the grass, and drank in the odor of the fields of my Homeland. "Good to be home, eh?" It was one of the soldiers, not a Jew, at my side.[27]

Three years earlier, Begin had married Aliza wearing a Betar uniform, with Jabotinsky at their side. Now, in the spring of 1942, Jabotinsky was dead and European Jewry was being eradicated. But Aliza was alive, and Menachem, wearing the uniform of the Free Polish Army, had arrived in Palestine.[28] He was twenty-nine years old and, for the first time in his life, felt he was home.

4

We Fight Therefore We Are

> Thus they spread calumnies among the Israelites about the land
>   they had scouted, saying,
> "The country that we traversed and scouted is one that devours
>   its inhabitants."   —*Numbers 13:32*

Begin arrived in Palestine in April or May 1942.[1] A year later, he had still not heard from his parents or brother, so he did what many other survivors of the war did. He went to the Zionist Information Office in Jerusalem, where Jews whose families had stayed behind in Europe could seek help in locating their missing relatives. The form that Begin completed still exists; it lists his father's age (he was seventy-four; Begin wrote seventy-five), his mother's name, and the names of their son Herzl and young grandson (Begin's brother and nephew).[2] But it was all for naught;[3] four years later, shortly after the establishment of the Israeli state, Begin learned what had happened to them from a former resident of Brisk, whom he met on a trip to the United States:

> Five hundred Jews were led one day to the banks of the Bug River near Brisk, *ir va-eim be-yisrael* (a mother city of the Jewish people). My father was among them. He started to sing the "song of faith" on the way: "I believe with unbroken faith in the coming of the Messiah." He also called on the [others] to sing "Hatikvah." Everybody sang. The Germans pushed them into the river and opened fire on

them. The Bug River reddened from the blood of Jews. My father and teacher, my elderly father, was with them. My mother was hidden in the hospital by a doctor-friend, who was [the hospital's] director. One day all the sick were taken from their bed and slaughtered. My mother was among them. Oyya Li.[4] *Yitgadal ve-yitkadash shemei Rabbah.*[5]

The Nazis had erased virtually his entire family. What had happened to his father and brother, and then to his mother, no less than the ideas of the Herzl for whom his brother had been named, would shape virtually everything he would do for the rest of his life.

B y the time Begin arrived in Palestine in 1942, the *yishuv* was already a complicated affair. The League of Nations had given quasi-governmental authority to the Jewish Agency, which was headed by Ben-Gurion. But the Agency, which was expected to cooperate with the British in implementing the Mandate, was thus forced to play a dual and often contradictory role—cooperating with the British while simultaneously seeking to establish a "Jewish national home."

No less complicated was the Jewish paramilitary complex. By the early 1940s, there were three different Jewish military groups in Palestine, each with its own agenda. The Haganah had been founded in 1920 as a spin-off of Jabotinsky's Jewish Legion, designed to protect Jewish settlements from Arab raids until the arrival of the Mandatory police. Although not officially recognized by the British, the Haganah saw its role as supplementing the protection offered by the British troops rather than as being a stand-alone Jewish militia with its own aims and agenda. Though there was some disagreement among Haganah members on the subject, the prevailing view held that the organization existed to protect Jewish people and property, not to pursue political aspirations.[6]

Under Ben-Gurion, the Haganah practiced a policy of restraint (*havlagah*) in response to Arab violence, particularly during what became known as the Arab Revolt of 1936–39. The Haganah generally maintained alliances with the British authorities and shied away from taking the offensive in military operations. The Haganah, though, did play a critical role in aiding and abetting illegal Jewish immigration to Palestine.

The second group in the Jewish paramilitary complex was the Etzel, founded with Jabotinsky's encouragement and under his informal leadership, when nonsocialist members of the Haganah split to create their own defense organization; in 1936, Jabotinsky finally officially accepted overall leadership of the organization.[7] Many members of the Betar youth movement in Palestine were also members of the Etzel. The Etzel's motto was *Rak Kach*, or "Only Thus," and its logo was a clenched fist raised in defiance; only through armed struggle would the Jews win their independence. During the 1936–39 Arab Revolt's increasingly frequent Arab attacks on Jewish settlements, the Haganah continued to espouse a policy of restraint, but some members of the Etzel decided that the time had come to strike back; for the most part, though, they maintained Jabotinsky's policy of avoiding civilian casualties.

A third, more hard-line group, the Lechi, would be created in 1940.

Ironically, though the Free Polish Army had brought Begin to Palestine, he was not yet technically free. He had made a commitment to Anders's Army, and refused to desert. "A deserter from whatever army is still a deserter," he declared, "and any man who deserted an army that was fighting Hitler could under no circumstances stand at the head of a national militia."[8] Begin thus spent close to two years in Palestine working for Anders's Army, all the while building relations with the Etzel and with the Betar cells there.

Betar and Etzel members regularly sought his advice. Soviet prison had clearly done nothing to extinguish the charisma that drew people to him; this was the same Menachem Begin who had quickly risen up the ranks of Polish Betar. Indeed, four months after his arrival in Palestine, probably simply because he was a Revisionist and an unabashed disciple of Jabotinsky, the Haganah intelligence services considered Begin a sufficiently significant player to have him tailed, and they opened a secret folder recording his activities.[9]

As Begin quickly began to make his mark, the same issues that had once animated his disagreements with Jabotinsky rose to the fore once again. The question of whether to cooperate with the British or to oppose them remained a complex matter for the entire *yishuv*. In 1936, largely in response to the ongoing Arab Revolt, which threatened to upend any semblance of law and order in the Mandate, the British appointed the Palestine Royal Commission, more commonly known as the Peel Commission, to investigate possible solutions to the uprising and the underlying tensions between the Jewish and Arab populations. When its report was published in 1937, the Peel Commission recommended that Mandatory Palestine be partitioned into a Jewish and an Arab state. By and large, the territory was to be divided by population; sections with predominantly Arab populations were to be given to the Arab state, while those with a Jewish concentration would go to the Jewish state.

Twenty years earlier, in 1917, the Balfour Declaration had stated, "His Majesty's government view with favor the establishment in Palestine of a national home for the Jewish people." The Peel Commission's recommendation, like several other British position papers that had been issued in the interim, was thus an affirmation of that long-standing policy. But in order to placate the Arab population, Peel also recommended limiting Jewish immigration to 12,000 immigrants per year over five years, at precisely a moment in which it was clear that the danger to European Jewry was growing and that those who were willing to flee would need a refuge.[10] The Peel Commission's limitation on Jewish immigration essentially condemned even those Jews who might have escaped the Nazis to death. And to make matters even worse, limiting Jewish immigration would also forestall progress toward the establishment of a genuinely viable Jewish state.

In what was to become an ongoing pattern, the Arab community rejected the Peel Commission report out of hand, refusing to even discuss it. In the Jewish community, the proposal was highly controversial as well. Contrary to what is commonly heard in today's discussions of Israel's prospective borders, one did not have to be a Revisionist to believe that the natural borders of the Jewish state should echo the borders of the biblical one. The Zionist establishment saw the Peel Commission proposal, which put forth an essentially nonviable Jewish state, as a capitulation to Arab violence and, in essence, a substantial curtailment of the promise of the Balfour Declaration; nevertheless, the Twentieth Zionist Congress ultimately voted to accept the principle of partition while rejecting the specific borders suggested by the Peel Commission.

The British were hardly finished backtracking from the commitments of the Balfour Declaration, however. Especially in a time of war, the British simply could not afford to lose Arab cooperation and the access that cooperation provided to the oil that flowed from Iraq to Haifa. Therefore, in 1939, even as centuries of European anti-Semitism morphed into outright genocide, Great Britain issued the "Macdonald White Paper," in which "His Majesty's Government therefore now declare unequivocally that it is not part of their policy that Palestine should become a Jewish State,"[11] in effect reneging on Balfour's promise.

If the Peel Commission had made a sovereign Jewish state unattainable by limiting immigration and envisioning borders that would be unsustainable, the White Paper now undid the very commitments to Jewish national sovereignty that had been reflected in both the Balfour Declaration and the Peel Commission's report. The White Paper thus put the Etzel in a torturous position. Should they continue fighting the British, who were now opposed to the state the Zionists so desperately sought to create? Or should they join forces with the British in fighting Nazi Germany and its allies, since whatever indirect harm the British policies were inflicting upon Jews, a Nazi victory in Europe would surely be worse?

Ultimately, the Etzel decided to accede to Ben-Gurion's suggestion that the Jews "fight the White Paper as if there was no war and fight the war as if there were no White Paper."[12] They collaborated with the Haganah in organizing and facilitating illegal immigration to Palestine in defiance of the British, but cooperated with the British in the struggle against the Third Reich. The Etzel maintained that the *yishuv* should not fight the British if such a fight would hinder British efforts to defeat the Third Reich.

This stance, among other reasons, caused several of the Etzel's members to break away and form their own Jewish militant group. The Lechi, or "Stern Gang," named after its founder, Abraham (Ya'ir) Stern, was smaller and more extreme than the Haganah and Etzel. The Lechi saw Great Britain as the real enemy, since it was the British who were occupying Palestine. The Lechi, therefore, also targeted British officials and diplomats rather than just institutions. They were also much less committed to avoiding civilian deaths than the Etzel.[13] After Stern's death in 1942, Yitzhak Yezernitzky, along with Yisrael (Eldad) Scheib and Nathan Friedman-Yellin, two of Begin's friends from Poland who had accompanied him to Vilna, assumed leadership of the group. Yezernitzky later Hebraized his name to Yitzhak Shamir, and eventually became Israel's seventh prime minister.

B egin had never shared the prevailing Jewish gratitude to the British Empire for the Balfour Declaration. In 1943, awaiting news of his parents—who like millions of European Jews had been barred by the British from finding sanctuary in Palestine—he was more convinced than ever that if the Jews were intent on creating their own sovereign state in their ancestral homeland, there would be no choice but to treat the British as the enemies that they were. Given what was unfolding in Europe, the Jews, more than ever before, needed a country of their own; and the British—who were preventing homeless Jews from entering Palestine and were thus complicit in the ongoing deaths of thousands of Jews—would depart Palestine only if staying became too costly and painful.

Toward the end of 1942, Yechiel Kadishai, who would one day become Begin's personal secretary, was serving in the British Army. Stationed in Ismailia, he was given a furlough of several days and returned to Tel Aviv.

There, the *yishuv* was receiving the first incontrovertible indications that Hitler was exterminating Polish Jewry. Kadishai attended a meeting with other young Jewish men to discuss what could be done.

In the middle of the meeting, Kadishai recalled, a man in his late twenties, wearing the short pants uniform of Anders's Polish Army and glasses with small, round frames, entered the room and sat quietly at the side. In the middle of the discussion, the late arrival spoke up and said that there was only one thing that Jews in Palestine could do to save Polish Jewry; they had to attack the British until they allowed Jews to enter Palestine. As long as Jews knew that they had nowhere to go, there was no impetus for them to flee Poland, the latecomer said. Hitler had not yet gotten to Hungarian or Romanian Jewry, and they could certainly be saved. Even part of Polish Jewry would manage to flee, if only they knew that they had somewhere to go.

The meeting ended inconclusively, but as they were departing, Kadishai—who had been struck by the audacity of the man who'd joined the meeting late—asked a friend who it was who had spoken up about the British. "He was the head of Betar in Poland," Kadishai's friend told him. "He was imprisoned by the Soviets, and eventually made his way here. His name is Begin."[4]

It was not exactly a meeting, but it was an encounter that the young, quick-witted, and affable Kadishai would never forget. Kadishai, who was wearing a British uniform but had spent virtually his entire life in Palestine, and Begin, the newcomer in the uniform of the Polish Army, shared a world of commitments.[5]

I t took very little time after Begin's arrival in Palestine for the members of the Etzel to decide that he was the right person to lead the organization. In some ways, Begin was a surprising choice, and not everyone was in favor. He was, and would remain, a cultural outsider in significant ways. His stint in the Polish Army notwithstanding, he had never been in battle and did not think of himself as a "real" soldier. He retained the ethos of an immigrant, wearing a battered suit in a land in which muscular, suntanned, shorts-wearing Jews were emerging. Unlike Ben-Gurion (Grün), Levi Eshkol (Shkolnik), or Yitzhak Shamir (Yezernitzky), he saw no reason to Hebraize his name or to push a plow so he could claim that he, too, had helped build the land. He was who he was, and was not at all uncomfortable being the outsider.

Those who wanted Begin to head the Etzel prevailed;[16] Ya'akov Meridor, who as second-in-command had reluctantly assumed leadership of the Etzel after David Raziel's death in Iraq, wholeheartedly encouraged Begin to take over. On December 31, 1943, Begin was given a twelve-month leave from the Free Polish Army, and on January 26, 1944, he received his official letter of temporary discharge.[17] On that very same day Begin officially announced his acceptance of the post of commander of the Etzel.

A mere five days after Begin's announcement, on February 1, 1944, Begin and the Etzel announced their armed struggle against the British in Palestine:

> We are nearing the final stage of the war. We are facing a decision that will change the fates of generations to come. The cease-fire announced at the beginning of World War II has been broken by the British. The rulers of our land did not take loyalty, concessions, or sacrifices into account; they have fulfilled and are still moving forward with their plan; the elimination of national Zionism . . . We shall draw our conclusions fearlessly . . . No more cease-fire in the land of Israel between the people and the Hebrew youth and the British administration, which hands over our brothers to Hitler.[18]

The decision to cooperate with the British during the war had been taken before the knowledge of the full horror of the Nazi genocide had reached Israel; now that "the blood of our people cried out to us from the foreign soil on which it had been shed,"[19] and the British continued to keep Palestine's gates shut, Begin felt that the time had come to break the alliance. "Had we anything to lose?"[20]

Begin instantaneously became an outlaw and was forced to go underground in order to avoid arrest by the British, who eventually declared him Terrorist No. 1 and offered a bounty of £10,000 for his capture. He directed the affairs of the Etzel from a secret house with his wife, Aliza, and their young son, Benny, who had been born a year earlier. In the Chassidoff quarter of Petach Tikvah, Begin first masqueraded as a bookish law student, and then assumed the identity of Rabbi Sassover. He moved his family to a dilapidated street in Tel Aviv, participating in weekly Talmud lessons and attending daily prayer services. Begin's command of traditional Jewish sources was so impressive that he could offer comments on biblical and Talmudic passages to taxi drivers and others while in this disguise. In some ways, Rabbi Sassover was a fitting alter ego. A Sassover, just like Begin, would see the Bible as the legitimate "deed" to the land of Israel; this was in some way the sort of persona who was unabashed about his love for an ancient Jewish way of life, and who, in the form of Rabbi Zvi Yehuda Kook (the son of the chief rabbi of Palestine, Avraham Yitzhak Kook), would inspire the Gush Emunim settler movement many years later. It was during the period that Begin assumed the persona of Rabbi Sassover that his and Aliza's second child, Chasia, was born and named after Begin's mother. The little synagogue he attended joyfully celebrated the birth of "Rabbi Sassover's daughter."

When the Tel Aviv neighborhood in which he was hiding as Rabbi Sassover became too dangerous and the risks that the British would find him seemed too great, Begin assumed the identity of someone whose passport he had found abandoned in a library. He became Dr. Yonah Koenigshoffer, residing in the heart of Tel Aviv; at that time, their third child, Leah, was born. She was named after Aliza's twin sister, who had perished in the Holocaust. Begin would later recall that when "Rabbi Sassover" shaved his beard to become "Dr. Koenigshoffer," his son Benny didn't recognize his clean-shaven father.[21] All told, Begin was underground for just over four years, from February 1944 through April 1948, from the resumption of the Etzel's armed struggle against the British until just shy of Israeli independence.

The Etzel's primary goal in the revolt was to make the price of remaining in Palestine untenably high for the British. It was also designed to undermine one of Britain's primary justifications for its continued presence in Palestine; for quite some time, the British had argued that the Jews of the *yishuv* needed protection from the Arabs, which only the British could provide. For Begin, the revolt was an opportunity to demonstrate that the Jews were capable of defending themselves. To strike at the core of the perception of British legitimacy over Palestine, the Etzel did not need to appear stronger than the British—it just needed to prove itself capable of flustering the British and of shaking the international community's confidence that the British could administer the Mandate.

In November 1944, the Lechi, more extreme than Begin's Etzel, imperiled the entire Zionist enterprise when two of its militants assassinated Lord Moyne, the British resident minister of state in Cairo, responsible for administering all British possessions in the Middle East. The Lechi, which operated small cells of no more than nine men so that captured fighters would not be able to reveal the identities of more than a few comrades, sent two men to Cairo to kill Moyne. The two, Eliyahu Hakim and Eliyahu bet Tzuri, who became known as the "two Eliyahus," had never met before arriving in Cairo. On bicycles, they followed Moyne for days, and ultimately shot him and a bodyguard at his home. They were sentenced to death for the assassination. They refused lawyers, and demanded—though they knew the request would not be honored—that they be tried by an international court, since the "crime" was a response to the British murderous refusal to allow Jews to escape Europe to Palestine. They were hanged in March 1945.[22]

The executions did not assuage Britain's fury. Even the reasonably pro-Zionist Winston Churchill, who had consistently distanced himself from the policy formulated in the White Paper,[23] warned:

> If our dreams for Zionism are to end in the smoke of assassins' pistols and our labors for its future to produce only a new set of gangsters

worthy of Nazi Germany, many like myself will have to reconsider the position we have maintained so consistently in the past.[24]

The *yishuv* leadership condemned Moyne's killing;[25] even the Etzel leadership admitted that the killing had set back the Zionist struggle, and it disassociated itself from the assassination.[26] Particularly telling was the fact that Begin did not issue an immediate call to avenge the hanging of the two Eliyahus, a call that he would make when other Jews were hanged by the British.

But neither Begin nor the Etzel would escape the repercussions of the assassination. The British saw the Lechi's assassination of Moyne as an opportunity to destroy the Jewish underground; so, too, perhaps, did the *yishuv* leaders, some of whom still believed that British sympathy and goodwill were indispensable for the establishment of a Jewish state. Now, Ben-Gurion and other leaders of the *yishuv* believed, they had an opportunity to do in both the Etzel and the Lechi.

Ben-Gurion and the Haganah unleashed the *Saison*, or "hunting season." For four months, from November 1944 until March 1945, Haganah forces or Haganah-informed British forces arrested Etzel and Lechi militants, confiscating their weapons and sabotaging their operations.[27] Jews were turning in other Jews—a situation that Begin found horrifyingly shameful. The *Saison* paralyzed the Etzel,[28] but Begin neither called off the revolt nor took action against the Haganah:

> We examined [the situation] from the viewpoint of the whole of Jewry. The extermination of Jews in Europe was in full swing. The gates of the Holy Land were barred to any who sought sanctuary. Where then was the political change that could justify the cessation of our struggle? . . . We decided not to suspend, nor to promise to suspend, our struggle against British rule; yet at the same time we declined to retaliate for the kidnappings, the denunciations and the handing over of our men . . . We said there would be no civil war but, in fact, throughout the whole country a one-sided civil war raged.[29]

It would not be the last time that Begin would play a central role in preventing civil war despite Ben-Gurion's obvious desire to destroy him.

Begin's insistence that the Etzel not respond to the Haganah's *Saison* was a reflection of his unique ability to couple his passionate tribalism (his belief in the importance of the Jewish people and his commitment to Jewish political sovereignty) with a deep-seated humanism for which he was never fully given credit. He was, and would remain, a moderate, whose reputation was often tarnished by those on the extremes, to either side of him. The Lechi acted alone because Begin insisted on limiting the fight against the British to targets in what would become the Jewish state; Labor Zionists and their Haganah branch hoped that they could placate the British by turning against Begin. It would take Begin decades to break Labor's stranglehold on Zionist politics and power, yet when he did, it was he—not Ben-Gurion—who would be characterized as the antidemocrat.

Begin would later say that if he were to be remembered for anything, it would be for avoiding civil war between Jews. The *Saison* was the first time that Begin's ongoing commitment to "Civil War—Never!" was put to the test. As would be the case in the future, he more than passed.

It was largely a shift in British political fortunes that brought about a rapprochement between the various Jewish groups. In July 1945, Clement Attlee's Labour Party won in a landslide victory, defeating Churchill. Churchill had been a steady friend to the Zionists and had denounced the 1939 White Paper; Attlee, on the other hand, quickly appointed Ernest Bevin, an unabashed anti-Zionist who favored establishing a single binational state of Jews and Arabs over the entire Mandate.[30]

Immigration quickly became *the* critical issue. The White Paper's immigration quota of 75,000 had been nearly exhausted, and Britain's new leadership seemed unlikely to open the gates of their Mandate to additional Jewish immigration anytime soon, despite the mass of refugees waiting in European DP camps, desperate for permission to enter Palestine. If the Jews did not band together, they would fail. In October 1945, the Haganah, Etzel, and Lechi signed an agreement to coordinate their activities against the British, with the Etzel and Lechi agreeing to operate under the Haganah leadership.[31] The three groups would collectively decide on and coordinate attacks and operations under the direction of "Committee X"; not surprisingly, however, the Haganah (and by extension, Ben-Gurion and the Jewish Agency) was to have veto power. Rather than attack any individual British soldier or politician, the intent was to attack critical strategic points, destroying the infrastructure and symbols of power that legitimated the British Mandate. The Haganah, though it would certainly not have characterized matters that way, was absorbing Begin's philosophy.

This period of coordination, known in Hebrew as *Tnu'at Ha-Mered Ha-Ivri*—the United Resistance Movement—yielded some of the Zionists' most successful sabotage operations. During "The Night of the Railways," for instance, the Palmach (the Haganah's elite fighting force) blew up railways used by the British to move troops and supplies in no fewer than 153 different places, while the Etzel and Lechi together blew up the central train station in Lod.

On the night of June 16 and 17, 1946, the Palmach staged eleven coordinated attacks on eleven different bridges across Palestine. All the bridges were on Palestine's borders or near ports and were thus critical to the British ability to move goods and men between the Mandate and the world beyond its borders. Ten of the eleven bridges were successfully destroyed.[32] The operation cost the British Mandate more than £4 million, an astronomical sum at that time.

The British had no alternative but to strike back, and hard. Since the operation had been executed by the Palmach, the British decided to retaliate against the Haganah and the leadership of the *yishuv*. Nothing short of that would restore order in Palestine and reestablish a semblance of legitimacy for the Mandate.[33]

Their response came in the form of Operation Agatha, known in Hebrew as *Ha-Shabbat Ha-Shkhora* ("The Black Sabbath"),[34] which took place on

June 29, 1946. The main Jewish cities—Jerusalem, Tel Aviv, Ramat Gan, Haifa, and Netanya—were placed under lockdown. Some 17,000 British soldiers were dispatched in those cities and throughout thirty more Jewish villages and *kibbutzim* to arrest perceived troublemakers, confiscate weapon caches, and locate incriminating documents.

The British operation was highly successful. British soldiers arrested approximately 2,700 men, including prominent leaders of the *yishuv* such as Moshe Sharett (who would serve as Israel's second prime minister) and David Remez (a future minister in Ben-Gurion's governments), and confiscated numerous weapons. Some of the documents confiscated by the British during Operation Agatha confirmed the existence of a direct link between the official *yishuv* leadership and the unified revolt; among the documents that the British recovered was the actual agreement signed by the leadership of the Haganah, Etzel, and Lechi, as well as cables that confirmed the Jewish Agency's role in the leadership of the United Resistance Movement.[35]

Word reached the *yishuv* leadership that many of those documents were being stored at what was essentially the headquarters of British Mandatory Palestine—the iconic King David Hotel. The *yishuv* was relatively certain that the British had sufficient documents in storage at the hotel to arrest, and possibly execute, a number of leaders of the *yishuv*, including Golda Meir.[36] In retaliation for the British crackdown, and in order to destroy the incriminating evidence, Begin's Etzel proposed staging an attack on the hotel. On July 1, 1946, Moshe Sneh, then head of the Haganah, sent Menachem Begin a secret note authorizing the bombing of the King David.[37] The operation, it was agreed, would be carried out by the Etzel.[38]

The King David Hotel had served as the British Mandate's military and administrative headquarters since 1938, although a third of the rooms continued to be used as guest accommodations. The Etzel had considered an attack on the King David as early as 1945, even prior to the

United Resistance Movement.[39] Amichai Paglin, chief operations officer of the Etzel, known by his code name, "Gidi," had even buried six complicated truck-mounted bombs of his own making near the olive groves south of the King David, hoping to detonate them on the king's birthday; the Haganah had learned of the plot, however, and the Jewish Agency had informed the British.[40]

This time, Moshe Sneh conceived of the plan as part of a double attack: the Etzel would blow up the King David Hotel, and the Lechi would bomb the adjacent David Brothers Building, which housed the Palestine Information Office. After Operation Agatha, the symbolic value of attacking the King David Hotel took on greater magnitude. Sneh argued: "They attacked our government body and sought to paralyze it; we will attack and paralyze their government bodies."[41]

Prior to the United Resistance Movement, the Haganah had opened their radio addresses with the biblical injunction "Thou shall not kill," a not so subtle rebuke of the Etzel's terrorist methods. The Etzel radio station responded by quoting another biblical passage: "Life for life, eye for eye, tooth for tooth, hand for hand, foot for foot, burning for burning, wound for wound, stripe for stripe."[42] Now, the head of the Haganah, the mastermind of the *Saison*, had come around to the Etzel point of view, and the Haganah high command unanimously approved the operation.

"Committee X," in charge of all United Resistance Movement operations, narrowly approved the operation by a vote of three to two.[43] When Begin received the official authorization from Sneh, he quickly mobilized his men.

Paglin planned the attack; he had joined the Etzel in 1943 and had become its chief of operations after Yerucham "Eitan" Livni, the first man to fill the post, and father of the Israeli politician Tzipi Livni, was captured. Begin left Paglin to work out the specifics. Paglin briefed Begin as the plans crystallized, assuring Begin that "every possible precaution" had been taken to avoid needless casualties.[44] The Etzel men who would eventually carry out the attack began staking out the hotel. One spent evenings strolling through the hotel grounds arm in arm with Yael, an

Etzel woman named after a biblical heroine from the book of Judges who helped save the Israelites by seducing and then driving a spike through the head of an enemy general. Two other Etzel women accompanied the men to the hotel's underground bar; after a night of dancing and drinking champagne, they reported that the entire south wing appeared to be supported by the nightclub's four concrete pillars.[45]

The King David Hotel received its milk from Jewish and Arab suppliers, and so the Etzel fighters planned to dress up as milkmen and place the 350 kilograms of TNT in the huge milk jugs they would bring into the hotel. Once inside, the men would place them in strategic locations and ignite the detonating mechanism.

Throughout Begin's tenure as Etzel commander, he had demanded that his commanders avoid civilian deaths. It was the legacy of Jabotinsky, who had first introduced preemptive action in Palestine while strategically avoiding civilian deaths. As many Jewish, Arab, and British civilians worked in the building alongside British soldiers, the Etzel planned to make a warning call sufficiently in advance to allow for a complete evacuation of the building before the detonation. Paglin suggested a forty-five-minute warning; Sneh objected that forty-five minutes was too long, that in that time the British could "save documents as well as people." Paglin and Sneh agreed on a compromise: half an hour. In addition, the explosives-filled milk containers were to be accompanied with a warning in English, Arabic, and Hebrew.[46]

Planning for the attack continued apace. It was initially scheduled for July 19, but on July 17, the Haganah's Sneh, without providing a reason, urged Begin to delay the strike, and Begin reluctantly agreed. Unbeknownst to the Etzel, Chaim Weizmann had threatened Sneh that he would publically resign as president of the World Zionist Organization, a move which would surely split the *yishuv*, if Sneh did not do everything in his power to stop the United Resistance Movement operations, or at the very least rein in the Haganah. Committee X voted three to two to reverse its earlier decision and to cancel the previously approved attacks. Sneh resigned as Haganah commander.[47]

Hiding in Tel Aviv, however, Begin became convinced that the Haganah's leaders were nothing more than cowards who were ultimately unwilling to fight for a Jewish state. Two days later, on July 19, the day initially chosen for the attack, Sneh, whose resignation had apparently not appreciably altered his role, again asked for a delay, once again with no explanation. He hoped to fly to Paris to meet with Ben-Gurion and to convince him to overrule Weizmann; then, with Ben-Gurion's blessing, they could proceed with the operation without tearing the *yishuv* apart.

Begin, again unaware of Committee X or of Sneh's political considerations, agreed to one last delay. He had pledged to coordinate the Etzel's attacks with those of the other two underground groups and to abide by the Haganah's leadership; as long as he could, he would honor his pledge. Yet he also knew that too many people were in on the plan, and every day that went by increased the chances of British detection and disastrous failure. Begin gave Sneh three days, and called the operation for July 22. When Sneh asked for yet another delay, Begin did not even bother to respond.[48]

Begin ignored yet another such plea by Sneh on the morning of the attack,[49] despite the fact that under the agreement of the United Resistance Movement, the Haganah had been given veto power over any suggested operation.[50] No longer would he permit what he saw as the Haganah's cowardice to delay a plan on which the Irgun had been working for months.[51] The Lechi had also ignored Sneh's final appeal and was planning to bomb the David Brothers Building, three minutes after the explosion of the King David Hotel.[52]

The seven milk jugs were filled with explosives, and the mechanism was set to detonate thirty-five minutes later.[53] The Lechi, however, was not ready for its part of the operation. It requested a delay, but Paglin refused. The Lechi canceled its attack; the Etzel was now alone.[54]

"Father Antippa," the elderly Greek who supervised the typists in the King David Hotel, received a warning call; he sent a policeman to the basement but found nothing.[55] The attack had been delayed by one hour due to a delay in delivering the explosives; it is possible that that first warning call came too early.

The fuses were set at 12:13 to explode thirty minutes later. Two bombs that had been designed to explode on Julian's Way, adjacent to the hotel, which would have cut the King David off from the rest of Jerusalem, failed. They detonated, but did not ignite containers filled with kerosene that had been placed nearby. Nonetheless, they attracted enough attention that the air sirens went off. Many of those in the King David took the sirens to mean that the worst was over, that the British were now in control of the situation.[56]

At 12:22, twenty minutes before the bombs were set to detonate, Adina, an Etzel courier, called the King David: "The building is going to blow up. You must evacuate immediately. You have been warned." She relayed the message in Hebrew and in English and hung up. The assistant manager transferred the call to a British officer who, jaded by the almost daily bomb threats the hotel received, dismissed the warning.

At 12:27, Adina called the French Consulate, housed next to the King David; she told them she had warned the hotel and suggested in French and Hebrew that they open their windows so as not to be harmed by the blast. They did as they were told. At 12:31, Adina called *The Palestine Post*, tipping them off and asking them to warn the hotel again.

At 12:37 p.m., six minutes before scheduled, the explosives detonated, creating a blast equivalent in pressure to a direct hit by a 500-kilogram aerial bomb.[57] Many occupants died immediately, dozens more were buried under the rubble. The death toll estimate mounted by the hour.

A distraught Begin followed the aftermath on the BBC, listening to the radio from his secret apartment in Tel Aviv. The BBC began to play a funeral march and Begin became increasingly agitated; Chaim Landau, the Etzel member sitting with Begin at the time, became so worried about Begin's frame of mind that he pulled a tube out of the radio, silencing it.[58]

Paglin told Begin that everything had gone according to the plan, but the British had refused to evacuate the building. Begin told him:

"I understand that the casualties were out of your control. You should not blame yourself. We all share responsibility."[59] Both in the *yishuv* and among the Etzel, Begin assumed full responsibility for the attack and the heavy human cost. In public, however, he released a statement unequivocally blaming the British for the horrific casualty count. Speaking in biblical terms of "Hebrew soldiers" and "self-sacrifice," he insisted that

> the tragedy, that took place in the civil offices of the occupying government, was not caused by Hebrew soldiers who fulfilled their role with strength and self-sacrifice, and followed carefully the instructions given to them regarding the time frame necessary to wait to allow for an evacuation of the building from civilians; it was caused by the British exploiters themselves who did not heed the warning and did not evacuate the building on the orders of their military "experts" who took it upon themselves to remove the explosive devices even though the slightest touch to those explosives would have caused them to detonate. But against this touch [of the explosives] were put large warning signs in three languages . . . Therefore the responsibility for the loss of civilian lives falls on them (the British) and only on them.[60]

Ninety-two people died as a result of the attack. Twenty-eight were British, forty-two were Arabs, and seventeen were Jews, including one of the Irgun militants carrying out the operation. The dead also included two Armenians, one Russian, and one Greek.

The attack fueled the fires of British hatred for the Zionists. Newspapers in both Great Britain and the United States warned that the bombing had set the Zionist cause back significantly, since it would erode any incentive that the British might have had for compromising with the Jewish authorities. Recognizing that danger, the Jewish Agency denounced the act as a "dastardly crime perpetrated by a gang of desperadoes,"[61] avoiding any mention of the fact that the *yishuv*'s leadership had known of the attack and had originally approved it. The King David bombing spelled the end of the United Resistance Movement.

Under fire, Ben-Gurion and the Haganah denied any involvement. Begin assumed full responsibility, an astonishing display of nobility given Ben-Gurion's obvious mendacity. The Haganah, Etzel, and Lechi had all agreed that after the Black Sabbath, British rule needed to be upended and their tactics needed to change. When the plot went awry, however, it was Begin who was left to take the fall.

The Mandate would end long before Begin would shake the accusation that he was nothing more than a terrorist. But Begin never apologized for his use of force. As he would write later:

A revolution, or a revolutionary war, does not aim at instilling fear. Its object is to overthrow a regime and to set up a new regime in its place. In a revolutionary war, both sides use force. Tyranny is armed. Otherwise it would be liquidated overnight. Fighters for freedom must arm; otherwise they would be crushed overnight.[62]

Just seven months after the King David bombing, in February 1947, the British announced their intention to depart Palestine. Nine months after that, the United Nations voted to create a Jewish state. And in May 1948, less than two years after the bomb-laden milk canisters exploded and demolished a wing of the very symbol of British presence in Palestine, the Union Jack was lowered, the last British soldiers set sail from Palestine, and the Jewish state was born.

5

A Brutal Act

So they hanged Haman on the tree that he had prepared for
Mordecai.   —*Esther 7:10*

At the height of the 1936–1939 Arab Revolt, Palestinian Arabs had
ambushed a taxi, then raped and cut up the body of one of the female
Jewish passengers. The British never arrested anyone for the attack.

Shlomo Ben Yosef had had enough. He and two Betar members, Shalom
Zurabin and Avraham Shein, found an old revolver and a grenade. On
April 21, 1938, acting on their own, the three ambushed an Arab passenger
bus driving from Safed to Rosh Pina.[1] The grenade failed to explode and
their gunshot missed the mark. No one was harmed, and the bus with its
terrified passengers drove on. But the British sentenced Ben Yosef and
Shein to death. Zurabin was determined to be "mentally unbalanced,"
while Shein, who was under eighteen, eventually got his sentence com-
muted to life imprisonment.[2]

With regard to Ben Yosef, however, the British were determined. They
ignored pleas from the *yishuv*, the Diaspora, and others around the world
(including the Polish government, Ben Yosef's birth country).[3] Ben Yosef
walked to the gallows singing the Betar anthem.[4] In the years that followed, until the British withdrew, twelve Jewish underground fighters
would be hanged by the British; they were referred to as *olei ha-gardom*
("those who went up to the gallows"). The Zionist establishment and the
Revisionists responded in opposite fashions. The Revisionists publicly

mourned Ben Yosef; Ben-Gurion, on the other hand, ordered that the black flag that had been placed over the Histadrut building be removed. "I am not shocked that a Jew was hanged in Palestine," he commented. "I am ashamed of the deed that led to the hanging."[5]

Eight years later, on March 6, 1946, with Begin's revolt under way, the Etzel attacked Sarafand (in Hebrew, Tzrifin, now an IDF base), the British military headquarters in the Middle East some twelve miles south of Tel Aviv. In the stunning operation, some thirty to forty Jewish fighters stormed the largest military base in Palestine, overwhelming the British defenders and raiding the ammunition depots. All the fighters, except for two, successfully escaped, but Michael Ashbel and Yosef Simchon were captured and on June 13 were sentenced to death.[6] Because they rejected the legitimacy of British courts in Palestine, Ashbel and Simchon refused to petition for clemency and prepared for the gallows.

By 1946, however, circumstances were not what they had been when Shlomo Ben Yosef was hanged. Now Begin was in Palestine, and after the horror and humiliation of the Holocaust, he was not about to let Jews hang in the name of British justice; it was the British, after all, who were keeping the shores of Palestine closed even as thousands of Jews had nowhere to seek shelter now that the Europe they had known was destroyed. It was a matter of *hadar*, in many ways. Those who offered the Jews no safe harbor could not also hang the Jews who were battling for independence.

But Begin had learned from the Ben Yosef chapter that appeals to British clemency and legal pleas would be of no avail. Thus, still hidden in Tel Aviv, he warned the British through the official Etzel radio station: "Do not hang the captured soldiers. If you do, we shall answer gallows with gallows."[7] The message was clear: We are no longer victims; we are your equals. Whatever you do to our fighters, we will return in kind.

Several days after Ashbel and Simchon's sentencing, the Etzel kidnapped five British officers. They issued a statement saying that if the

British executed the Etzel men, their five officers would be hanged. Days of intense and secret negotiations ensued, which ended with the British commuting Ashbel's and Simchon's sentences to life imprisonment. "For the first time in the history of the British occupation," Begin wrote, "the head of the British occupation army authorized a verdict, and the head of the British occupation annulled a verdict, without anyone asking him to do so."[8] The Etzel had won the first round.

Then, on December 27, 1946, sixteen-year-old Binyamin Kimchi was flogged eighteen times. An Etzel fighter, Kimchi had been caught holding up a bank in Jaffa to "retake" tax money that the British had collected.[9] He was sentenced to eighteen years in prison and eighteen lashes.[10] Lashes were not an uncommon punishment in the British Empire, used primarily for petty criminals, but they had been outlawed among British soldiers since 1881.[11] The sentence of lashing was thus designed to send the Etzel a message in response to their victory in the first round: Your militia is no more than a gang; your soldiers are no more than petty criminals.[12] The Etzel promptly posted a warning in Hebrew and English:

> Warning! A Hebrew soldier, taken prisoner by the enemy, was sentenced by an illegal British Military "Court" to the humiliating punishment of flogging. We warn the occupation Government not to carry out this punishment, which is contrary to the laws of the soldier's honour. If it is put into effect—every officer of the British occupation in Eretz-Israel will be liable to be punished in the same way: *to get 18 whips.*[13]

The British disregarded the Etzel warning, but news of the game of chicken that was challenging the empire spread nonetheless. The threat of reprisal was a bigger story than the verdict itself. A *Washington Post* article reported Kimchi's sentence under the headline "Irgun Reprisal Due in Order for Whipping."[14]

Kimchi received his eighteen lashes on December 27;[15] the Etzel responded swiftly. The very next evening, they kidnapped a British major sitting with his wife in a hotel lounge in Netanya, flogged him eighteen times, and returned him to his hotel still stripped to his underwear. In Tel Aviv, another Etzel group kidnapped two British sergeants outside a hotel, tied them to a tree in a public park, and lashed them eighteen times. In Rishon LeTzion, yet another group abducted a British sergeant from the café in which he was sitting and whipped him with a rope—also eighteen times.[16]

The honor of the empire was at stake. The British imposed curfews on the major Jewish cities and began searching for the perpetrators. Yechiel Drezner (a.k.a. Dov Rosenbaum), Mordechai Alkoshi, and Eliezer Kashani, three Etzel fighters, were found carrying whips and arms and were promptly arrested.[17] The following day, Begin reiterated his warning:

> Despite our public warning, the Nazo-British General Barker authorized the humiliating flogging punishment that was imposed on the Hebrew soldier by the illegal British "Court" . . . As we had warned and as a reaction to the barbaric act of these oppressors, British officers were flogged on Sunday, Vav of Tevet in Netanya—the place of the last British pogrom—Tel Aviv and Rishon LeTzion . . . We now warn: if the oppressors dare to injure the body, or the personal or national honor of young Hebrews, we will not respond with the whip: we will respond with fire.[18]

Begin was speaking both to the Jews of Palestine and to the British. To the Jews, he was evoking a powerful sense of Jewish history and of Jewish belonging. The British general was "Nazo-British." He referred to the Etzel men as "Hebrew" soldiers; Moses, the Bible had recounted, was stunned into action when he saw an Egyptian beating a "Hebrew man, his brother."[19] These men, too, were "Hebrew soldiers." The date was the sixth of Tevet, the Hebrew date on the lunar calendar. And what was at stake was "national honor"—the *hadar* of which the Betar anthem spoke.

The British now knew that Begin was not bluffing. When another Jewish youth was sentenced to flogging by the Mandatory military court a week later, the high commissioner for Palestine remitted the judgment despite the boy's verdict having already been confirmed by the general officer commanding.[20] Dresner, Alkoshi, and Kashani were kept imprisoned, but they were not hanged. The Etzel was slowly changing the conduct of the British Empire. Begin had won another round.

He understood that the image of the Jew was changing. "No Jew or Arab was ever flogged again by the British in Palestine," Begin boasted years later.[21] "We received congratulations from Irishmen, from Americans, Canadians, Russians, Frenchmen." Most important for Begin, "our brother-Jews throughout the world straightened their backs."

Begin had learned well the lesson that the British inadvertently taught when they capitulated to Arab violence: power is rewarded. But the Jewish Agency's spokesperson, predictably, deplored the Etzel's floggings: "The British Empire is not threatened by the acts of the Etzel, but the Jewish people may well be."[22] Across the Mediterranean, the British were outraged; no British soldier had been flogged in Palestine before.[23] Less than a week after the incident, a synagogue was set on fire in London, with the words YOU WHIP—WE BURN chalked on a stone pillar outside the fire-damaged building.[24] An editorial in *The Palestine Post* predicted:

> [T]he action of the terrorist group in kidnapping and punishing four others for a matter with which they have not the remotest responsibility or concern, can only result in setting in motion a vicious spiral of act and counter-act, of mounting intensity leading to the disruption of all the civilized values which ordinary people are desperately clinging to.[25]

But the plan that a young Begin had first articulated in that meeting attended by Kadishai, in which he had said that the only way to help the Jews of Poland was to attack the British, was beginning to work; Britain was rocked by calls to withdraw from Palestine.[26]

Shortly thereafter, in January, the British military headquarters issued "nonfraternization" orders for its troops in Palestine: the soldiers were prohibited from entering any Jewish or Arab public place save movie theaters, which could be attended only in groups of three or more.[27] On January 31, they announced the evacuation of all nonessential civilian British residents of Palestine.[28] The soldiers remained without their families, banned from partaking in the local entertainment, enduring constant fear of terror for the purpose of defending the British in a land for which they lacked any coherent long-term plan. The Etzel's methods were taking their toll.

Some months earlier, in April 1946, Dov Gruner had been caught by the British following an Etzel operation that seized weapons from the Ramat Gan police station, one of the most fortified structures in Mandatory Palestine. Thirty weapons and seven thousand rounds of ammunition had been taken, but the Etzel had also lost two men and Gruner had been shot in the face and captured.[29] On January 1, 1947, two days after the Etzel's retaliatory flogging of British troops, Gruner was sentenced to death.[30]

The Etzel resorted to a method they had assumed was guaranteed to work; they kidnapped a British officer and a British judge, again threatening "gallows with gallows." After days of uncertainty, the British postponed Gruner's execution indefinitely, and the Etzel released their captives. The British claimed the execution had been postponed due to a pending appeal to the Privy Council; in fact, however, no such appeal was in motion.[31] The British were desperate to save face. Drezner, Alkoshi, and Kashani (the three Etzel fighters captured during the "night of the whippings") were now joined by Gruner on death row; but according to Begin, the Etzel had been led to believe that all death sentences would be pending until Gruner's situation was clarified.[32]

On April 14, Gruner and the other three fighters were secretly transferred from the Jerusalem prison at the heart of the *yishuv*, where a hanging was more likely to stir up violent protest, to a heavily guarded compound in Acre, a northern Arab city. Two days later, on April 16, 1947, the four were hanged.[33] In violation of explicit British policy, no clergyman was brought to accompany them. All four went to the gallows singing "Hatikvah."[34]

Dov Gruner had composed a last letter addressed to Begin in which he quoted Jabotinsky's Betar anthem and thanked Begin for his encouragement during imprisonment:

You may rest assured that whatever happens I shall not forget the teachings on which I was weaned, the teachings to be "proud and generous and strong" [a quote from the Betar anthem] and I shall know how to stand up for my honour, the honour of a fighting Hebrew soldier . . . The right way, to my mind, is the way of the Irgun, which does not reject political effort but will not give up a yard of our country, because it is ours. And if the political effort does not have the desired result it is prepared to fight for our country and our freedom—which alone ensures the existence of our people—by all means and in all ways. That should be the way of the Jewish people in these days; to stand up for what is ours and be ready for battle even if in some instances it leads to the gallows. For the world knows that a land is redeemed by blood. I write these lines forty-eight hours before the time fixed by our oppressors to carry out their murder, and at such moments one does not lie. I swear that if I had the choice of starting again I would choose the same road, regardless of the possible consequences to me.[35]

At the news of the hanging, Begin immediately ordered the Etzel troops to attach field courts-martial to every unit. "Should any enemy troops fall into our hands," Begin explained, "they would be liable to die—as our four comrades had died." But the British Army, undoubtedly knowing of Begin's outrage, kept a very low profile. "Our units went out on the roads, on the streets in the towns. But the military were literally not to be found."[36]

In the meantime, more Etzel men were awaiting execution in Jerusalem. Meir Feinstein had been arrested following an Etzel attack on the Jerusalem railway station; he had lost his arm in the ensuing clashes, and was eventually captured, tried, and sentenced. Moshe Barazani, a Lechi fighter, was found in possession of a hand grenade; in Palestine, merely carrying a hand grenade was a capital offense.[37] Feinstein and Barazani were determined to do what Gruner and the others could not; they could die but take some British with them. It was the biblical model of Samson, who had vowed to "perish with the Philistines." The two wanted to die in the model of "our ancient hero."[38]

A hand grenade hidden in an orange was smuggled to Barazani and

Feinstein;[39] the plan called for them to explode it near the British officers who would carry out the hanging. But the British brought a rabbi to be with the two men, and the rabbi, unaware of their plan, promised to return in the morning and to remain with the prisoners through their last moments. Not wanting to take another Jewish life with them, Barazani and Feinstein abandoned their plan to die "Samson's death." On April 21, 1947, after the rabbi retired for the night, the sound of the singing of *Adon Olam* from the two men's cell was suddenly silenced by a loud explosion. Feinstein and Barazani had detonated the grenade. They had befriended their British guard, and Feinstein had presented the guard with his personal Bible moments before the explosion. In the dedication to the guard, whose life they saved by detonating the grenade when he was not present, Feinstein had written: "It is better to die with a weapon in hand than to live with hands raised."[40]

L ess than two weeks after Feinstein and Barazani took their own lives, on May 4, 1947, the Etzel conducted one of its most daring operations and broke into Acre Prison. Like the Bastille, the prison was a symbol of imperial power—its freedom to arrest suspects at will, hold them indefinitely, convict them, and, when it saw fit, execute them.

Acre Prison, housed in a Crusader-era fortress, held many of the Etzel's men captured over the course of numerous previous operations. Begin was determined to get them out. Forty-one prisoners were selected for liberation; thirty were Etzel members and eleven were Lechi.[41]

At a prearranged signal, Etzel fighters outside detonated the explosives, creating a breach in the wall. The prisoners inside blew up internal heavy iron bars using explosives that had been smuggled in earlier. A battle erupted in the prison courtyard, but the prisoners marked for release made it out. They boarded prepared trucks and sped off. The British police force followed in hot pursuit, but was impeded by the mines the Etzel had placed along the road in anticipation of the chase.

The Etzel did not anticipate, however, that British soldiers would be bathing south of Acre. Hearing the commotion, the soldiers dressed quickly, gathered their arms, and set up a roadblock. A skirmish ensued, and nine Jewish fighters were killed—seven from the Etzel, including Michael Ashbel, who had been saved from the gallows less than a year earlier, and two from the Lechi. In the end, the Etzel successfully freed twenty-seven of the forty-one prisoners it had originally designated for liberation; six of the prisoners died in the battle, and eight others were wounded and recaptured by the British. In the confusion, more than two hundred Arab prisoners (the majority of the Arab prisoners in the jail) also escaped.[42]

Another major element of the plan went wrong. Avshalom Haviv, Meir Nakkar, and Ya'akov Weiss, who had been standing watch over one of the Etzel posts, did not hear the signal to board the truck and stayed behind.[43] After a lengthy fight, they were captured by the British, tried, and sentenced to death by hanging.[44] (Two more Etzel members were captured during the operation but escaped the death penalty due to their youth.)[45]

Begin went to work on two fronts. Though he would not appeal these cases to the British courts, which he considered illegitimate, matters had changed on the political front. On April 2, 1947, the United Kingdom had referred the question of the future status of Palestine to the United Nations, in effect admitting defeat and acknowledging that it would not long retain the Mandate. On May 15, 1947, the United Nations Special Committee on Palestine (UNSCOP) was formed. Since UNSCOP was designed to be part of the process of ending British dominion over Palestine, Begin did not consider it illegitimate in the way that British courts were. Hopeful that the situation could be resolved bloodlessly, the Etzel submitted an appeal to the United Nations to annul "the 'sentences' of the illegal military courts," and a separate appeal to UNSCOP to subpoena the three prisoners so that they could testify for UNSCOP's fact-finding mission, which would delay the execution.

Begin was not terribly optimistic that this would work, however, so he also instructed his men to kidnap more British officers, who could then be traded for the Etzel fighters.[46] They nabbed two British policemen, but the Haganah quickly uncovered the scheme and led the British to the location where the policemen were being hidden. The Etzel tried again, but the British soldiers, on high alert, proved frustratingly elusive. The Etzel was persistent, and on July 12, almost a month after Begin issued the directive, it captured Clifford Martin and Mervyn Paice in the coastal city of Netanya.[47]

The prey was hardly ideal. The two men were noncommissioned officers and were sitting in a café, out of uniform. Martin's mother was Jewish and Paice was sympathetic to the Zionists and had collaborated with the Haganah.[48] A reader of *The Palestine Post* wrote to the editor that "one of the kidnapped men is Melvin [*sic*] Paice, my good friend who has visited our farm in Beer Tuvia . . . I know him as an educated man, noted for his human approach and understanding of our cause."[49] And they were only sergeants, the lowest rank of soldier the Etzel had hitherto captured.[50] The British were going to be much less worried about sergeants than they had been about majors. By the time the news that the captured soldiers were mere sergeants reached Begin, who was still hiding in his Tel Aviv apartment, it was too late to turn back.[51]

For twelve days, Netanya was a ghost town as British soldiers searched house-to-house trying to find their captured soldiers.[52] The Etzel had to keep the sergeants in a bunker of three cubic meters, with no light and minimal air, under a diamond factory; the roof was covered with almost a meter of sand to stifle noise. A canvas bucket in the corner served as a toilet.[53]

While the Etzel fighters awaited the gallows and the British scoured Netanya in search of their men, the S.S. *Exodus* arrived in Palestine. Part of the *yishuv*'s efforts at increasing immigration in defiance of the White Paper, the *Exodus* was crammed with more than 4,000 immigrants. The ship's passengers slept on shelves with barely enough space to lie down, a painful reminder of the concentration camps where many of them had suffered.[54]

Under the aegis of the Haganah, the *Exodus* arrived at the port of Haifa at the end of July. The British immediately seized the ship and ordered it back to sea. When it reached Europe, the passengers, who had boarded the ship in order to flee that continent, refused to disembark; they were forcibly removed from the ship in Germany and sent to displaced persons' camps. The episode, which highlighted the homeless condition of the Jewish people, became a rallying point for Zionists the world over. Golda Meir wrote in her autobiography:

> Before the shocked eyes of members of UNSCOP they forcibly caged and returned to Germany the 4,500 refugees who had come to Palestine aboard the Haganah ship *Exodus 1947*, and I think that by so doing they actually contributed considerably to UNSCOP's final recommendations. If I live to be a hundred, I shall never erase from my mind the gruesome picture of hundreds of British soldiers in full combat dress, bearing and using clubs, pistols and grenades against the wretched refugees on the *Exodus*.[55]

Pressure on the British increased, but pressure mounted from London, as well. When Begin had first announced, more than a year earlier, that he would answer "gallows with gallows," the British annulled Ashbel's and Shimshon's death sentences and decided to forgo flogging the Jewish youth out of fear of retaliation. Churchill was revolted: "This is the road of abject defeat, and though I hate this quarrel with the Jews, and I hate their methods of outrage, if you are engaged in the matter, at least bear yourselves like men."[56]

Ironically, Churchill's view was the same as Begin's. "If you're in it to win, you fight to win." Begin's approach was precisely the attitude that Britain and America had taken in their defense of freedom as they fought the Nazis.

This time, indeed, the British "bore themselves like men"; despite the fact that the Etzel was still holding Martin and Paice, the three Etzel fighters—Weiss, Haviv, and Nakkar—were hanged on July 29, 1947.[57] Begin's plan had failed, and now that there was nothing to be gained from holding Martin and Paice any longer, calls for their release were issued throughout the *yishuv*. The Jewish National Council (Va'ad Leumi), the "executive branch" of the official *yishuv* administration, released a statement:

> The *Yishuv*, which has been hurt and shocked by the Government's lack of response to all the appeals of clemency and by the execution of the three young men sentenced to death for the attack on the Acre Prison, will regard any act of reprisal taken against the two inno-cent Britons as a bloodthirsty deed contrary to all human standards and as an unforgivable sin against the *Yishuv* and the Jewish people.[58]

That evening was the thirteenth day of the Hebrew month of Av, Menachem Begin's thirty-fourth Hebrew birthday. From his bunker in Tel Aviv, he made what he later called "the most difficult decision of my life."[59] The next day, the bodies of the two British sergeants were found, lifeless, hanging from a tree in Netanya.[60]

Begin had given the order. The clearing in which they were hanged was mined ("two hanged men was one fewer than three"[61]); a British captain was injured when he tried taking one of the bodies down.[62] A note attached to one of the bodies, signed by "the court of the Irgun Zva'i Leumi in Eretz Israel," explained that the two men had been executed fol-lowing the decision of an Etzel court that had heard their testimony and rejected their plea for pardon.[63] The end of the note read:

> The hanging of the two British spies is not a retaliatory act for the murder of Hebrew prisoners-of-war, but it is an ordinary legal action of the court of the Underground which has sentenced and will sentence the criminals who belong to the criminal Nazi British army of occupation.[64]

The sergeants' charges virtually mirrored those of the executed Irgun-ists: "Being a member of an armed force illegally occupying Palestine; illegally carrying weapons in the uniform of the enemy; being members of a force conspiring to oppress the rightful citizens of Palestine."[65]

The British were humiliated, furious, and despondent. Colonel Nichol Grey, inspector-general of the Palestine Police Force, remembered:

We could have gotten over losses of life or property . . . But the Empire cannot withstand blows to prestige, and the floggings, the Acre prison break in and the hanging of the sergeants—these were blows to prestige. The first one made a joke out of us. The second, which took on a symbolic importance similar to the fall of the Bastille, underscored we were no longer capable of ensuring law and order in the land, and the hangings set us, the rulers, on the same level [of authority] as them, the terrorists.[66]

Riots broke out in Palestine and Britain. Demoralized British police officers, risking their lives in a territory it was increasingly obvious their government could not continue to hold, went on a rampage; armored police cars fired upon two civilian buses and grenades were thrown into a coffee shop; properties were destroyed, and many were injured.[67] Five Palestinian civilians died in the violence.[68] In Britain, the rioting continued for five days in what were essentially pogroms; Jewish-owned shops were attacked to the cheers of crowds, Jewish cemeteries were vandalized, and synagogues were burned down.[69]

Begin defended the decision to hang the sergeants, but it haunted him until the end of his life. In a rare interview, granted in July 1991, he acknowledged: "I admit it was a brutal act." And yet he could not fail to note that it accomplished one significant objective. "After the brutal act," he noted, "there were no more hangings of Jews in Palestine."[70]

6

Deadly Road to Jerusalem

All the Israelites turned back to Ai and put it to the sword.

—*Joshua 8:24*

On August 31, 1947, UNSCOP released its report; it recommended ending the Mandate at the earliest possible time, and creating two new states, one Jewish and one Arab.[1] Violence between Zionists and the British Mandate subsided, while violent clashes between Arabs and Jews increased.[2] The Arabs rejected the recommendation out of hand. Officially, they objected to the Jews, who constituted 37 percent of the population, being given 55 percent of the land.[3] But everyone understood that the objection was more basic; they had no intention of accommodating any Jewish state in the region, no matter what its borders. For their part, the Zionists, led by the ever-pragmatic Ben-Gurion, accepted the proposal despite the sacrifice it entailed of what they saw as the natural borders of Israel and the original pledge of the Balfour Declaration. Indeed, Ben-Gurion worked hard to persuade other Zionist leaders, who had their misgivings, to back the proposal. They did, and the Zionist bloc vigorously lobbied for the resolution. On November 29, the United Nations voted on Resolution 181, which called for the partition of Palestine into Jewish and Arab countries and for the withdrawal of all British troops by the fall of 1948.

The borders of the proposed Jewish state were geographically absurd and virtually indefensible. Nonetheless, the Jews had supported the measure, and around the world, Jews still recovering from the horrors of the

Holocaust listened tensely to the roll call. The resolution, which required a two-thirds majority, passed narrowly, 33 in favor, 13 opposed. All of the independent Arab nations voted against. Great Britain abstained.

In Palestine, Jews danced in the streets; Ben-Gurion, however, was sober: "I could not dance, I could not sing that night. I looked at them so happy dancing and I could only think that they were all going to war."[4]

Begin, too, found himself unable to sing or dance. He knew that war was looming. But Begin had yet another reason that he would not and could not celebrate: he categorically rejected the "Partition Plan." In a radio address the following day, he declared:

> In the name of the divine promise that was given to the fathers of the nation—in the name of the saintly men who, in every genera- tion, gave their lives for Zion and its redemption . . . in the name of [our nation's] unquestionable historical right . . . the partition of our homeland is illegal. It will never be recognized . . . Eretz Israel will be returned to the nation of Israel in its entirety. Forever.[5]

In fact, Ben-Gurion had also opposed the division of the land (though, as the pragmatic leader of the state, he had no choice but to acquiesce), and both were correct in their prediction of intensified war. Within weeks, six to eight thousand volunteers from the Arab world, mostly from Syria, Iraq, and Egypt, answered the call to *jihad* and began drifting across the border. More than four thousand Jewish and non-Jewish volunteers, the overwhelming majority of whom were former Allied soldiers, came from abroad to help the Zionists.[6]

The war, which was waged first by Palestinian Arabs, and then, after May 14, by the armies of neighboring Arab nations that amassed to destroy the new Jewish state, was brutal and complex, fought on numer- ous fronts, with wins and losses on both sides. Because the fighting popu- lations were intermingled throughout northern and western Palestine, Arabs often controlled routes to Jewish neighborhoods and vice versa; thus, Jewish fighters could besiege Arab villages and Arabs could cut off food and supplies from Jewish settlements.[7]

The Jewish portion of Jerusalem was dependent on Haganah-protected convoys for food and reinforcements. By late March 1948, the city was on the verge of collapse. In the last week of March, 136 supply trucks had tried to reach Jerusalem; only 41 succeeded. The supply lines ran through Arab-controlled areas, and unless the Jews managed to secure these routes, all of Jerusalem would almost certainly fall to the Arabs. In Jerusalem and elsewhere on the war front, matters were dire.[8]

Diplomatically, things were not much better; even American support for the partition plan was eroding. In February, President Truman informed his secretary of state, George Marshall, that "in principle" he approved of putting all of Palestine under U.N. trusteeship. In March, the U.S. ambassador to the United Nations, Warren Austin, declared before the Security Council that "the [Partition Plan] cannot now be implemented through peaceful means . . . We believe that a temporary trusteeship for Palestine should be established under the Trusteeship Council."[9] Although Truman quickly reversed that position and reiterated his unwavering support for partition, the message to the Zionists was clear: their having won the November 1947 vote at the United Nations was no guarantee that the Jews would have their state. If they wanted their Jewish state, they would have to defend it themselves.

Everything they had accomplished over the past bitter years was now hanging in the balance. And even the territory the Jews had been granted had to be defended. Arab armies were amassing, determined to destroy the newly created state. Israel's leaders were now engaged in an all-out war, defensive in the sense that it had been foisted on them, but a war of conquest at the same time, in that every inch of land was now contested.

In March, Jerusalem was still starving and on the verge of collapse. Ben-Gurion decided to act. In a desperate move, the Haganah scraped together 1,500 fighters for Operation Nachshon, named after the biblical figure who, according to Jewish tradition, jumped into the Red Sea before it had parted to get the Israelites to follow him. The intended goal was "to open the road to Jerusalem by means of offensive operations against enemy bases."[10] Capturing the road would move the Jewish forces one step closer to uniting the strategic areas of the country. The Haganah took the lead in planning the operation; the Etzel and Lechi would participate in the offensive, but Begin probably did not play a role in its planning.

By April 6, the Haganah had effectively secured the main Arab band at the western end of Jerusalem, and the following day, a sixty-three-vehicle convoy with food, reinforcements, fuel, and ammunition arrived in Jerusalem unscathed. But the Haganah's gains were short-lived. On April 7, a battle for Castel—a village just a few kilometers outside Jerusalem on the road to Tel Aviv—erupted once again, this time more violently than before. The original directive, issued on April 2, had explicitly forbidden the Haganah troops from demolishing the village. The follow-up order to recapture Castel on April 8, however, seemed to recognize that the Jews would not win that way; the new order specifically ordered the destruction of houses. The war was getting dirtier.[11]

The Etzel believed it needed to capture Deir Yassin, another village on the outskirts of Jerusalem on the road to Tel Aviv, because it lay next to a flat stretch of land that could be used as an airfield and would be strategically useful for the looming battle for Jerusalem. It decided to join forces with the Lechi to capture the village. Deir Yassin and the nearby Jewish neighborhood of Givat Sha'ul had signed a mutual nonaggression pact in August 1947. Deir Yassin residents had subsequently turned away Arab volunteers who had come to join in the fighting. But David Shaltiel, commanding officer of the Haganah in the Jerusalem area, approved the initiative. Capturing Deir Yassin fit in with the strategic objectives of Operation Nachshon of securing the western entrances to Jerusalem. The pro-Labor newspaper, *Davar*, reported that sniper fire had come from the village; this may have contributed to the Haganah's decision to support the Etzel operation, but that claim has never been fully verified.[12]

Either way, there was no expectation of resistance; most of the captured Arab towns in the area had put up little, if any. The Etzel and Haganah believed that the mere sound of automatic gunfire would quell any opposition to their mission and would cause the Arabs to flee.

Matters did not unfold that way. At dawn on April 9, Etzel and Lechi fighters, along with dozens of recent ill-trained and ill-equipped volunteers, set out for the village. In accord with Begin's long-standing insistence on warning civilians—as advocated by Jabotinsky—they planned to send a truck, driven by the Lechi, to broadcast a warning in Arabic, telling civilians to leave or to take shelter.

On the way to the village, however, the Lechi and Etzel forces—which had planned an attack from two sides—were separated without means of communication. The Etzel fighters entered the village from the east and south at approximately 4:30 in the morning, and were immediately targeted by sniper fire from villagers' homes. A firefight unfolded. Meanwhile, the Lechi truck, driving toward Deir Yassin, got caught in a homemade tank trap and could not get as close to the village as planned. Its loudspeakers blared: "You are being attacked by superior forces . . . The west exit of Deir Yassin leading to Ein Karim is open for you! Run immediately! Don't hesitate! Our troops are advancing! Run toward Ein Karim!" But the warning came after the battle had already started, and was barely audible over the blasting of automatic weapons.

Encountering unexpected resistance from the villagers and quite possibly Iraqi volunteers, the ill-trained Etzel fighters, utterly unprepared for house-to-house combat, made the hasty decision to throw hand grenades into the homes from which sniper fire was emerging. When the Etzel second-in-command, Yehuda Lapidot, realized the futility of trying to clear homes by that method, he asked Commander Mordechai Raanan for TNT to blow them up. A dozen or more houses in the village were then destroyed.

By four o'clock in the afternoon, the town had been captured, though at a devastatingly high price. Of the Etzel and Lechi fighters, 5 had died and 31 were injured.[13] Among the villagers, the carnage was widespread; when the Haganah command arrived at the bloody scene in the late afternoon, they were horrified and withdrew.

Begin, still hunted by the British and therefore in hiding in Tel Aviv, received only scant, confused initial reports about the success of the mission. Over the airwaves, he proclaimed the success of a mission in which "for the first time, soldiers of the IZL and of LEHI and of the Palmach together took part."[4] But soon, different reports began to emerge, claiming that 240 or 254 Arabs had been killed, with women and children among the dead. There were also reports of mutilation, rape, and looting; of babies being ripped from their mothers' arms; and of Arabs rounded up in trucks and transported to the edge of the village to be shot at point-blank range. Ironically, all the parties had a reason to falsify the extent of the carnage. The Arabs were seeking international support, the Haganah and the Jewish Agency now had an opportunity to discredit the Etzel and Lechi, while some of the commanders of the Etzel and Lechi embraced the exaggerated figures and the tales of atrocities, hoping that the rumors would frighten Arabs from other villages into fleeing. Some elements of the Haganah may also have hoped that the Arabs would flee.

Rumors and disinformation spread like wildfire. These were the reports that reached the international community. Though it was hardly the bloodiest of the battles in the war, the episode was quickly dubbed the "Deir Yassin Massacre," the name that it retains in most accounts to this very day.

Ben-Gurion, the Haganah, and the Jewish Agency rushed to express regret. As was the case in the aftermath of the King David bombing, they also denied responsibility for what had transpired. The Haganah High Command condemned the attacks, expressing "deep disgust and regret." The hatred for Begin and the power struggle between Ben-Gurion and Begin now reigned supreme. Libelously, Shaltiel now denied that the Haganah had approved the operation, calling the massacre "a premeditated act which had as its intention slaughter and murder only." Ben-Gurion sent a letter of apology to Jordan's King Abdullah.

Begin defended the decision to take the village and insisted that the civilians had heard the broadcast of warning but refused to leave. Typical for him, he took personal responsibility for the casualties, publishing a wall poster released shortly after the event that said, "We express our great sorrow that among the wounded were women and children." When he was shown the correspondence from the Haganah that had given the

Etzel the green light to proceed with the operation, Begin took to the air-waves to lambast the Haganah as hypocrites. "Deir Yassin was captured with the knowledge of the Haganah and with the approval of its Commander," he told the public.

Nonetheless, Deir Yassin stuck to Begin and the Etzel just as, years later, the settlement movement, though green-lighted in its earliest incarnation by the reigning Labor government, was seen as the work of Begin's party. Ben-Gurion was masterful at splitting off and attributing to Begin—as he had to Jabotinsky—the use of force, the conquest of territory, retaliation for violent acts, and forcible opposition to the British that he wished to disavow even as he deployed Begin's men and internalized the Etzel's worldview.

In the American Jewish community, Begin's protestations that the tragedy was unintended and that Ben-Gurion also shared responsibility fell on deaf ears. Six months after the battle, Begin planned a trip to the United States to raise money for his new political party, Herut (Freedom). On December 4, 1948, two dozen prominent American Jews sent a letter to the editors of *The New York Times* accusing Herut of terrorist inclinations. Not surprisingly, Deir Yassin occupied a central place in their letter, and their version of what had happened bore almost no resemblance to what had actually transpired:

[On April 9] terrorist bands attacked this peaceful village, which was not a military objective in the fighting, killed most of its inhabitants—240 men, women, and children—and kept a few of them alive to parade as captives through the streets of Jerusalem. Most of the Jewish community was horrified at the deed, and the Jewish Agency sent a telegram of apology to King Abdullah of Trans-Jordan. But the terrorists, far from being ashamed of their act, were proud of this massacre, publicized it widely, and invited all the foreign correspondents present in the country to view the heaped corpses and the general havoc at Deir Yassin. The Deir Yassin incident exemplifies the character and actions of the Freedom Party.

The letter was signed by, among others, Albert Einstein and Hannah Arendt. A narrative that was largely invented by the Jews was broadcast to the world and continues to haunt Jews and Israel to this day.

Inside Israel, Begin's long-standing enemies began to call him "The Butcher of Deir Yassin." He never entirely shook this epithet. After his election in 1977, the Palestine Liberation Organization revived it as part of its protesting his premiership. When he later received the Nobel Peace Prize, some members of the international press claimed that the award was unjustified, given his actions during the King David bombing and Deir Yassin.

Accounts of what actually occurred are still hotly contested. Many years after the battle, Yehuda Avner, Begin's advisor and friend, spoke to Yehuda Lapidot, who had been the Etzel's second-in-command at Deir Yassin. Lapidot continued to insist that there had been no deliberate massacre and the Arabs had resisted much more fiercely than anyone had anticipated. He believed that though the truck with the loudspeaker had fallen into a ditch, the Arab residents did hear the message but chose to fight rather than flee. The Etzel men did have to demolish many houses on their way to the house of the *mukhtar* (village elder), said Lapidot, but they brought the Arab residents out in trucks and released them on the Arab side of the city. He denied that anyone was shot in cold blood, though other Etzel and Lechi fighters admitted that they had shot civilians (including women and children) on sight, while denying categorically the reports of mutilation and rape.[15]

Benny Morris, an internationally recognized and respected Israeli "New Historian," who wrote numerous accounts of Israeli military excesses, believes that the accusations of rape were simply false. Most contemporary historians estimate the number killed at 100–120.[16] Even Arab historians have changed their narrative; in 1987, two Palestinian scholars associated with Birzeit University near the West Bank city of Ramallah released a report after multiple interviews with witnesses. They put the number of dead at 107, and made no mention of rape in their report.[17] Their conclusions were not unlike Begin's.

Four days after Deir Yassin, a medical convoy on its way to Hadassah Hospital was attacked near Mount Scopus, which was home to both Hebrew University and Hadassah Hospital. In a departure from usual practice, the British did not send an armored car to accompany the caravan, though it is not clear why. They might have been shorthanded; Benny Morris suggests they might also have decided to give the Arabs an opportunity to settle the Deir Yassin score.[18] In the attack, seventy-nine people were killed by gunfire or were burned (many beyond recognition) when their vehicles were set on fire; twenty of them were women. Among the dead were the director of the hospital, Dr. Chaim Yassky, and Dr. Moshe Ben-David, who had been selected to head the new planned medical school on Mount Scopus. The area surrounding Mount Scopus ultimately fell to the Arabs, and the Israeli enclave there was encircled by the Jordanians until the end of the Six-Day War in 1967.

Despite the Hadassah convoy massacre, the tide of the war began to turn. Terrified by the rumors of what had happened at Deir Yassin, many Arabs feared the Etzel as never before and evacuated their villages preemptively, adding to a mass exodus of Arabs from Palestine. An attack by the Haganah against an Arab village called Saris was facilitated, according to British intelligence, by Deir Yassin: "the violence used [at Deir Yassin] so impressed Arabs all over the country that an attack by Haganah on Saris met with no opposition whatsoever." According to the Haganah Intelligence Service, the Deir Yassin attack was a "decisive accelerating factor" in the completion of Operation Nachshon.[19]

Not long thereafter, the road to Jerusalem was open.

On April 24, 1948, with the British departing, Begin ended his years of hiding and emerged into the open. When asked what the hardest part of being in hiding was, he responded that it was coming out of hiding and having his son, Benny, who had been hearing terrible things about Menachem Begin, learn that the very same Menachem Begin was actually his father.[20]

On May 10, he gave a radio address in which he announced his new political party, Herut, named after the underground newspaper of the same name. By May 12, Jaffa had surrendered; Jerusalem was the last remaining frontier. On May 14, 1948, the last of the British troops departed Palestine. That same day, David Ben-Gurion, now interim prime minister, announced the creation of the State of Israel. Many of the country's leadership gathered in Tel Aviv for the declaration; Begin was not included.

Since May 14 was a Friday and the ceremony concluded shortly before Shabbat, Begin waited until the next night, May 15, to broadcast his own speech:

> this event has occurred after seventy generations of dispersion and unending wandering of an unarmed people and after a period of almost total destruction of the Jew as Jew. Thus, although our suffering is not yet over, it is our right and our obligation to proffer thanks to the Rock of Israel and His Redeemer for all the miracles that have been done this day, as in those times. We therefore can say with full heart and soul on this first day of our liberation from the British occupier: Blessed is He who has sustained us and enabled us to have reached this time.

It was notable language, especially given the fact that the Declaration of Independence, which Ben-Gurion had read aloud the previous day, did not explicitly mention God. (Begin, when he would later become prime minister, donned a *kippah* and went to the Western Wall. Ben-Gurion, instructively, chose to leave his head uncovered as he proclaimed renewed Jewish sovereignty after two millennia of exile.) Begin continued:

> We shall go on our way into battle, soldiers of the Lord of Hosts, inspired by the spirit of our ancient heroes, from the conquerors of Canaan to the Rebels of Judah. We shall be accompanied by the spirit of those who revived our nation, Ze'ev Benjamin Herzl, Max Nordau, Joseph Trumpeldor, and the father of resurrected Hebrew heroism, Ze'ev Jabotinsky. We shall be accompanied by the spirit of

David Raziel, greatest of our Hebrew commanders of our day; and by Dov Gruner, one of the greatest of Hebrew soldiers . . . God, Lord of Israel, protect your soldiers. Grant blessing to their sword that is renewing the covenant that was made between your chosen people and your chosen land. Arise, O Lion of Judea for our people, for our land. On to battle. Forward to victory.

Victory, though, would be more elusive than he might have imagined. Begin and Ben-Gurion were both celebrating the rebirth of Jewish sovereignty, but Begin had not been invited to the Declaration of Independence, and had had to deliver his address from Paglin's apartment in Tel Aviv. That fact was of great symbolic significance. The ongoing bitterness and mistrust between the two men would soon threaten the very enterprise they had both worked so tirelessly to achieve; just weeks later, they and their respective fighters would lead the newborn nation to the brink of civil war.

7

A Civil War with the Enemy at Our Gates

"... alone I crossed this Jordan, and now I have become two camps." —*Genesis 32:10*

Israel's War of Independence had erupted long before independence. The Arab violence of the 1930s had never fully ceased, and once the United Nations voted on November 29, 1947, for partition and the creation of Jewish and Arab states, Palestinian Arabs opened full-scale war. When David Ben-Gurion declared independence on May 14, 1948, the war was well under way and Arab armies throughout the region, including Iraq, announced their determination to join the fray and to destroy the Jewish state. The war would last until mid-1949; a full 1 percent of the new state's population would be killed.

But there were also lulls in the fighting. Beginning on May 29, 1948, just two weeks after the Declaration of Independence was signed, the United Nations declared a cease-fire between Israel and the Arab forces. The cease-fire, which would last twenty-eight days, called for a full arms embargo; neither side was permitted to import arms or secure its military positions. Ben-Gurion knew that though his fledgling state was desperate for arms, violating the cease-fire would jeopardize Israel's international standing. He also suspected (correctly) that the Arab armies would violate the embargo, but it was Israel's legitimacy, not theirs, that was his concern.

Ben-Gurion had other military problems, as well. He had to cobble together one united army out of the Haganah and its Palmach strike force plus the Etzel and the Lechi. Begin had emerged from hiding and had fighters still loyal to him; he was emerging as a national player. Furthermore, after years of mistrust, the Etzel and Lechi were wary of giving up their independent identities and of serving under the very Haganah commanders who had once hunted them down during the *Saison*. As Begin himself acknowledged, "It was not an easy matter to send our comrades to an army whose officers had hated the underground, persecuted it, besmirched it, kidnapped its members and handed over its officers . . . The men who were about to take command of our members had been systematically trained to hate them."[1]

Begin's Etzel and the Lechi proposed to Ben-Gurion that their fighters would constitute distinct units within the new army, so that they could maintain internal control over their own weapons and ammunition. David Ben-Gurion flatly refused. That there would ultimately have to be one military force in the new country had been clear to everyone. Begin and Ben-Gurion had been discussing both the merger and a proposed agreement under which the Etzel could retain autonomy until independence. It would be difficult for the Etzel to stomach having to report to former enemies, but it was a compromise for others, as well. Some left-wing politicians were deeply critical of the merger: "This is an agreement with murderers, the heroes of Deir Yassin," complained Moshe Erem, a member of the Marxist Mapam party.[2]

Two weeks after independence, Begin announced the unofficial agreement the two had made, though he did not refer to the army's official name, calling it instead the "United Forces."[3] The Israel Defense Forces were created on May 31, and the next day, a few days after the U.N. cease-fire was declared, Ben-Gurion and Begin finally signed the official agreement about the IDF's absorption of the Etzel. The agreement stipulated that Etzel members would enlist in the newly created IDF; their arms and equipment, as well as installations for the manufacture of arms, would be turned over to the army; there would be no special Etzel units within army brigades; separate purchasing activities were to be terminated; and most important, the Etzel would cease operating as a distinct military unit within the State of Israel.[4]

Begin signed the merger agreement, dissolving the force that his master and mentor had inspired, with Jabotinsky's own pen.[5]

Much of the agreement, however, was vague. For example, the agreement included the phrase "within the State of Israel," but it was not clear whether that included Jerusalem, which at that point was not a part of Israel. Earlier that spring, the Old City and the eastern part of Jerusalem had ended up in Arab hands, cut off from the "New City," despite weeks of cooperative struggle from the Etzel and Haganah and despite the efforts of Operation Nachshon to liberate the city. Ben-Gurion had given up on retaking Jerusalem, while Begin still had fighters stationed there.

The compromise was a step forward in the creation of a unified Israeli army. Both the Haganah and Etzel had sprung from Jabotinsky's mind, but the new unified force would now bear Ben-Gurion's mark. The agreement was signed with great reservations, in large measure because neither party knew precisely to what it had just agreed.

Even as Begin was negotiating with Ben-Gurion the conditions under which he would fold the Etzel into the IDF, however, Etzel fighters in Jerusalem were running dangerously low on ammunition. Etzel branches abroad, which had taken on a quasi-independent identity, thus continued to gather arms to send to Israel, to their fighters and particularly for the defense of Jerusalem. Shmuel Katz, who was then at the helm of the Etzel's Paris office, later recalled:

> We would not disband entirely. We never forgot Jerusalem, where the Israeli Government refused to claim sovereignty, where the Old City had fallen and the New was in danger. There the Irgun would have to continue its independent existence to struggle for the inclusion of the whole city in the Jewish State. Until then, a remnant of the Irgun abroad had to be kept in being.[6]

Katz, like other Etzel members, saw the arms embargo as grossly unfair, since the British could still ship arms to Iraq, Jordan, and Egypt, and those arms were almost certain to make their way into the hands of the Palestinian Arabs.[7]

Hillel Kook, who had changed his name to Peter Bergson, was at the helm of Etzel operations in America. He was responsible for Etzel fundraising and acquiring arms in the States, and he also organized committees in support of the Jews of Europe during World War II. One of his major projects postwar included facilitating "illegal" immigration to Palestine (a project to which the Haganah was also deeply committed). Cognizant of the Etzel men's desperate situation, Kook and a few other members of the Etzel leadership outside Israel purchased a U.S. Navy tank-landing ship that had been used in World War II; it was not unlike the immigration ships that sailed from Europe as part of Aliyah Bet.

They named the boat the *Altalena*, after Jabotinsky's pseudonym when he was a journalist (it was the Italian word for "swing" or "seesaw").[8] Its commander was Eliyahu Lankin, a senior Etzel member who would become a member of the Knesset and, later, Israel's ambassador to South Africa. At first, the ship sailed around the Mediterranean in the guise of a cargo ship doing regular business. Then the ship docked in Port-de-Bouc, France, the same port from which the doomed *Exodus 1947* ship had set sail, to pick up weapons and immigrants destined for Israel. Several countries contributed to the arms aboard the *Altalena*, but none more than France, which, apparently hoping to curb British influence in the Middle East, gave munitions valued at 150 million francs.[9] Some 940 immigrants, all survivors of the war, also boarded the ship.

Despite the crowded conditions, morale on the ship was high. Those who sailed on the *Altalena* remember days of strict discipline and nights of singing Hebrew folk songs.[10] Having barely survived the war with nowhere to hide, these men and women were finally headed home to the new Jewish state. Victims no longer, they had arms with which to defend both themselves and their newly founded state. There was, several of them recalled, a renewed Jewish sense of pride and dignity; *hadar* had been restored.[11]

But the ship's departure had been delayed, and by the time it was ready to sail, the U.N. cease-fire was in place. Importing arms to Israel was explicitly forbidden under the agreement. The Etzel leadership in Paris made the unilateral decision to send the *Altalena* to Israel, without informing Begin that it had sailed. Begin, they knew, was expressly committed to upholding the cease-fire: "No matter what our attitude to the truce, we may not take upon ourselves responsibility for the possible consequences of its breach."[12] They later acknowledged that they had acted without authorization; they simply claimed that had they transmitted a cable, the plan could have been discovered and the boat confiscated, or sunk. Everything depended on secrecy.

The ship raised anchor on June 11, nearly a month behind schedule.[13] Begin did not learn that it had sailed until the next day, when Radio London (a BBC station) reported the story.[14] He immediately instructed his cable operator, Zipporah Levy, to send a message to the ship. "Keep away. Await further instructions," she typed out, time and again. But she received no reply. She had accidentally mistyped the radio code, and she woke up Begin in the middle of the night to nervously report her mistake. Distraught and agitated, he told her to retype it, and she worked feverishly for hours, trying to get the message through to the ship. Ultimately, she concluded that either there were technical difficulties or those on board were not deciphering the message properly; Lankin, the ship's captain, later admitted that since the message could not be deciphered, he had ignored it and continued the voyage as planned.[15]

Increasingly agitated, Begin gave orders for a telegram to be sent to the Paris office of the Etzel; the ship simply could not approach Israel's shores. "Why did she leave?" Begin wrote to Katz in the telegram.[16] But again, he received no reply.

There was no choice but to tell Ben-Gurion and the leadership of the Provisional Government what was unfolding (though since the story had already been reported on the BBC, they were likely aware of at least some of the developments).[17] A few days later, Begin held a meeting with government officials, emphasizing that the ship had set sail without his permission. Ben-Gurion understood well both the problem of the arms embargo but also the value of the munitions on board. He was clear: Israel needed to keep the arms; but to avoid endangering the Tel Aviv port he instructed the ship to approach shore at Kfar Vitkin, north of Tel Aviv, which was relatively hidden from potential U.N. observers.

The larger question was what to do with the arms once they reached the coast. Begin offered to give most of them to the Haganah, with 20 percent allocated for Etzel fighters in Jerusalem and for some of the new Etzel fighters in the IDF. Ben-Gurion was furious: the mere suggestion that weapons would go to Etzel fighters in a newly united IDF would subvert Ben-Gurion's goal of one united army. He would not bargain about percentages.[18] Israel Galili, the Haganah's chief of staff, offered to buy the weapons and turn them all over to the army, but Begin refused.

By June 18, the ship was in Crete, dangerously close to Israeli waters, with no agreement reached.[19] Finally, Galili agreed that 20 percent of the weapons would be used in Jerusalem, without stipulating who would wield them. He remained deeply distrustful of the Etzel, and on June 19, he played to Ben-Gurion's own misgivings, saying, "A new and dangerous situation has arisen, a demand for a kind of private army, with private weapons, for certain units in the army."[20]

The next day, June 20, Ben-Gurion called an emergency meeting of the cabinet. Etzel soldiers were leaving their units and heading toward Kfar Vitkin to await the ship. They had apparently heard that Begin, who had until recently been in hiding for years and whom many of them had never seen, would also be there. Old Etzel loyalties were warming again. Ben-Gurion told his ministers—falsely—that Begin had hidden the *Altalena* plan until the ship was already at sea. His long-standing mistrust of Begin was reaching the boiling point. Said Ben-Gurion:

There are not going to be two States and there are not going to be two armies. And Mr. Begin will not do whatever he feels like. We must decide whether to hand over power to Begin or to tell him to cease his separatist activities. If he does not give in, we shall open fire.[21]

The council published an official announcement that read:

The Provisional Government and the High Command of the Defense Forces wish to make clear that they are determined to stamp out immediately this traitorous attempt to deny the authority of the State of Israel and of its representatives. The Provisional Government and the High Command will not permit the enormous efforts made by the Jewish people in this country to secure their independence and sovereignty, while fighting a bloody conflict forced on them by external enemies, to be undermined by an underhanded attack from within. Jewish independence will not endure if every individual group is free to establish its own military force and to determine political facts affecting the future of the State. The Provisional Government and the High Command call on all citizens and soldiers to unite in the defense of national unity and the authority of the people.[22]

Begin, who had not initiated the purchase of the ship, who had radioed it to remain far from the coast, and who had informed Ben-Gurion of its impending arrival, was convinced that he had acted entirely honorably. But Ben-Gurion, whose hatred for Begin knew few bounds and who believed that the Etzel had not genuinely joined the IDF, saw disloyalty to the new state all around him. He was convinced that this was simply another Begin threat to his leadership; if he had to, he would use force.

The council decided that when the ship landed, the "officer in charge should endeavor to avoid the use of force, but if his orders are not obeyed, force will be employed." Galili interpreted the cabinet vote as a decision to rid the Etzel of its arms. He decided to use the Air Force to bomb the ship, but the pilots—many of them volunteers from abroad—refused to carry out the mission. "We came here to fight for the Jews, not against the Jews," they said.[23]

Meanwhile, on the beach, Begin instructed the ship to come back after nightfall to avoid U.N. security forces. One aide wondered if they might be heading into a trap, but Begin did not share the concern. After dark, the ship inched close to shore; Begin boarded in order to visit the soldiers and was greeted with applause.[24] The work of unloading tons of arms began, but proceeded exceedingly slowly.

Soldiers (from Haganah and Palmach units) appeared on the beach and instructed Begin (who had since disembarked) to hand over the cargo to the army. Though Galili and Begin had reached the tenuous agreement that the IDF would get all the weapons but the 20 percent that would be used in Jerusalem, Begin understood that the weapons for Jerusalem would be under the Etzel's command, while the IDF assumed that they would control them. The two groups also neglected to stipulate where the arms would be stored after unloading. The Etzel was planning to store the weapons in Etzel-controlled locations, while the Defense Ministry, of which Ben-Gurion was at the helm at the time, insisted that the arms be turned over to the army immediately. Begin told his men to keep unloading. One boy, watching the exchange, grew worried and muttered aloud that he thought the Haganah would shoot at them. Begin reassured him confidently, "Jews do not shoot at Jews!"[25]

The next day, Haganah fighters showed up on the beach in full force. The Holocaust survivors and non-Irgunists aboard the *Altalena* were allowed to disembark. Then, General Dan Even, the brigade commander in the IDF, issued an ultimatum to Begin:

By special order from the Chief of the General Staff of the Israel Defense Forces, I am empowered to confiscate the weapons and military materials which have arrived on the Israeli coast in the area of my jurisdiction in the name of the Israel Government. I have been authorized to demand that you hand over the weapons to me for safekeeping and to inform you that you should establish contact with the supreme command. You are required to carry out this order immediately. If you do not agree to carry out this order, I shall use all the means at my disposal in order to implement the order and to requisition the weapons which have reached shore and transfer them from private possession into the possession of the Israel government.

I wish to inform you that the entire area is surrounded by fully armed military units and armored cars, and all roads are blocked. I hold you fully responsible for any consequences in the event of your refusal to carry out this order. The immigrants—unarmed— will be permitted to travel to the camps in accordance with your arrangements. You have ten minutes to give me your answer.

In Galili's eyes, the ultimatum offered Begin "an honorable way out"; but the sides were continually misreading each other, and Begin deeply resented the mere notion of an ultimatum and what he considered the absurdly short time frame given to him. He did not bother to respond. Nor did he take the army's threats seriously: "We must unload the arms here before the United Nations arrive. I do not believe the army has bad intentions toward us." Dramatically underestimating Ben-Gurion's Machiavellian partisanship, he told one of his officers, "The problem is only the U.N."[26]

Late in the afternoon of June 21, the Etzel commanders tried to persuade Begin to take the ship to Tel Aviv. Things were going badly at Kfar Vitkin, which was an old Haganah stronghold, and they might well get worse. Just then, rifle fire broke out. To this day, it is unclear who fired first. Shlomo Nakdimon, an Israeli journalist who has written extensively about the events surrounding the *Altalena*, suggests that the IDF soldiers opened fire against orders and in the confusion the Etzel returned fire. But Hillel Kook, who was at the beach at Kfar Vitkin, said that the Etzel shot first, aiming their shots into the sea as a sign that they were prepared to fight.[27]

Ya'akov Meridor, who years earlier had convinced Begin to assume command of the Etzel and who was now a member of the Etzel High Command, noted that, when the firing began, Etzel fighters aboard the *Altalena* were instructed not to fire back.[28] As bullets flew overhead, Begin lay on the sand, adamantly refusing to retreat. Eventually, cursing in Hebrew and Yiddish and struggling to believe what was unfolding, Begin himself boarded the ship once again.[29]

To some members of the Etzel, it was clear that Ben-Gurion was trying to assassinate Begin, to end the rivalry once and for all. But there were other victims, as well. The Etzel had already suffered six fatalities and eighteen wounded, while the IDF had two dead and six wounded. Ben-Gurion, worried that protests over the killings of Etzel soldiers could get out of hand, refused to allow the Etzel to bury its dead in Tel Aviv.[30]

Jews were killing Jews; Begin's men insisted that he get away from the troops on the beach. At 9:35 p.m., the *Altalena* departed Kfar Vitkin with Begin aboard and set sail slowly for Tel Aviv, tailed by Israeli warships, and arrived at Tel Aviv at midnight. As the ship left Kfar Vitkin, Meridor, who had remained on the beach, waved the white flag of surrender at the Haganah troops surrounding him, though exactly on behalf of whom he was surrendering was not clear.[31]

For Begin and the Etzel, arriving at the Tel Aviv beach was a public-relations coup. The *Altalena* ran aground, but did so on the busiest stretch of the shore, in full view of hotel guests and beachgoers, reporters, and United Nations observers on hotel balconies.[32] In *The Revolt*, Begin would later claim that the Etzel had sailed the *Altalena* to Tel Aviv because "we could extricate ourselves from these siege conditions and I would be able to communicate directly with the Government and put an end to what I still hoped was a perilous misunderstanding somewhere."[33] He insisted that they came ashore specifically at Frishman Street not because it was in the public eye, but because it was the original docking point. Whatever the intent, though, the *Altalena* was now in full view of the city.

On the IDF side, Yigal Allon, a former Palmach commander, was in charge of the operation. Yitzhak Rabin arrived at headquarters in Tel Aviv by chance and was pressed into service. "It felt like a military putsch," Rabin would recall half a century later in an interview. But even five decades after the events, the Ben-Gurion-inspired mistrust of Begin had not fully abated. It was clear by then that there had been no putsch, but Rabin could not admit that. All he could bring himself to say was "If it was true, I don't know, but there was a feeling."[34]

Early on Tuesday, June 22, Ben-Gurion's government issued one final offer via loudspeaker from the beach in Tel Aviv: "Listen! Listen! A representative of the government and the army will board the ship and arrange to have the people taken off, help for the wounded and unloading of cargo."[35] Begin consented, so long as his representatives could come on board, too. But the Haganah refused.

Begin urged the people on shore not to fight. He began unloading weapons "for ourselves and for you. We have come to fight together," he shouted from the ship. "We shall not fire; we shall not fight our brothers."[36] But his pleas for calm were to no avail. The army opened fire, whereupon the Etzel fighters on the *Altalena*, ignoring Begin's orders to stand down, fired back. One Etzel officer yelled to the shore, "Why are you shooting at Jews?" Rabin responded, "When Jews stop shooting at us, we will stop shooting at Jews."[37]

But Ben-Gurion was committed to using force. That day, he sent a letter to several of his colleagues describing the Etzel's "surrender" and the need to forcibly subdue the ship. When the interior minister asked him if he would still insist that the navy contain the ship if it retreated into international waters, Ben-Gurion responded, "Absolutely."[38]

In the afternoon, a cease-fire was declared so that the wounded could be evacuated. Begin may still not have fully understood the severity of the situation; during the cease-fire, Begin and the Etzel men played songs of the underground from their loudspeaker, and broadcast messages such as "Hello Tel Aviv, from the Hebrew arms ship," and "Our Tel Aviv, in blue and white."[39] At 4:00 p.m., however, when the Palmach resumed firing, he must have understood how determined Ben-Gurion was.[40] Allon claimed they were firing warning shots with hopes that the *Altalena* would surrender; Begin was now convinced they meant to hit him personally and sink the ship.[41] In fact, when Haganah soldiers heard that Begin was on the ship, they apparently increased their fire.[42] Nonetheless, Begin continued to shout over the loudspeaker that his fighters would not return fire.

The Palmach was primed for action, in no small part due to Ben-Gurion's ultimatum. "The entire future of this country is in the balance," Ben-Gurion said to Allon. Yadin added, "You might have to kill Jews."[43]

The Palmach brought cannons to the beach. Hillel Daleski, then a recent immigrant from South Africa who had been in Israel for only two months, was told to prepare his cannon for firing on the ship. He was distraught, and protested to his commander, "I didn't come to the land of Israel to fight against Jews"; the commander's response was "An order is an order."[44]

Daleski's cannon fired, and missed, erring to the south. He and his men recalibrated, and fired again. The shot missed to the north. Then another miss. But the fourth shot hit the ship, and smoke began to billow out of its belly.[45] As more and more of the ammunition ignited, the fire spread and was soon out of control. It was clear that the ship was going to explode. Gunfire from the shore continued. Against Begin's wishes, the white flag of surrender was raised.

Those on board the *Altalena* were not the only ones in danger. There was widespread concern that when the massive stores of ammunition on the ship exploded, the blast might destroy buildings on the coast, as well; but by this point, there was nothing that anyone could do.

With the ship about to blow, the Etzel men on board insisted that Begin be taken ashore. He resisted (the accusation that he'd abandoned his Betar members in Warsaw still haunted him), but as soon as the wounded had been evacuated, his men insisted that he take a launch (he couldn't swim[46]). How exactly Begin got to shore is the subject of conflicting accounts. He later wrote that he jumped into the water, though reluctantly:

> If I continued to stand on the burning ship, it was not out of heroism, but because of a sense of duty. How could I leave the ship which was about to blow up? And there were wounded on board! And the catastrophe could happen at any moment! The commander said to me: "I promise that we shall all get off. Get off! Most of the wounded have been taken off already." So I jumped into the water.[47]

The ship burned behind him as he was taken to shore. Some witnesses, including both Begin and Rabin, recalled that Haganah soldiers intentionally shot at the water as the Irgunists were swimming to the beach, making the most of their last opportunity to kill them.[48]

All in all, including the fight in Kfar Vitkin, the death toll included six-teen men from the Etzel and three from the IDF.[49] Among the dead was Begin's childhood companion Avraham Stavsky, who had been acquitted of Arlosoroff's murder years earlier. Dozens were wounded. Between two hundred and four hundred people were arrested. One estimate puts the number arrested at five hundred.[50] Eight IDF soldiers who refused to fight against the Etzel were later court-martialed for insubordination.[51] Among the Etzel survivors of the attack on the *Altalena* was Yechiel Kadishai, the young British Army volunteer with the impish sense of humor, who had heard Begin advocating action against the British in that 1942 meeting shortly after Begin had arrived in Palestine. Kadishai had departed Pales-tine to participate in the Etzel's bombing of the British embassy in Rome in 1946; the *Altalena* had been his "ride home."

Hillel Daleski, the man who shot the cannon, went on to become an academic and received the Israel Prize (the country's highest award) for literature. Reflecting on the events of that day, he would later note: "If I could erase but one day from my life, I would erase that day."[52]

Begin was too public a figure to arrest. He made his way from the shore to his house, stumbling about soaking wet, without his glasses, which had been lost in the ocean, and without his shoes.[53] He looked utterly lost, spent. It was understandable. His family had been forced to flee Brisk during World War I, and had lost most of what they had. Then the Nazis killed his parents and his brother. The Soviets imprisoned him. The Brit-ish hunted him and forced him into hiding. And now Jews had tried to kill him.

He took to the airwaves and delivered an Etzel radio address that lasted over an hour. The man who had fearlessly stared down his Soviet interrogator and had forced the British to depart Palestine now wept, inconsolable. "It was me they wanted to destroy," he cried, as he outlined his version of the entire saga, beginning with his forewarning Ben-Gurion that the ship was on its way. He reviewed the agreements that he and Ben-Gurion had reached and which, he claimed, the prime minister had blatantly abrogated. Yet even so, he reminded his men time and again, "Do not raise a hand against a brother, not even today." In what emerged as a refrain, he insisted that Jew not fight Jew, for "it is forbidden that a Hebrew weapon be used against Hebrew fighters."

"Long live the Hebrew homeland! Long live the heroes of Israel—soldiers of Israel forever!" he concluded.[54]

Throughout, the theme he repeated most was that his men must not take revenge. "There must not be a civil war with the enemy at our gates!" he virtually shouted in his radio address. The next day he went to speak to a group of Etzel soldiers. One of them later recalled his precise words: "Not one bullet against the Jews! Our enemy is the Arabs!"[55]

In a pamphlet released the day after his address, Begin referred to Ben-Gurion's "dictatorial regime," warning that it would set up "concentration camps," and called the prime minister an "insane dictator" and "that fool, that idiot."[56] He called upon Ben-Gurion to release the men from jail. Many of the Etzel members would be released within a few weeks, except for some of the most senior commanders, including Ya'akov Meridor, Eliyahu Lankin, and Hillel Kook. Due to intense public pressure—especially from American Jewish groups, such as Kook's American League for a Free Palestine—they were released at the end of August.[57]

But Ben-Gurion was not yet done with Begin. On June 24, the Palmach stormed the Etzel's headquarters as part of a general post-*Altalena* raid seeking incriminating materials relating to the "rebellion." Arthur Koestler, a journalist and novelist who had met Menachem Begin when he was still masquerading as Rabbi Sassover, wrote in his journal that the Palmach men "smashed the furniture and tore up the files. On Begin's orders not to shoot at any price, the Irgun boys stood by white-faced and silent, watching the destruction."[58]

On June 23, the day after the *Altalena* was destroyed, the Provisional State Council convened at the JNF building in Tel Aviv.[59] The main topic of conversation revolved around the *Altalena* and the Etzel's "wayward" leader, Menachem Begin, who was, unsurprisingly, not present. Ben-Gurion summarized the events of the *Altalena* to his cabinet: he falsely claimed that he found out about the ship only the day before it arrived, on Saturday, June 19 (he had actually learned of this three days earlier, on June 16). He had been told, he said, that the Etzel had a ship loaded with arms and needed assistance in unloading it. The government told the Etzel to turn the ship over to it, but the Etzel refused. There was never an agreement that the Etzel would be given weapons for Jerusalem. He failed to mention either that there had been an agreement to divide the arms between the two groups or that the agreement had not stipulated whether the Etzel could have the arms at its disposal for the defense of Jerusalem.

In Ben-Gurion's words, the *Altalena* affair was an "attempted assault" by the Etzel, whose members were "dissidents." He outlined the ways in which the Etzel broke the terms of the agreements concerning the IDF and the terms of the cease-fire:

> In violation of the laws of the state and its own guarantees, IZL brought a ship carrying arms to the country. Even if there were no U.N.-imposed truce, this would be a very serious matter, for no country can tolerate the importation of even a small number of weapons by private citizens or organizations without the government's permission.

He described the Etzel's behavior as "an even greater danger because it places the state in jeopardy and creates a climate of civil war." Ben-Gurion also twice pointed out that he had summoned the emergency cabinet to approve military action before he acted—in other words, he had not acted alone. "My duty to ensure the security of the state and enforce the law was clear," he declared, "and I knew this could be done only by force. Nevertheless, I brought the matter before the entire cabinet . . . it was decided that the necessary military forces would be dispatched." As his speech continued, his language became more and more militant:

> I regret to say that some IZL soldiers left their battalions and went to Kfar Vitkin to join the revolt against the government. This was

swiftly quashed, however, and the IZL forces surrendered, hand-
ing over their weapons and military equipment and guaranteeing
to accept the government's demands. Alexandroni, our commander
on the Central Front, acted wisely and well, performing the task
with which he had been charged by the government with maximum
efficiency and minimum casualties . . . The IZL rebellion by soldiers
and civilians in Kfar Vitkin is now over . . .

The present incident may have ended, but the danger has not,
despite the fact that the army is strong enough to put down any
armed uprising . . . It is not by military might alone that the evil
will be uprooted . . . the dissidents derive support from various
sources, for many reasons.

Ben-Gurion latched on to the fact that Israel could not be fighting a
war on two fronts and lambasted the Etzel for its dangerous actions in the
midst of the war with the Arabs. The leader even referred to the Etzel as
"armed gangs" and "evil."

The audacity of armed gangs within the country in acting at this
moment jeopardizes what may be even more important than the
existence of the state itself—the ability of the Jews of this country
to defend themselves for the sake of their own future and that of the
nation. This danger will not pass until the inhabitants of the state,
and Jews throughout the world, realize the tragic consequences of
giving moral and military support to them, as a number of Zionist
organizations do . . . As soon as members of the dissident organizations join the army they are given the same military equipment as
any other soldier . . . Do not rely solely on the army, however. The
entire nation must eradicate the evil which exists among us.

Ben-Gurion justified the actions of the government in attacking the
ship:

If the government had exercised self-restraint and had not acted as it
did, it would have destroyed the war effort and the state . . . Blessed

be the cannon that blasted that ship. Obviously, it would have been preferable to avoid the use of arms entirely and have the ship delivered intact. However, in view of the fact that this was not done, the best thing was to sink it.

The cannon that sank the *Altalena*, he insisted, was so sacred that it deserved to "stand close to the Temple, if it is built."[60]

It was largely to defend himself against accusations that he and the Etzel were a "terrorist" group that Begin wrote *The Revolt* four years later. He knew that he needed to explain to the Jewish world why the revolt had been both necessary and just. And on the subject of the *Altalena*, he wrote that he was convinced Ben-Gurion had manipulated the situation in order to crush the Etzel; the prime minister, he implied, had precipitated the civil war precisely so that he could then quell it.

Begin was undoubtedly telling the truth, but as he saw it. The mistrust between the two was so deep that any potential misunderstanding was bound to spin out of control, and it did. Whether Ben-Gurion really believed that the *Altalena* incident represented a coup attempt by Begin, or whether he simply believed that the *possibility* of a coup existed and that he should quell it preemptively, or whether he saw the incident as an opportunity to rid himself of Begin once and for all, we cannot know with certainty. It is probably the case that Ben-Gurion himself did not know, either. The country was young, Israel was at war, he despised Begin and was fearful for his own political future. Given all those factors, neither man was likely to make tempered judgments. The tragic outcome was almost inevitable.

Begin listed numerous additional counterclaims against Ben-Gurion's accusations: If the Etzel had wanted to stage an armed revolt, he argued, why did it choose to land on a "bottleneck" of a beach with no escape route and in the public eye?[61] As for the accusation that the Etzel was going to stash the arms in a private hidden storeroom, Begin countered that since the end of the underground era, hidden storerooms no longer existed.[62] Finally, Begin accused Ben-Gurion of failing to mention that the Haganah had also broken the U.N. cease-fire on the same day that the *Altalena* landed, when the *Inco* unloaded a shipment of arms at Bat Yam.[63]

During the June 23 deliberations of the Provisional Government at which Ben-Gurion spoke, Rabbi Meir Berlin from the religious Zionist Mizrahi party announced the resignation of two Mizrahi ministers, Rabbi J. L. Fishman and Haim Moshe Shapira. They demanded that the Provisional Government appoint a commission to investigate what had happened. Their request was denied.

For Ben-Gurion, the entire episode was a victory on many fronts. He and the Haganah were able to scapegoat Begin even as they profited from the arms that the Etzel had brought to the fledgling state. In Ben-Gurion's narrative, Begin became the symbolic terrorist, bearing the sins of Zionism into the desert like a proverbial goat from Azazel. Though it was Begin who ordered his men to put down their arms and Begin who would be exiled to the political desert for decades, Ben-Gurion's "holy cannon" would emerge the hero of the story as it was commonly told.

Begin's reputation suffered terribly. Some ridiculed him for his weeping during his speech. Others focused on what they considered his inept management of a complex situation. He acted like a "Yiddishe mamme," recalled Shmuel Katz.[64] But Begin was characteristically unrepentant. His son, Benny, would later recall that some kids at school bullied him about the tears that his father had shed on that radio address. "I don't recall if I was proud of those tears," he said, but "my father was proud of those tears."

His reputation was also tarnished in the United States. *The New York Times* referred to him as a terrorist, while the day after the *Altalena* sank, a *Washington Post* article called the Irgunists "rebels" who planned to bring arms and ammunition into Israel in violation of the U.N. truce.[65]

Ironically, it was the Lechi—and not Ben-Gurion—that indirectly forced Begin to finally shut down the Etzel. When members of the Lechi

assassinated the United Nations Security Council mediator in the Israeli-
Arab conflict, Folke Bernadotte, in September 1948, in Jerusalem, Ben-
Gurion ordered both the Lechi and the Etzel disbanded. This time there
was no resistance. On September 20, the Etzel was ordered to enlist all of
its fighters into the IDF and to hand over all military equipment and fire-
arms within twenty-four hours under the threat of immediate military
action. Begin acquiesced. By November 7, Ben-Gurion had succeeded
in unifying the various Jewish military forces, dissolving the Palmach's
headquarters as well, and the IDF became Israel's sole fighting force.

I n his masterful account of the American Revolution, Joseph Ellis notes
that in the wake of other national movements—the French, Russian,
and Chinese revolutions, as well as the multiple movements for national
independence in Africa, Asia, and Latin America—the leadership class of
the successful revolution proceeded to decimate itself in bloody reprisals
that frequently assumed genocidal proportions. But the conflict with the
American revolutionary generation remained a passionate yet bloodless
affair.[66]

It was largely thanks to Begin that the Jewish state followed the
American model, and not the French. Later in life, he would write, "After
my death I hope that I will be remembered, above all, as someone who
prevented civil war." For Ben-Gurion's part, it was only in 1965 that he
admitted, following a government inquiry into the *Altalena* affair, "Perhaps I was mistaken."[67]

8

Say "No" to Forgiveness

"You may not accept a ransom for the life of a murderer who is
guilty of a capital crime; he must be put to death."
                                                    —*Numbers 35:31*

The civil war may have been (mostly) avoided, but the State of Israel,
just formed, was a house deeply divided. The burned-out, exploded
hull of the *Altalena* remained at the Tel Aviv shore for a year. Worried that
it was becoming a shrine to the memory of the Etzel men who had died
and to the ongoing charisma of Menachem Begin, Ben-Gurion ordered it
towed out to sea and sunk.

Months earlier, Ben-Gurion had set the first Israeli elections for the
Knesset for January 1949. Menachem Begin moved his energies from
the underground to the political arena, and founded the Herut party. A
new phase of his life was now beginning. Old hatreds, though, did not
fade quickly. On the side of what remained of the *Altalena*, someone
painted giant letters that read, HERUT: YOU WILL END UP LIKE THE
ALTALENA.

The elections confirmed Begin's ongoing role as the outsider. Ben-
Gurion's Mapai party won handily, receiving forty-six of the Knesset's
120 seats, while Begin's Herut earned only fourteen. Begin, along with
Hillel Kook, Yochanan Bader, Shmuel Katz, Ze'ev Jabotinsky's son Ari,
and other loyal Irgunists, became members of the Knesset in the main
opposition party.

The relative stability of the political system notwithstanding, the new Jewish state had gotten off to a rough start. Its borders had expanded dramatically beyond the seemingly indefensible boundaries of the 1947 Partition Plan, but what Israel had eked out was an armistice, not peace; its neighbors still refused to recognize it. The Armistice Line, as it was called, would eventually be called the "Green Line," the standard to which the international community would demand that Israel return after the 1967 war expanded the borders even further; but in 1949, no one saw the line as permanent or legitimate.

Territorially, Israel now had control of the coastal plain, the Galilee, and the Negev, while Jordan retained the West Bank and Egypt controlled the Gaza Strip. Jerusalem was divided, with the western half in Israeli hands but the eastern side, including the Old City with its Jewish Quarter and Western Wall, under Jordanian control. The Jordanians also controlled the areas surrounding Mount Scopus, home to Hadassah Hospital (an Israeli convoy, accompanied by UN personnel, was allowed access once every two weeks), and the Mount of Olives, the site of one of Judaism's oldest and most hallowed cemeteries.

Economically, matters were equally difficult. New immigrants, many of them destitute, poured in. Some half million survivors of the Nazi drive to eradicate European Jewry came to Israel's shores during its first years of existence, and they were joined, in turn, by around 700,000 Jews from Arab lands, summarily evicted from their homes and countries when the Arab-Israeli war began. Israel's population was growing rapidly; by the end of 1951, only three years after independence, its Jewish population had doubled.[1] Its economy strained under the burden of the massive influx of new citizens. To add to the misery, a drought in 1950–51 further strained the state's already meager resources.

As the economy faltered, immigrants were housed in corrugated huts in poverty-stricken neighborhoods created specifically for them, and the state had no choice but to rely on foreign aid. The American Jewish community and a variety of Diaspora organizations had been directing financial support to the *yishuv*, and then Israel, for years, but Israel needed more. Without a significant source of new money, there was no guarantee that the country could survive.

D espite the crises, or because of them, David Ben-Gurion's Mapai party retained its dominance in the 1951 elections, winning forty-five seats, while Begin's Herut declined to a mere eight, with just 6 percent of the vote.[2] Dejected, Begin announced that he would leave politics, and on August 20, 1951, less than a month after the election results came in, he formally submitted his resignation letter to Herut.

Begin had planned to spend his self-imposed seclusion at home in Tel Aviv with his growing family, but those plans were upended when David Ben-Gurion announced that he was planning to explore an arrangement whereby Germany would pay reparations to Israel for the deaths of six million Jews. The shadows of the Shoah still hung darkly over Israeli life, and Ben-Gurion's reparation plan now reopened wounds that had barely begun to heal.

Israelis were deeply divided. Some agreed with Ben-Gurion that the matter ought to be explored, but for many, the very notion that the Germans might atone their guilt by giving the Jews money—the German name for reparations, *Wiedergutmachung*, meant, literally, "making good again"—was appalling. Opponents immediately intuited that the best person to lead the fight against the plan was Menachem Begin, and went to draft him to their cause. In doing so, they were unknowingly precipitating another bitter battle between Ben-Gurion and Begin that this time, too, would come perilously close to ripping the country apart.

The suggestion that Germany ought to provide financial compensation for the horrors that the Nazis had perpetrated was not entirely new. As early as 1945, individual Jews and Jewish organizations had been making legal claims against Germany,[3] seeking financial compensation for Jewish property lost or destroyed before and during the war.[4] In 1948, the newly formed Jewish Restitution Successor Organization managed to have property worth some $250 million restored to its original Jewish owners; heirless assets worth more than $25 million were also recovered.

But this restitution affected relatively few people. Most Jews remained ineligible for restitution or indemnification, and more important, the system did nothing to acknowledge the enormous debt that the German people owed to the Jews as a whole.[5] Nor, of course, did it do anything at all to help secure the future of the still fledgling Jewish state.

In March 1951, the government of Israel under Ben-Gurion's leadership presented a specific claim in a letter to the Allied powers occupying Germany. Israel asked for compensation for the costs of absorbing the half million European immigrants who had arrived on its shores, seeking $3,000 for each of the immigrants, for a total of $1.5 billion.[6] The note made clear that the money demanded was based "only on the expenditures incurred and anticipated in connection with the resettlement of the Jewish immigrants from the countries formerly under Nazi control."[7] To whatever extent possible, the request was phrased in a way to make it clear that this was compensation for Israel's resettlement costs, not a settlement for what Germany had done to the Jewish people.

Ben-Gurion did not consider these reparations to be a step toward the normalization of political relations between Israel and Germany. Indeed, from the very moment of its founding, Israel had established a "lack of contact" principle as the dominant facet of the new state's relations with Germany. Israeli passports read, "This document is not valid for Germany."[8] That was precisely why Ben-Gurion presented his claim to the Four Powers occupying Germany rather than to the Germans directly.

Germany, however, was well on its way to sovereignty and the Allies refused to serve as proxies for the Germans in negotiations with Israel. In a reply that would have been unimaginable from Germany just a few years earlier, Konrad Adenauer, the postwar German chancellor, and his government responded to the letter on September 27, 1951, saying that they were "ready, jointly with the representatives of Jewry and the State of Israel, which has received so many homeless refugees, to bring about a solution of the problem of material restitution."[9]

As word spread that Israel might actually negotiate directly with the Germans (the Allies having insisted on that), Israelis erupted in fury. *Ma'ariv*, one of the country's leading newspapers, published a cartoon depicting a German holding a blood-soaked bag of money, extending his arm to give it to an Israeli. To get to the Israeli, however, he had to cross a bridge built over a mass grave, cut off in the middle by the chimney of a crematorium. Some of the most vociferous objections came from the Revisionists and the fighters of the now defunct Etzel. A headline in *Herut* from December 1951 asked, "How much will we get for a burned child?"[10]

The Herut leadership almost certainly understood that this was also an opportunity for a political redemption of sorts; if handled well, the explosive issue of German reparations could afford Begin a chance to end his retirement and to emerge as the leader of a movement that would speak to a broad political spectrum, unifying a wide array of otherwise adversarial political actors.

Begin resisted at first. But Yochanan Bader, who had originally suggested that Begin join the Free Polish Army and was now a fellow MK from the Herut party and editor-in-chief of the *Herut* newspaper, came to see Begin at his home to urge him to reenter the fray. Bader recalled, years later, how he persuaded Begin to return to the field: "Menachem, this is not just a historical issue," Bader told him. "This is your moral obligation to your family, your obligation to your murdered mother."[11]

The invocation of Begin's murdered family had the desired effect, and Begin relented. That very evening he wrote an article, published in *Herut* on January 1, 1952, warning that the government's authorizing the reparations would result in "eternal shame on the Knesset."[12] His rhetoric would become infinitely more heated in the weeks ahead.

So, too, would his constantly tumultuous relationship with Ben-Gurion. By this point, Ben-Gurion's curious appellation for Begin in the Knesset plenum—"The man sitting next to MK Bader"—was well-known. The disdain was mutual, and an incendiary topic such as reparations would only fuel the fire. The battle between the two titans was, to some extent, a battle for the past versus an engagement with the future, a romantic preoccupation with Begin's *hadar* pitted against the pragmatics of Ben-Gurion's nation-building. In a series of speeches and debates throughout that winter, Begin focused on the victims whose memories were being "sold," while Ben-Gurion countered with concern for the survivors for whom the funds would provide enormous relief.

Ever the pragmatist, Ben-Gurion argued that international admiration would come with an economically flourishing Jewish state; Begin, however, insisted that the Jewish state would lose all respect it had painstakingly acquired if Israel—the international face of the Jewish people—now took money from its former oppressors. Ironically, Begin and Ben-Gurion had changed places; Begin was no longer the Diaspora-minded throwback. The "no deal" and "no money" position was also an argument for self-reliance and the cutting of old ties.

By early 1952, Begin was so thoroughly consumed by the reparations issues that he swallowed his pride and began a gradual return to the political arena. For the first time since he had quit political life in August 1951, he appeared in public on January 5, 1952, in Mugrabi Square in Tel Aviv, before some 10,000 supporters. Some of those in the crowd were carrying Torah scrolls, and Begin himself donned a black *kippah*, undoubtedly to make clear that this was no mere political issue. At stake was the dignity of the entire Jewish people; this was a matter not of politics, but of sanctity.

Always inclined to biblical metaphors, Begin evoked the memory of Amalek, the nation that had sought to destroy the Israelis in the desert by preying on the weak, in his address. Germany, like Amalek, was pure evil. The Torah commanded the Jewish people to obliterate the very memory of Amalek; thus, the last thing the Jewish state ought to be considering now was a financial agreement with Germany.

Some Israelis, such as Abba Kovner, a former partisan fighter, took the Amalek analogy even further than Begin, and actually advocated revenge against the Germans, plotting unsuccessfully to poison the water supply of several major German cities. For others, Nazi victims, although not guilty, had "gone like sheep to the slaughter," and their deaths constituted a sort of un-Zionist shame. Young Israelis derisively referred to survivors as "soap." Herzl had seen Zionism as a European movement that would make the Jews safe from European anti-Semitism, but in that regard, Zionism had failed. The reparations fight brought all the paradoxes of Zionism's hybrid origins to the fore.

Begin's rhetoric went beyond the use of painful biblical metaphors—he virtually threatened insurrection. "There will be a turning point in the country's history if the agreement is approved," he warned. "Our people will not pay taxes anymore."[3]

But his protestations went unheeded. On January 6, Ben-Gurion announced the government's intentions to open the debate on accepting reparations from Germany. The acrimonious national dispute reached its climax on January 7, the day the Knesset was scheduled to vote on the issue. Tens of thousands of people from all over Israel had gathered in Jerusalem's Zion Square to protest the debate in the Knesset, then housed only a hundred yards away on King George Street. On a cold and rainy day, Begin addressed his listeners before walking down the street to the Knesset:

> The most shameful event that has ever occurred in the history of our people is about to take place this evening. At this bitter hour, we will recall our hallowed fathers, our slaughtered mothers, and our babies who were led by the millions to the slaughter at the hands of the Satan who emerged from the very bottom of hell to annihilate the remnant of our people.[14]

With that, Begin reminded his listeners of the enormity of the Holocaust in their national narrative. Yes, Ben-Gurion and the Israeli-born sabras might want to move beyond the Holocaust, but both the horror and the recovery were necessary parts of the Jewish people's story. This was a point-counterpoint in which both sides had important light to shed on the question, taken directly out of a proverbial Talmudic argument. Begin continued:

> They are on the verge of signing an accord with Germany and of saying that Germany is a nation, and not what it is: a pack of wolves whose fangs devoured and consumed our people, [and] even though

that blood was spilled like water, it was not for naught. It gave us the strength to rise up against the British enslaver. Because we always asked ourselves how we were better than our slaughtered forefathers, and why they are dead and we alive. That blood, the holy and sanctified [blood], taught us to fight and lead us onto the enemy's battlefield. And it is thanks to that blood that Ben-Gurion, that little tyrant and big maniac, became prime minister . . .

And then the man who had helped avert civil war seemed to threaten it: "There will not be negotiations with Germany, for this we are all willing to give our lives. It is better to die than transgress this. There is no sacrifice that we won't make to suppress this initiative."

Calling attention to the armed police presence, Begin declared his willingness, and that of his supporters, to die for their cause. He then dissolved the distinction between negotiating with Germans and becoming a Nazi:

Mr. Ben-Gurion has sent policemen here carrying—according to information we have just received—grenades and tear gas made in Germany, the same gases that choked our fathers; he has jails and concentration camps. Ben-Gurion is indeed older than I am, and I am more experienced in standing up to a wicked government. And therefore I am announcing: Evil is standing before a just cause—and it will shatter like glass against a rock . . . You will collect taxes by force, services by force, nothing will be given [to the state] by our own free will. We will not have enough prisons to hold the protesters.

Ben-Gurion's police were the Gestapo. Ben-Gurion's prisons were the despised camps of old. In a warning that was to haunt him for the rest of his life, Begin referred back to his decision to lay down arms during the *Altalena* incident, a decision of which he remained proud:

When you fired your cannon on me [during the *Altalena* episode,] I gave the order "no!" Today I will give the order "yes!" . . . You will no longer be a Jewish government, and you will not have moral legitimacy in Israel.

It may have been a cri de coeur blurted out in the passion of the moment. It may have been an intentional threat with no intent to follow through. And it may have been a genuine warning. We cannot know. But Begin's threat—moments before the Knesset debate was to begin—to resort to armed resistance against Ben-Gurion would lead opponents to argue that the "real" Begin was the hunted "terrorist" from his Etzel days, animated by antidemocratic impulses. It would be decades before Begin would begin to escape the cloud of this accusation, to which he had, unquestionably, left himself wide open.

But Begin had positioned himself at the intersection of the Jewish and the democratic in ways that continue to reverberate in Israel. Addressing himself to the "thousands of religious Jews" gathered outside the Knesset, he declared that "we have been denigrated" by the willingness of religious members of the Knesset (many of whom had supported Begin during the *Altalena* incident) to make a deal with Germany. The "we" is telling; not strictly observant, Begin attached himself here to the religious segment of society, accusing Ben-Gurion and the supporters of reparations of selling themselves "to the golden calf: Go forth, my brothers, and do not be afraid of the gas grenades, tell the Jewish policemen: You too are Jewish, we cannot agree to this. Do not raise your hands, because we are not fighting over bread, we are not fighting against rationing; we are fighting for the soul of the people and the honor of the nation."[15]

"The soul of the people and the honor of the nation" was, for Begin, what the conflict was about. The State of Israel was but four years old, and what he wanted to know was whether it had a soul. This was his Jewish version of "give me liberty or give me death." Life itself was not an ultimate goal; life was worthwhile only if the Jews who had narrowly escaped extinction still stood for something.

At 5:30 in the afternoon, Begin completed his speech and strode the short distance up the street toward the Knesset building to take part in

Begin sometime in the 1930s, in his Betar uniform (*Government Press Office, State of Israel*)

The Begin family in Poland in 1933. Left to right: Herzl, Chasia, Menachem, Ze'ev Dov, and Rachel (*Government Press Office, State of Israel*)

Begin in a Betar uniform (right) saluting Jabotinsky (center), circa 1933 (*Government Press Office, State of Israel*)

Mug shot of Begin, prisoner #3983 in Lukishki Prison, Vilna, September 1940 (*Jabotinsky Institute Archives*)

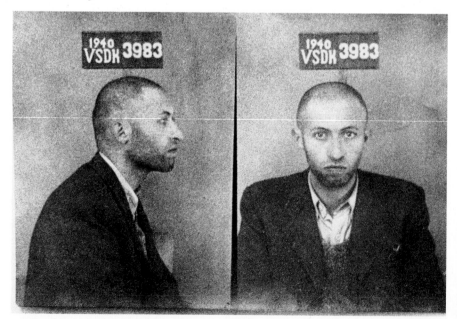

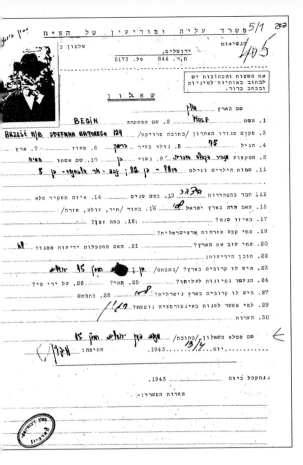

Official document that Begin filled out in Palestine to determine the fate of his family in Poland, April 13, 1943 (*Jabotinsky Institute Archives*)

Begin (front row, left), in his Polish Army uniform, in Palestine in 1942, with Aliza to his left and several Betar colleagues (*Government Press Office, State of Israel*)

Begin, in disguise as Rabbi Israel Sassover, with wife, Aliza, and son, Benny, in Tel Aviv, 1946 (*Jabotinsky Institute Archives*)

Begin appears at the extreme left of this wanted poster distributed by the Palestine Police Force in 1947. (*Jabotinsky Institute Archives*)

THE PALESTINE POLICE FORCE.

WANTED!

REWARDS WILL BE PAID BY THE PALESTINE GOVERNMENT TO ANY PERSON PROVIDING INFORMATION WHICH LEADS TO THE ARREST OF ANY OF THE PERSONS WHOSE NAMES AND PHOTOGRAPHS ARE SHOWN HEREUNDER

قوة البوليس الفلسطيني

مكافآت

גמול

פרסים ישולמו ע"י ממשלת פלשתינה (א"י) לכל אדם אשר ימציא ידיעות שיובילו למאסרם של האנשים ששמותיהם ותמונותיהם נתונים להלן.

British soldiers removing bodies in the aftermath of the King David Hotel bombing, July 1946 (*Imperial War Museum, U.K.*)

The burning *Altalena*, as seen from the Tel Aviv beach, June 1948 (*Jabotinsky Institute Archives*)

Begin speaking at the Herut convention in August 1948 (*Hans Pinn/Government Press Office, State of Israel*)

Begin shakes his fist during a speech in the Knesset in 1961 (foreground, from left to right: David Ben-Gurion, Golda Meir, and Yosef Burg). (*Fritz Cohen/ Government Press Office, State of Israel*)

Begin kisses Aliza's hand after the Likud election victory that made him prime minister, May 17, 1977. (Yediot Ahronoth/*David Rubinger*)

Begin in Afula, welcoming Vietnamese refugees who have been taken in by Israel, 1980 (*Chanania Herman/Government Press Office, State of Israel*)

Begin (front row, second from left) and Aliza watch as the 1978 Salute to Israel Parade proceeds up Fifth Avenue in New York City. (*Yaacov Saar/Government Press Office, State of Israel*)

Begin listens to the *megillah* reading on Purim at the Israeli ambassador's residence in Washington, D.C., 1978. (*Moshe Milner/Government Press Office, State of Israel*)

the deliberations. Hundreds of those gathered in the square followed him. Despite their best efforts, the police were unable to block the protesters from reaching the Knesset and they eventually fired their tear gas. Inside, Begin was in the process of being sworn into office (this was his first official appearance since his departure from public life). But outside the building, matters grew more ominous as his supporters surrounded the Knesset. Amid the yelling and the cacophony from the clashes raging outside, Begin took the podium. He dismissed out of hand the government's contention that these Germans with which it would be negotiating were different Germans from those who had carried out the Final Solution:

> Maybe you will say that the Adenauer government is a new German government, that they are not Nazis? You probably know Adenauer, [so] I ask: In which concentration camp was he interned when Hitler was governing Germany, to which prison was he sent because of the bloodthirsty rule of the Nazis? . . . I will remind you of some facts: Sixteen million Germans voted for Hitler before he came to power. There were twelve million Communists and Social Democrats in Germany. To where did they disappear? The German army had twelve million soldiers, the Gestapo millions, the S.A. and the S.S. millions. To where did they disappear? From a Jewish perspective there is not one German who is not a Nazi, and there is not one German who is not a murderer. And it is to them that you will go get money?[16]

Meanwhile, outside, the rioters whom Begin had riled up with his powerful oratory hours earlier were now throwing rocks at the Knesset building, attempting to break into the hall. Begin continued unfazed, and turned now to the issue of *hadar*, Jabotinsky's notion that pride and dignity were critical for the Jews:

> The Gentiles did not just hate us, they did not just murder us, they did not just incinerate us, they were not just jealous of us—most important, they belittled us. And in this generation that we call

the last generation of submission and the first generation of redemption—in this generation in which we attained a measure of respect, in which we have moved from slavery to redemption—you are coming, because of a couple of millions of impure dollars, because of impure merchandise, to rob us of the little respect that we have managed to obtain.

A volley of stones soon broke through the windows, interrupting Begin's speech. MK Hanan Rubin was hit in the head. The tear gas the police had used now filtered into the debate hall. Through the broken glass of the now shattered windows, the MKs could see cars outside going up in flames.[17] Begin nevertheless continued, now addressing Ben-Gurion directly:

I am turning to you not as an adversary against an adversary; as adversaries there is a chasm between us, there is no bridge, there cannot be a bridge, it is a chasm formed in blood. I am turning to you in the final moment as a Jew to a fellow Jew, as a son to an orphaned nation, as a son to a bereaved nation: Stop, don't do this![18]

Perhaps because he was eager to garner every vote that he could, and perhaps aware that he was going to be accused of antidemocratic demagoguery in light of what he had said earlier to the assemblage in Zion Square, Begin then turned to the Arab members of the Knesset. The power of his oratory outside notwithstanding, he wanted to emphasize that he was unquestionably and fully committed to the rule of law. He made this point by asking the Arab MKs not to vote on this decision: "You have a formal right to vote on this matter; but you ought to distinguish between a formal right and a moral right. This is our matter, the blood of our mothers, brothers, and sisters is intermingled with it; allow us to decide on this matter."

Ben-Gurion, of course, was entirely unswayed by Begin's speech. This was, after all, the same Ben-Gurion who had told the Knesset during the *Altalena* deliberations that he would sink the ship even if it sailed back into international waters. He surely never even considered taking Begin's arguments seriously. Instead, referring to the throng outside, he asked, "And who brought these hooligans here?"

That was too much for Begin, who countered angrily, "*You* are the hooligan!"[19]

But as far as the Speaker of the Knesset was concerned, Begin had now crossed a red line. He demanded that Begin apologize for insulting the prime minister, or he would be removed from the podium. Begin, not surprisingly, refused to stand down, insisting that if he "won't speak, then nobody will speak here."

At 6:45 p.m., scarcely an hour after Begin's return to politics, his speech had brought the Knesset plenum's debate to an utter halt. The army was called in to restore order, and precisely as Begin had predicted in Zion Square, some 140 protesters were arrested. Hundreds of injured policemen and protesters had to be taken to hospitals. The police, again proving Begin's prediction correct, raided the Herut headquarters in Jerusalem and set up roadblocks on the road from Jerusalem to Tel Aviv to ensure that the protest could not resume.

It was not until 9:00 p.m. that Begin agreed to publicly apologize to Ben-Gurion and was permitted to continue his speech:

> One more event occurred before the elections; Mr. Ben-Gurion will remember it. He commanded that I be shot at with a cannon. I was standing in a ship that was going up in flames, I saw my brothers, my boys, my students, dropping dead; my brothers, my boys, my students had machine guns, mortar shells, rifles. I gave the order—in front of the enemy—not to raise their hand, and they listened. In this Knesset, during three years, what decisions you made that crushed our spirits! We left after those decisions with a bowed head, very sad, maybe we had failed in our mission. And after those decisions we went, my friends and I, to that same youth that you are now insulting. That [generation of young men] is risking its life for his nation and for his country, it gave of its blood, twelve of them

went to the scaffold and "Hatikvah" was on their lips until the last second—I went out to this war-trained youth and told them: "This is our Knesset, this is our government. The majority rules, let's go to the people and try to convince them. If we don't succeed, what can we do? This is our nation."[20]

Ben-Gurion was obviously not going to be moved by a man he considered a demagogue, a man who invoked martyrdom and "the sanctification of God's name" at the podium in a country of new post-European Israelis. The two men, beyond even their personal enmity, simply saw the Jewish world through profoundly different lenses.

For Ben-Gurion, the Jewish state was about looking forward, acknowledging the horrors of the European past but moving beyond it. For the prime minister, the Diaspora Jew for whom Begin still mourned was the Jew as he had been described by Chaim Nachman Bialik in his painful epic poem *The City of Slaughter.*[21] In that poem, Bialik describes traditional European Jews as weak-kneed and pale-faced men from the yeshiva, Jews of an era now gone, men who cowered behind casks as they watched Cossacks rape their wives, their mothers, their daughters. It was the poem in which Bialik "accused" these helpless Jewish men of not only having no courage, but because they were so weak, no soul.[22]

Bialik was no longer alive (he had died in Vienna in 1934), but his acidic description of what Europe had been—Gentile viciousness coupled with Jewish weakness—echoed everywhere in Israeli society. Ben-Gurion harbored no romantic memory for the Jewish world that had been lost. It was time, he believed, to jettison completely that European model of what a Jew had been, and to replace it with a vigorous and—if reparations could be passed—economically self-sufficient Israeli. For all of Ben-Gurion's love of the Hebrew Bible, he felt no particular warmth for the Jewish world that had unfolded between the *Tanach* (Bible) and the Palmach (the Haganah's elite fighting unit), as the commonly invoked rhyme put it.

Begin could not have been more different. He was a product of a traditional father he revered, and of the religious schools—the *cheder* and the yeshiva—as well as secular institutions. Although he certainly did not romanticize the Diaspora experience, he could never disparage all that it had been, either. Begin's father, after all, was also a fighter, not in spite of his Jewishness but because of it. Begin had lived longer in Poland than Ben-Gurion had, and in worse times, and he had overseen a militant Jewish organization there. And though certainly familiar with the ethos of passivity Bialik had characterized (Jabotinsky had himself translated the poem into Russian in 1904[23]), he may well have known that soon after the publication of the poem, Jewish self-defense groups were created in Kishinev, too.[24]

Begin was no less committed to the Jewish future, but for him, the past animated the future. Whatever strength Israel might eventually muster, it would do so because the Jewish past would forever remind Jews of why they needed a state. And just as he believed that the Jewish past was more heroic, so he believed the Jewish future would not be exempt from ancient enmities. More religious than Ben-Gurion, by both temperament and training, he was also far less messianic.

For Begin, *vehi she'amda*, the line from the Passover Haggadah—which his father had recited each year in tears—that declares "in every generation, they rise up to destroy us," resonated far louder than any accusation Bialik might have leveled at the Diaspora Jew. Murderous anti-Semites were the villains, and there was no point blaming the Jews for the "shame" of studying in a yeshiva. Begin rejected the impotent Jew of the Diaspora no less forcefully than Ben-Gurion did; it was he, after all, not Ben-Gurion, who had called for the revolt against the British. But Begin—like the Sephardic Jews and religious Zionists who would one day form the backbone of his political party—could not imagine and would never accept a Jewish narrative in which all that Jewish Europe and the Sephardic Diaspora had accomplished was derided.

On January 9, the Knesset voted 60–51 to proceed with the negotiations with Germany. Begin dropped his resistance once the vote was taken. It was, in some respects, reminiscent of how he defended his right to arms on the *Altalena*, and then conceded defeat once the outcome was clear. But his incendiary words spoke louder than his democratic actions, and he was banned from the Knesset for three months.[25] The reparations, combined with other foreign aid sources, were used to improve housing, create an Israeli fleet and national airline, build roads and telecommunication systems, and establish electricity networks.[26]

But the memory of what Germany had done would remain a powerful part of Israeli culture. Yad Vashem, Israel's internationally known Holocaust museum and memorial, was first established in 1953 by a law in the Knesset. In 1960, the Israeli intelligence agency, the Mossad, captured Adolf Eichmann, one of the organizers of the death camps and a close advisor to Hitler, and brought him to Israel. His execution in 1962—after the hugely publicized trial in a civilian court that preceded it—was a great catharsis for Israel, but the ten years that had passed since the reparations debate had been, for a young country, an eternity. In 1965, Israel received ambassadors from Germany, which marked the beginning of what would become a solid and mutually respectful political relationship. But the reparations debate had always been about Israel more than Germany.

I n many respects, the reparations debate afforded Begin an opportunity to undo much of the damage done to his reputation during the *Altalena* tragedy. During the debate, and afterward, Begin had emerged as the defender of the Jewish soul of the Jewish state. He was redefined as the political voice for whom the dignity of Jewish memory and its inseparability from Jewish survival mattered more than anything else. In some respects, the episode cleared the way for the role he would eventually play as the most Jewish of Israel's prime ministers.

9

Of Whom Were We Afraid?

"You shall have one standard for stranger and citizen alike."
—*Leviticus 24:22*

By 1962, the Jewish state was no longer on the brink of economic collapse or civil war. The 1956 Sinai Campaign, Israel's second major war, convinced the international community, including the United States, that the fledgling country was no passing phenomenon; until that war, many nations had assumed it would survive a few years and collapse. Israel captured the Sinai Peninsula and Gaza Strip from Egypt, and though it soon returned them as a result of American pressure, the crisis secured Israel's freedom to navigate through the Straits of Tiran and, more important, changed not only the world's view of Israel, but Israelis' perceptions of themselves. The Jewish state was coming of age.

The "Kadesh Campaign," as the 1956 war was known, revealed that Ben-Gurion had absorbed more than a bit of Jabotinsky's "Iron Wall" doctrine. Israel had struck preemptively, and Ben-Gurion had come to understand that—just as Jabotinksy had said—Egypt would understand nothing but force. Nevertheless, stark differences remained between Ben-Gurion's worldview and that of Begin, and nothing revealed them as much as a little-known crisis that gripped the country in 1962.

Israel's Declaration of Independence asserted that a "Constitution [shall] be adopted by the Elected Constituent Assembly not later than the 1st

October 1948." But October 1948 came and went with no constitution ratified, and as the dust from the War of Independence settled, it became
clear that Ben-Gurion had little intention of expending the political
capital that would be needed to get one passed. Rejecting the American
model that positioned a constitution as a central pillar of democracy, he
advocated for the signing of Basic Laws, which would one day, collectively, make up the basis of a constitution.

In large measure, Ben-Gurion was hoping to avoid a showdown with
the religious parties; he understood that defining the limits of the Jewish
religion in a newly founded Jewish state would unleash political battles
with which he simply could not contend at that point. He preferred to
acquiesce to the agreed upon status quo—in which the Sabbath would
be honored in public spaces, food served by government offices and the
army would be kosher, and Haredi men would not be drafted into the
army—without defining the principles upon which the status quo was
based. That unspoken acquiescence meant that he had to dodge the issue
of the constitution.

Naturally, Begin objected to Ben-Gurion's tacit decision not to move a
constitution forward. Begin was, of course, loath to forgo an opportunity
to take a shot at what he saw as Ben-Gurion's limitless quest for power.
Without mentioning Ben-Gurion explicitly, he said in a July 1956 Knesset
speech:

> The day will come when a government elected by our people will
> fulfill the first promise made to the people on the establishment of
> the state, namely: To elect a founding assembly whose chief func-
> tion—in any country on earth—is to provide the people with a
> constitution and issue legislative guarantees of civil liberties and
> national liberty . . . For the nation will then be free—above all, free
> of fear, free of hunger, free of the fear of starvation. That day will
> come.[1]

But Begin the lawyer and the man committed to the rule of law also
disagreed with Ben-Gurion as a matter of principle. He argued that with-

out a constitution the power of the majority party (Ben-Gurion's, in this case) would go unchecked, and as a result, the failure to adopt a constitution would also endanger individual and minority rights. "We have learned," he said in 1952, "that an elected parliamentary majority can be an instrument in the hands of a group of rulers and act as *camouflage* for their tyranny. Therefore, the nation must, if it chooses freedom, determine its rights . . . in order that the majority thereof, that serves the regime more than it oversees it, should not negate these rights."[2]

He held these views consistently, for the duration of his career. In a February 1962 Knesset debate regarding the repeal of the Emergency Regulations that had been instated shortly after Independence, he again invoked the importance of defending the rights of Israel's Arabs:

Some say that it is impossible for us to provide full equal rights to Arab citizens of the state because they do not fulfill full equal obligations. But this is a strange claim. True, we decided not to obligate Arab residents, as distinguished from the Druze, to perform military service. But we decided this of our own free will and I believe that the moral reason for it is valid. Should war break out, we would not want one Arab citizen to face the harsh human test that our own people had experienced for generations . . . We believe that in the Jewish state, there must be and will be equal rights for all its citizens, irrespective of religion, nation, or origin."[3]

Begin's stance on the constitution and its related issues came as a surprise to many, especially in the Mapai camp, who had been taught to see him as nothing more than a fascist. Even *Haaretz* paid Begin a grudging compliment when it opined, "It is strange to see how a political movement that by its very nature usually tends to strengthen the executive force is asking here to represent pure liberalism."[4]

But Begin did not push the constitution as feverishly as one might have expected. He, too, was conflicted about the battle that would emerge with the religious parties; as a lover of the Jewish tradition and a man committed to the rule of law, he was probably himself somewhat conflicted on what the principles ought to be and did not want to fight the battles that would undoubtedly have emerged.

Internal Herut politics were also at play. Eri Jabotinsky, then living in the United States, represented an arm of the Revisionists who believed that Israel ought to separate itself from the "obsolete ancient civilization" of Judaism. Begin obviously disagreed vociferously, but given his precarious political condition in Israel, he could not afford a split in his own ranks. For an array of reasons, therefore, he made perfunctory remarks about the importance of a constitution, but, like Ben-Gurion, did little to move one forward. Sadly, in what was a grave mistake on each of their parts, Ben-Gurion and Begin both left those battles for future Israeli generations to contend with.

The 1962 crisis known as the Soblen Affair not only highlighted the radically different ways in which Ben-Gurion and Begin thought Israel should react to international pressure, but—like the constitution issue—also revealed a great deal about Begin's commitment to coupling Israel's Jewish commitments to the rule of law, a point that was particularly critical in light of his provocative rhetoric during the debate on reparations.

Robert Soblen, a Jew who had been born in Lithuania but naturalized as an American citizen in 1947, practiced psychiatry in New York.[5] In July 1961, he was convicted by American courts for espionage on behalf of the Soviet Union and sentenced to life in prison.[6] Unlike other, more famous cases (such as that of Julius and Ethel Rosenberg), no one doubted that Soblen was guilty. But perhaps because he suffered from lymphatic leukemia and perhaps because the United States hoped that he might give up secrets in exchange for a furlough, Soblen was granted a brief bail before beginning his sentence. He was to surrender himself to the authorities on June 28, 1962.

The wily Soblen exploited his temporary freedom and left the country the day before his sentence was to start. Using his deceased brother's

Canadian passport, he fled the United States and went to Israel. On June 29, two days after he landed, Soblen was arrested by the Israelis.

At that time, Israel had no extradition treaty with the United States. But the Americans wanted Soblen back; they wanted the information he had yet to divulge and they wanted him to serve his sentence. Prime Minister Ben-Gurion saw no reason to scuffle with the Americans over him. The justification for sending him back to the United States, Israel claimed, would be his illegal entry into the country with a passport that was not his, and not his illegal activities in America. Ben-Gurion wanted to stay out of what he saw as an entirely domestic American issue. The Israelis therefore announced that they would keep Soblen in custody for ten days as they investigated the legality of his entry into the county, and would then act.

The Israelis, however, did not wait ten days. Soblen was expelled from Israel on July 1, only two days after his arrest, under the orders of Minister of the Interior Moshe Shapira. In the custody of a U.S. marshal, Soblen was placed on an El Al flight bound for New York by way of Athens and London.

Thirty minutes before his plane landed in London, Soblen stabbed himself in the stomach and slit his wrists, turning what was to have been a brief stop for fuel into an extended stay for medical care. Once he had recovered in an English hospital from his attempted suicide, Soblen initiated legal actions to prevent his extradition to the United States, and sought to remain in Britain. The request was denied, whereupon the British demanded that the Israelis take their ward and fly him to the United States.

Not surprisingly, the story captured international attention. In the United States, *The New York Times* front page on June 29, 1962, announced, "Soblen Flees to Israel and Is Arrested; U.S. Asks Return, Seizes $100,000 Bail."[7] Three days later, the *Chicago Tribune* proclaimed, "Soblen Tries to Kill Self!"[8]

Having failed to kill himself, Soblen tried to immigrate to Israel under the 1950 Law of Return, which guaranteed every Jew the automatic right to immigrate to Israel. The Law of Return was the state's response to the stories of the *St. Louis* and the *Exodus*, boats loaded with Jewish refugees whom no country would take in and which then were turned back, or of the *Struma*, which was sunk with its almost one thousand homeless Jewish passengers still on board. The Law of Return was the legislative representation of a new existential condition for Jews the world over; never again would Jews wander without a place to go.

While Soblen convalesced in England awaiting word from Israel, the subject of his eviction from Israel erupted in the Knesset. Once again, Ben-Gurion and Begin were at odds. Begin accused both Ben-Gurion, his nemesis, and Moshe Shapira of having acted illegally, bypassing Israel's justice system in order to pander to the Americans. Since Israel and the United States had not signed an extradition agreement, he insisted, Israel was under no legal obligation to return Soblen to the Americans. Yet Soblen had been forced onto the El Al flight to the United States with a U.S. marshal, who allegedly told authorities in Britain that Soblen was "his prisoner."[9] In addition, even though the legal basis for Soblen's expulsion was said to be the illegal manner by which he entered the country, Soblen had not been allowed to remain under arrest while his lawyer petitioned the Israeli courts. Rather, Soblen's lawyer, Ari Ankorion, had been told explicitly that Soblen was to be expelled only when he was *already* on the flight out of Tel Aviv.

Like many of Begin's speeches, his impassioned plea to the Knesset on Soblen's behalf was rich with Jewish allusion. By now, members of the Knesset knew that when Begin would address the plenum, they would witness an extraordinary oratorical and rhetorical display. For Begin, violating an Israeli law to gratify another nation to which Israel had no legal obligation constituted a form of national betrayal, which was to say a form of Jewish betrayal. In his speech to the Knesset on July 11, Begin addressed himself to the minister of the interior, who had also studied in a yeshiva in Europe, and spoke to him in language that evoked classic Talmudic dialogue:

You know, Mr. Shapira, that I view you with both respect and affection, but I beg you to understand: If Reuben deceives Simeon and uses his signature, and in so doing acquires a certain amount of money, should Reuben appear before the court to justify his actions, he cannot, for the sake of his acquittal, make the claim, "But I succeeded!"[10]

Similarly, Begin insisted, the Israeli authorities could not claim that the ends justified the means in their handling of Soblen.[11] When legal procedure has been violated, the outcome is tainted by definition. Begin had come a long way from his threats against Ben-Gurion in the reparations debates. Perhaps because of the damage he had done to his own reputation then, *he* was now the one arguing that the rule of law was sacrosanct.

Some people suspected that Begin was also animated by his enduring hatred for the British, who had hunted him like a criminal, put a price on his head, and hanged his fighters. But in the Knesset, at least, he never once mentioned the British. His arguments were strictly focused on reverence for Israeli law, which in Begin's rhetoric became an extension of Jewish law.

Half a dozen times in a relatively short speech, Begin stressed that deporting Soblen without notifying his attorney was a violation of the rule of law and of Soblen's due process. A "government that respects law and justice," he declared, should have been willing to take its case to court "with heads held high, a pure heart, and clean hands."[12] This government's hands, he thundered, were anything but clean.

Begin provided no explicit source for his quote about "clean hands and pure heart," which comes from Psalm 24, but for most of his listeners, there was no need to. He had chosen a psalm recited by the entire congregation upon returning the Torah to the Ark. Without mentioning Judaism or prayer book or synagogue, Begin made Israeli law synonymous with the Torah, while suggesting that Ben-Gurion's secular pragmatism was a form of sacrilege. He may also have had in mind Ben-Gurion's speedy withdrawal from the Sinai Peninsula after the 1956 victory, succumbing even then to American pressure.

In his Knesset speech, Begin also referred to a well-known verse from Proverbs, "It is through trickery that you shall wage war."[13] But he added that wars are waged only against enemies, and "the law is not an enemy."[4] Here, too, the legacy of the *Altalena* smoldered.

As to why the government had not publicized its decision to deport Soblen, Begin asked rhetorically, "Of what were we embarrassed? Of whom were we afraid?" There was nothing to be embarrassed about, Begin insisted, no one before whom the Jewish state had to cower. Years earlier, Begin had written derisively of British hangings, noting: "There is no precedent in history of a government carrying out a death sentence in such fear and in such secrecy." Ben-Gurion, it seemed to him, was mimicking the shameful behavior of the detested British.

The Soblen case evoked for Begin, once again, the matter of *hadar*, the head held high, of which the Betar anthem had spoken. In Soviet prison, Begin had refused to deny that he was a Zionist or a member of Betar. There was nothing wrong with being a Zionist, he insisted; the fact that it annoyed the Soviets did not make it a crime. Now, too, Israel had acted appropriately when it arrested Soblen and insisted that it would hold him for ten days; the fact that holding Soblen might have annoyed the United States did not make it wrong. Ben-Gurion and Shapira had brought shame (the opposite of *hadar*) on Israel for no reason at all.

Israel afforded the Jewish people the opportunity to transcend their historical role as subservient semicitizens, Begin wanted his listeners to understand. In the past, any action distasteful to the local authorities or neighbors could endanger the Jews' property, even their lives; Jews always had lived in fear. Now they did not. Israel's significance lay in changing that existential dimension of Jewish life.

Begin alluded to that as he ridiculed Ben-Gurion's incomplete legal education:

> The prime minister has told us that as a young man, he studied law. But Mother History did not permit him to complete his studies. I do not know how much time you studied, Mr. Ben-Gurion, but whatever time you studied should have been sufficient for you to learn that every man must be given an opportunity to present his

case before a court. There is a law of expulsion, a law of extradition, and many other laws. But there is *in a state governed by the rule of law* a Law of Laws: the obligation to allow every man to take his case to court.[15]

The sting was not only the ridicule of what he believed was Ben-Gurion's legal amateurism. The real slap was the reference to Mother History. In kowtowing to the Americans, Begin suggested, it was Ben-Gurion and not Begin the Diaspora Jew who was truly trapped in a history of old. Jews were now sovereign in their ancestral homeland, and no foreign power could dictate to Israel how to behave. If the Americans wanted Soblen, they could wait for the Israeli courts to rule on the matter.

Ben-Gurion, of course, was hardly left speechless. He provided a legal defense of his position in an article published in the newspaper *Davar*,[16] where he focused on the need to prevent the Law of Return from allowing Israel to become "a haven for cheats and crooks." The man willing to chase the *Altalena* into international waters in order to destroy it had no qualms about tossing out undesirables without due process. While Begin's argument was that by failing to honor due process—in its haste to placate the Diaspora—the Jewish state would itself become criminal, Ben-Gurion's justification was that Diaspora Jews would stop their voluntary support for the Jewish state if they saw it welcoming Jewish criminals.

In some sense, both Begin and Ben-Gurion were operating out of pre-state ideas. Begin could hardly have harbored much love for a man like Soblen, who spied for a country that had once imprisoned and tortured Begin. But Begin had once been branded a criminal himself, and he believed that fleeing Jews deserved the benefit of the doubt when the culture that incriminated them was itself suspect. For Ben-Gurion, the opinion of Diaspora culture—a small but essential portion of which had voted for the partition of Palestine (which Revisionists such as Begin rejected out of hand)—was essential for Jewish survival.

Ben-Gurion could argue—with much justification—that building a state was a practical matter that trumped all else. But debate and rhetoric were hardly incidental matters. The Jewish state was also built by words—quite literally as it revived an ancient language. In Israel today, terms such as "purity of arms"—indeed the very use of "to ascend" as a verb describing the move to Israel—are more than mere practical terminology but carry the weight of biblical injunction and rabbinic morality.

Begin, with his grounding in the scriptural and liturgical, used the Soblen affair—and many other debates—as an opportunity to read into the Knesset record, and into the national soul, a set of principles that continue to reverberate to this day.

The debate raged on. On July 30, the cabinet voted unanimously to reject Soblen's application for a visa under the Law of Return. The next day, on July 31, members of the opposition questioned the minister of transportation regarding his part in forcing Soblen onto an El Al flight to leave the country. They debated for so long that they delayed the vote confirming the budget, and for several hours on August 1, Israel found itself without a ratified budget.

By this point, however, the handling of Soblen's case had become a full-blown Israeli political controversy, and it was now politically impossible for Israel to collude in his extradition to the United States. On that score, Ben-Gurion had lost. The Israelis agreed to take Soblen back to Israel and then permit him to fly to Czechoslovakia, for which he did have a visa. A *Baltimore Sun* article from August 4 announced dramatically, "Airline Refuses to Fly Soblen to U.S.: El Al Defies British Directive on Israel Government Orders."[7]

Ultimately, though, the British and Americans arranged to have Soblen brought to New York on a Pan American airplane. But shortly before the flight, Soblen took an overdose of barbiturates, fell into a coma, and was pronounced dead on September 12, 1962.

The entire episode was soon forgotten. Today, hardly anyone even knows about it. But it served Begin's purposes. He had stood up to Ben-Gurion, made an impassioned plea for what he believed was right, and in the process further established his role as the Jewish conscience of the Jewish state.

10

The Style of a Good Jew

"And you shall remember all the ways which the Lord your God
has led you these forty years in the wilderness, that he might
humble you, testing you to know what was in your heart."

—*Deuteronomy 8:2*

In June 1963, Prime Minister Ben-Gurion resigned suddenly, in the aftermath of a failed Israeli covert operation that become known as the Lavon Affair. He left public life for Kibbutz Sde Boker, deep in the Negev Desert, and turned over the reins of government to Levi Eshkol.

Almost as soon as Eshkol took over, Begin raised with him an issue that had long given him no rest. Ever since the establishment of the state, Ben-Gurion had refused to permit Ze'ev Jabotinsky's reburial in the national cemetery on Mount Herzl in Jerusalem. Jabotinsky had specifically requested in his will that the Israeli government—when it came into being—bury him in Israel, and Begin had embarked on a mission to see that wish fulfilled after 1948. It was for Begin a personal quest, but also a political one that would strengthen Herut's legitimacy.[1]

Now that the "Old Man," as Ben-Gurion was commonly called, had left the political stage, Begin could inch closer to the center of power without his nemesis blocking his way. With Ben-Gurion out of the picture, there were no other Israeli titans to replace him, and with personal animosities no longer obstacles, Labor and Revisionist Zionists could also begin to work more closely together. The two sides of the Jordan might never come together under one flag, but the divided elements of Zionism could now begin a tentative reintegration. Menachem Begin and Levi Eshkol worked together on Ze'ev Jabotinsky's reburial.

The reburial was important to Begin for other reasons, as well. In *White Nights*, he had often reflected more on the suffering of others than he did on his own. In one poignant passage, Begin describes leaving behind a Jewish friend named David Kroll, whom he had met on the train to the labor camp. Kroll, a middle-aged man who had left behind his mother and his new wife when he was arrested, was among the small number of Jewish prisoners who banded together in a tight-knit group. When Begin was relocated to another labor camp in August or September of 1941, Kroll stayed behind, mistakenly believing that the recently signed pact between the Soviet and Polish governments would allow him, as a Polish citizen, to be set free. Instead, he apparently died at the labor camp while awaiting his freedom. Begin wrote, "Somewhere in the frozen north, his bones lie buried. My people will remember the name of David Kroll among the rest of its martyrs who died for Zion and for Jerusalem." Begin may not have been able to give either his parents or his fellow prisoner a proper burial, but he would now attend to the final resting place of his inspiration, mentor, and father figure.

Begin, who had been married in his Betar uniform and who forever believed in the paramount significance of public pomp, orchestrated a series of ceremonies that afforded his master great honor. When Jabotinsky's body was exhumed in New York and then taken to the airport, Times Square was temporarily renamed Jabotinsky Square in his honor.[2] Eshkol met Jabotinsky's remains, and those of Jabotinsky's wife, at Orly Airport, from where the body was flown to Israel. Begin and three hundred Herut supporters met the entourage at Israel's airport, where former members of the Irgun placed Jabotinsky's sword on the coffin. The coffins were then brought to Tel Aviv, stopping in Ramat Gan and resting beside the monument to Dov Gruner, the Etzel fighter whose hanging by the British had so infuriated Begin. The following day, the coffins were brought to Mount Herzl, the national cemetery for fallen Israeli leaders and heroes; President

Shazar was the first to place earth on the coffin. Ben-Gurion, who had said he would attend the ceremony, apparently did not.[3]

A few days later, the Knesset met in a special session in Jabotinsky's honor. Once exiled from Palestine by the British, and his ideological heirs subsequently exiled to Israel's political margins, Jabotinsky was now officially part of the Israeli Zionist narrative. The Knesset Speaker, Kaddish Luz, spoke for a full hour, acknowledging the deep ideological divisions that still remained, and insisted that Jabotinsky's manifold accomplishments and sacrifices sufficed for him to merit being seen as one of the great leaders of Zionism and founders of the state.

The honor done Jabotinsky was an implicit recognition of Begin's legitimacy, as well, and Begin thus continued his march toward the heart of Israeli political life. He became a master of the unique Israeli parliamentary system, in which a coalition of at least sixty-one votes was needed to control the Knesset. He joined forces with the Liberal Party to form the "Herut-Liberal Bloc," called by its Hebrew abbreviation, Gahal.

The new party was meant to reflect Begin's long-held positions; indeed, speaking about the commitments of the newly created partnership, Begin said, "The freedom [Herut] movement will continue to insist on the idea of the wholeness of our ancestral homeland, which is to say, the Jewish people has a right to the Land of Israel, in all its historic borders, and that right is inalienable."[4] Begin had a new party, but his beliefs had not budged.

Gahal, Begin's new party, won twenty-seven seats in the 1965 election, but it was still not enough. Ben-Gurion's former party, now called the Alignment (an assortment of socialist parties dominated by the Labor Party, which replaced Mapai) took forty-five seats, but with Levi Eshkol at its head, the Alignment was struggling. Ben-Gurion, ironically, contributed to the erosion of his former party's domination by returning to politics and forming his own party, Rafi, but it won only ten seats in the election. Ben-Gurion was fading; Begin, in contrast, was slowly rising, and though he was still in the opposition, the political sands were shifting.

Ironically, it was Israel's enemies who moved Begin closer to the seat of real power. After Ben-Gurion left office, the borders with the Arab states, particularly Egypt, Syria, and Jordan, grew increasingly tense. By the spring of 1967, Syrian artillery had been firing on Israeli settlements for months; cross-border raids and aerial dogfights above the Sea of Galilee were frequent occurrences, and Cairo Radio blared, "Egypt, with all its resources, is ready to plunge into a total war that will be the end of Israel."[5] The Egyptian press, a mouthpiece for Egyptian president Gamal Abdel Nasser, warned that Egypt would "push the Jews into the sea."[6] Al-Fatah raids across the Jordanian border were a persistent problem.

When Nasser ordered U.N. peacekeepers to depart and then blocked the Straits of Tiran, war was inevitable. Though it did not promise to send troops of its own to defend Israel, the United States had specifically promised at the 1956 withdrawal from the Sinai that Israel would have the right to defend itself if Egypt limited Israel's access to the Gulf of Aqaba.[7]

Eshkol called for a national unity government on June 1, which meant that Begin, for the first time in his political career, was a member of Israel's cabinet. He was a minister without portfolio—which is to say not assigned any official ministerial responsibility such as finance, interior, or defense—but at last the perennial outsider was part of Israel's government during the greatest trial since 1948.

Begin made the most of the opportunity. In what many regarded as an astonishing move, though in fact it accorded deeply with his obsession with Jewish unity, it was Begin who floated the idea of asking Ben-Gurion to suspend his retirement and serve as prime minister during the period of emergency. Ben-Gurion declined, but his response captured an emerging sentiment. "If I knew Begin like I know him now," he would later say, "the face of history would have been different."[8]

Weeks of waiting produced virtually intolerable tension. More than 10,000 graves were dug in public parks and 14,000 hospital beds prepared, in anticipation of the massacre many believed was inevitable.[9]

At the same time, in the religious, Zionist camp, Jabotinsky's spirit revived. His remains were now in Israel, his ideological heir was in the government for the first time, and suddenly, a religious figure, Rabbi Zvi Yehuda Kook, the son of the former chief rabbi of the *yishuv* and the inspiration for what would eventually become the settler movement, gave an impassioned speech. Why, he asked, were the Jewish people content to have divided the land in 1948: "Where is our Hebron? Are we forgetting it? And where is our Nablus? Are we forgetting it? And where is our Jericho? Are we forgetting it? And where is our east side of the Jordan? Where is every lump and chunk? Every bit and piece of the four cubits of God's land? Is it up to us to give up any millimeter of it?"[10]

It was, metaphorically, an added verse to the Betar anthem, an echo of the verses that Jabotinsky had written, "the Jordan river has two banks—this one is ours, but so is that." The secular Jabotinsky had planted the seeds of the "Whole Land of Israel Movement"; now the passionately religious Rabbi Kook picked up where Jabotinsky had left off, responding to the impending crisis not with doom but with messianic fervor.

Elsewhere, though, desperation was omnipresent. Ben-Gurion had been a complicated man, but no one doubted his giant stature. Eshkol paled in comparison; both he and the country knew it. To make matters worse, it was not just the Arabs who threatened Israel. The Soviets were lurking just behind Nasser, and the United States, which Ben-Gurion had been so desperate to placate in the Soblen affair, was—as Begin had worried in 1956—now too busy with Vietnam to live up to its post–Sinai Campaign pledge to safeguard Israel's security.[11] The Jewish state was on its own; some Israelis could not help but notice that even in their sovereign state they lived and died at the mercy of enemies sworn to their destruction, just as had been the case in Europe. The lessons of Diaspora history that Begin had been preaching for decades suddenly rang true; what had happened to the Jews in the Diaspora could not be erased by a Jewish state. Eternal patterns of Jewish fate, Begin had long insisted, would endure wherever Jews lived. Nasser proved Begin right.

Unlike the pattern in Europe, however, the Israelis did not wait to go like lambs to the proverbial slaughter. In a now well-known preemptive attack, the Israeli Air Force struck first, destroying the Egyptian Air Force almost in its entirety as it rested on the tarmac. The outcome of the war, which lasted six days, was determined by the success and boldness of the decision to preempt, though the ensuing days would still entail much brutal and costly fighting. In under a week, Israel drove Egypt out of the Sinai, captured the Golan Heights from Syria, and, with the enthusiastic support and encouragement of Begin, reclaimed East Jerusalem and the Temple Mount. The Old City of Jerusalem, which Begin had hoped the *Altalena*'s arms and the Etzel's fighters might conquer in 1948, was now in Israeli hands. So, too, were Mount Scopus, the site of the horrific Hadassah Hospital massacre, and the Mount of Olives. Israel had tripled its size; while most Israelis referred to the conflict as the Six-Day War, Begin called it the War of Redemption and Salvation.[12]

The West Bank and Gaza Strip were also under Israeli control now, and with them came one and a half million stateless Palestinians. As Israel had no plan for what to do with either the territory or the people who lived on it, the Six-Day War unleashed an internal Israeli ideological and political conflict that has never been resolved.

Even in the first days of the war, with the battles still raging, Begin—newcomer to the cabinet though he was—revealed the style and commitments that would be his legacy. The minutes of the cabinet meeting of June 6, 1967, record an extraordinary request on the part of the man who had just begun to end his political exile. The cabinet was discussing how to handle Jordan's King Hussein, when Begin insisted that the Old City be taken, and without delay. And then he said:

And here I have a sentimental request. We keep using the term "capture," which from a military perspective is correct, but with regard to the Old City we should say "liberate." If that raises any doubts, we can simply state that the Old City of Jerusalem, the City of David, is in the hands of the IDF [without saying that it had been "captured"].[13]

And then, the Begin whose fascination with pomp and ceremony had been in evidence as early as his Betar days, continued:

If we do enter the Old City, and maybe this is simply a ceremonial matter, though in my eyes it is of supreme importance, immediately, if we can physically pull it off, from a military point of view, the prime minister and the members of the government, with the two Chief Rabbis, should go to the Western Wall and say *Shehechiyanu* [a traditional blessing to mark an achievement and good fortune] and "When the Lord brought back the exiles of Zion [Psalm 126]" and anything else that should be recited.

At the height of the war, in the midst of a tense cabinet meeting about existential matters, Menachem Begin saw the unfolding events not through a military or political prism, but through the prism of Jewish history. He had no compunction about stating, unequivocally, that this war was the latest battle in an epic war for survival that the Jewish people had been waging since time immemorial.

W ith the war still raging and the Old City not yet in Israeli hands, Begin was already determined that Israel's nomenclature should convey that this was ancestral Jewish land, not merely "captured" territory; and he wanted a ceremonial celebration to reflect that. Ten years later, he would return to that Wall, for a very different symbolic moment.

As in 1949 and 1956, Israeli victory did not bring peace. The Arab countries, along with Palestinian representatives, held a conference in Khartoum shortly after the war and emerged with a declaration that famously insisted there would be "no peace, no recognition, and no negotiations" with Israel. But to many Israelis, the victory felt decisive, even miraculous to some, and a feeling of invincibility began to set in. Begin, however, understood—better than most—that Arab reprisal was all but inevitable.

A year and a half after the war, in February 1969, Levi Eshkol died suddenly from cardiac arrest; the national unity government dissolved shortly afterward. But the 1969 elections that followed did little to bolster Gahal (the composite party of Herut and Liberals), which remained with twenty-six seats, while the Alignment (now in an alliance with another left-wing group, Mapam) increased its share of the Knesset to fifty-six seats. Golda Meir, who had replaced Eshkol as party leader, maintained the good relations with Begin, who referred to her as "our senior sister" and (perhaps the ultimate compliment from Begin) a "proud Jewess." But Begin preferred being his own man, and, spurred by a disagreement with Meir over the American-initiated Rogers peace plan (which would have required Israel to return the Sinai Peninsula, which it had acquired once again in the 1967 war), he returned to the opposition.

In September 1973, elections loomed again. Gahal merged with Free Center, State List, and the Independent Liberals to create the Likud—"Unity"—party. The merger came about largely through the efforts of the larger-than-life Ariel "Arik" Sharon, an outspoken and stubborn commander who had risen to celebrity status after a stunning victory in the 1956 counterattack in the Sinai. Sharon came by his nerve and bravado honestly; his grandfather had been a close Zionist ally of Ze'ev Dov Begin in Brisk (the two had defied the local rabbis to hold the memorial service for Herzl in 1904), and his grandmother had been the midwife at Menachem Begin's birth.[14] He and Begin would work together for the rest of Begin's life; Sharon, some would say, would eventually be responsible for Begin's downfall. For the time being, though, Sharon's work boosted Begin significantly. Boasting an impressive array of politicians, with Begin at the helm and the now ever-present Kadishai by his side, the new Likud party seemed poised to do well in the next election cycle. But before the elections could be held, Israel was once again plunged into war.

On the afternoon of October 6, 1973, on the holiest day of the Jewish calendar, Yom Kippur, Egyptian and Syrian forces launched a surprise attack against Israel. The army and government had disregarded critical intelligence that should have alerted them to the attack; now caught off guard, the IDF scrambled to send reservists to the Golan Heights and to the Sinai, which had been breached by Syria and Egypt, respectively.

While Israelis refer to the war as the Yom Kippur War, the Egyptian president, Anwar Sadat, had named it Operation Badr, after the Battle of Badr in 624 CE, Muhammad's first major military victory. In Muslim tradition, the Battle of Badr was no mere military success, but rather the triumph of good over evil, of faithful over infidel. This, Sadat stated with pride, was not an attempt to get the Sinai back; it was a war to utterly vanquish the Jewish state.

Once again, Israel's very existence hung in the balance. The Soviet Union, Begin's old foe that had surprisingly voted for the Partition Plan, had long been backing the Arabs, but the United States was agonizingly slow in responding with aid. Richard Nixon's secretary of state, Henry Kissinger, whose Jewishness was, according to Yehuda Avner, a "source of neurosis,"[15] was regularly subjected to Nixon's anti-Semitic rants. A man who called Israel's leaders "a sick bunch" and "the world's worst shits"[16] (and who, in the Richard Nixon tapes released in 2010, can be heard advising the president that "if they put Jews into gas chambers in the Soviet Union, it is not an American concern"),[17] Kissinger was hardly going to be an advocate for rapid, decisive American support for Israel. Rather, it was Ariel Sharon (who had been part of the more reticent Haganah and not the Etzel) who largely saved the day. In a daring move, he sent Israeli troops across the Suez Canal even though Egyptian troops had already crossed into the Sinai. In short order, he had Egypt's Third Army encircled, and could have obliterated it were it not for international pressure. The United States eventually began rearming Israel in response to Soviet arming of the Arabs, and the tide of the nearly fatal war slowly began to shift.

Given the horrific disadvantage at which Israel found itself in the first days of the war, the fact that the Jewish state ceded no territory and destroyed much of the Arabs' armies once again attested to great military accomplishment. But that was not how it felt to Israel's citizens. The deaths of some three thousand soldiers—Israel had lost only six hundred soldiers in the lightning victory of the Six-Day War—were blamed on Prime Minister Golda Meir and Defense Minister Moshe Dayan.

Begin, though he had actually supported the government's "sit still, do nothing" policy, rode the wave of hostility to Meir and her generals, born of a popular sense that they could have done more to foresee the war and prepare for it.[18] The Agranat Commission, formed to investigate the failures that led to the military calamity, had not yet been appointed. But even before its inquiry, the country was wracked by a sense that Meir had not adequately prepared the country for what some saw as an inevitable attack.[19] The rescheduled elections took place at the end of December. Begin's Likud took an impressive thirty-nine seats to the Alignment's fifty-one. He was still stuck in the opposition, but he was inching closer to real power.

Later that month, David Ben-Gurion died at the age of eighty-seven.

In April 1974, the Agranat Commission released its report on the government's role in the Yom Kippur fiasco. It scathingly criticized the inactions of high-ranking military officials who ignored military intelligence that should have alerted them to the imminent attack. Implicated by the tone if not the content of the report, Golda Meir resigned as prime minister ten days later, ending her political career. Defense Minister Moshe Dayan resigned as well, but would be brought back into the government as part of Begin's Likud cabinet. The commission also stated that David "Dado" Elazar, the IDF's chief of staff, "bears personal responsibility for the assessment of the situation and the preparedness of the IDF"; Elazar died of a heart attack two years later at the age of forty-seven. Begin's post-1967 pessimism about the long-term resolution of the Arab-Israeli conflict had proven prescient; the optimism of many in Labor that Israel was too dominant to ever be trifled with had proven itself vastly naïve about the persistence of Jew hatred, the perennial nature of which Begin never doubted.

With Golda Meir's departure, Yitzhak Rabin, who had been chief of staff in the 1967 war, became prime minister. He, too, would resign three years later, in the spring of 1977, when the Israeli press revealed that his wife had a small overseas bank account, a practice then prohibited by Israeli law. In the monthlong interim period before elections, the Alignment's Shimon Peres became prime minister.

The seemingly incessant change in the left's leadership (relative to the uninterrupted Ben-Gurion reign from 1948 to 1965) and its perceived incompetence, dishonesty, and elitism (very few Israelis in that era could even imagine having a foreign bank account), contributed to the decline in the labor parties' fortunes.[20] Increasingly, the left was perceived as the province of a European, white, educated elite, wholly out of touch with the needs of the lower classes.

Social unrest became a major issue. Israel's Mizrachi[21] population—Jews from North Africa, Yemen, and Iraq, among others, who had never gotten their full share of Israel's still meager bounty—was clamoring for change. Begin, though educated and Ashkenazi, had never been seen as part of that elite. His exile to the political opposition for so many years was a political asset; his long-standing emphasis on *Klal Yisrael* (the concept of a unified Jewish people) made him a multicultural populist in the midst of a socialist elite. For years, he had paid special attention to those Jews from Middle Eastern backgrounds who were often overlooked by the Ashkenazi upper echelons.

The Etzel, composed of Jews of many backgrounds, had never given any consideration to these ethnic differences. In *The Revolt*, published in 1952, around the same time that hundreds of thousands of immigrants were living in crowded transit camps (one of every two recent immigrants to Israel was then living in some sort of temporary housing structure), Begin had described how his fighters came from Tunisia, Yemen, Syria, Argentina, South Africa, Israel, Persia, and several other far-off countries:

> We were the melting-pot of the Jewish nation in miniature. We never asked about origins: we demanded only loyalty and ability. Our comrades from the eastern communities felt happy and at home in the Irgun. Nobody ever displayed stupid airs of superiority toward them and they were thus helped to free themselves of any unjustified sense of inferiority they may have harbored.[22]

In the Etzel, unlike the Knesset, Sephardic men attained the highest positions of power. The iconic fighters Feinstein and Barazani, who had killed themselves by hugging a grenade between them while singing *Adon Olam* rather than go to the gallows, were Ashkenazi and Mizrachi, respectively. United as equals in death, they represented an egalitarian attitude from which the labor faction seemed entirely divorced.

Even the trappings of Begin's Polish background—the black suit and tie that made him an anomaly among *yishuv* leaders—served him well with Israel's North African immigrants, who viewed his formal attire as a sign of respect and were stunned by Ben-Gurion's penchant for T-shirts and shorts.[23] In the early 1950s, Begin visited the *ma'abarot*, transit camps where recent immigrants from Morocco, Iraq, and Algeria were placed due to a drastic shortage of genuine housing. He called them "my brothers and sisters," promising to allocate funds provided by world Jewry to provide for immigrant housing.[24]

In 1955, Begin had attacked the government's idea for selective immigration from Morocco, a policy that would have meant the elderly and the ill would not be allowed to make *aliyah* due to the economic hardships that Israel was facing. On September 1, he addressed the Knesset on the life-and-death situation facing Moroccan Jews. As always, he spoke as the Jew, as the Jewish conscience of a state that was in dire danger of losing its soul:

> If you had not wasted millions building luxury palaces there would be money for absorption . . . The saving of life takes precedence not only over the Sabbath, but also the development of our economy for a more distant future . . . If there is a rescue plan, we will also assume the burden, because rescue supersedes everything else.[25]

It was, in many ways, a return to the rhetoric of the reparations conflict, in which Begin had insisted that dignity prevail over economic pragmatism. But this time, because the proposed law singled out Moroccan Jews, Begin also seized on the implicit discrimination against Sephardim. As early as his unsuccessful 1959 election campaign, Begin told a largely Sephardic audience that David Ben-Gurion had turned Israel into a divided country of "Ashkenazim and non-Ashkenazim."[26] Ambassador

Yehuda Avner, who would later work closely with Begin in his years as prime minister, called those speeches the beginning of "Begin's love fest with Sephardic Jews."[27] "Without sycophancy or pretense, he had won their hearts, knocking down the high walls of arrogance and sectarianism which had cut them off from mainstream Israel since their mass immigration two and three decades before."[28]

B egin's emerging image as an ethnic pluralist and as the Jewish conscience of a state that often seemed determined to shuck its Jewish veneer would also slowly shift the attitudes of Diaspora Jews, as well, many of whom had long seen him as a "terrorist" and the "Butcher of Deir Yassin." For those who had grown up in households where Ben-Gurion's socialist values reigned, Begin had long been the rebel who threatened the state during the *Altalena* crisis and who had the temerity to put Jewish pride over the common welfare by voting against reparations. To be sure, there were others to whom Begin's strategic attacks against the British spoke to their feelings of helplessness during the Holocaust. Hart Hasten, a Holocaust survivor and a close confidant of Begin's in later years, recalls that in the displaced persons camps in Europe, members of the left-wing youth group Hashomer Hatzair and members of Begin and Jabotinsky's Betar often came to loggerheads about the actions of the Jewish leaders in the *yishuv*. But in 1947, when he heard about Begin's decision to whip the British generals, "he was my hero," says Hasten, who subsequently settled in Indianapolis.

But Hasten's was a minority view for decades. The Etzel was barely mentioned in American textbooks and Jewish day school books, and Begin's name was little known to mainstream Jews. At a 1948 dinner in Begin's honor in Manhattan, not a single prominent American Jewish leader was in attendance.[29] Between 1948 and May 1977, American newspapers struggled with the question of how to describe the terrorist-turned-politician. Einstein and Arendt had called him a "fascist" in their 1948 letter to *The New York Times*, and the appellation stuck. In January 1952, a

Jewish Telegraphic Agency article referred to the "anti-government dem-
onstrations" in which Begin had been involved, an indication that the
events surrounding the reparations debate continued to hound him.[30]

As chairman of the Israel Bonds in Indianapolis, Hasten frequently
appealed to community leaders to invite Begin to speak at events. But
before one event in 1971, a high-ranking member of the Jewish Federation
told him not to expect a big crowd: "Everyone knows he's a fascist."[31]

Just months before the 1977 elections, Begin was invited to speak in
Milwaukee before hundreds of Jews at an event to be held at the Jewish
Community Center. But the Anti-Defamation League tried to cancel the
event, claiming that Begin was not a "mainstream Jewish leader." The
invitation was not rescinded, however, and Begin came to town to speak;
yet history was beginning to weigh on him. He had apparently come to
believe that he would never be elected prime minister, and he told his
American supporters that this would be his last election.[32]

The one notable exception to the American antipathy toward Begin
was Abba Hillel Silver, a leading American Reform rabbi and Zionist,
who was heard to say, "The Irgun will go down in history as a factor
without which the State of Israel would not have come into being."[33] But
until Begin was elected, friends and supporters such as Abba Hillel Silver,
Hart Hasten, and Canada's Nathan Silver were mavericks, often at odds
with the prevailing communal ethos.

Matters were not all that different in Britain; as in the United States,
Begin was often marginalized and vilified. As late as 1955, he had been
denied a visa to visit Britain on the grounds that the Israeli government would be displeased if he were admitted into the country, and
was referred to in government documents as an extreme nationalist and
Jewish terrorist. That view eventually tempered somewhat, but never
completely. Decades later, the JTA reflected on his relationship with the
United Kingdom:

> Of all who fought the British Empire, Begin has been least success-
> ful in winning the respect that the British are so wont to extend to
> their former enemies—Eamon de Valera, Jawaharlal Nehru, Jomo

Kenyatta, and even Anwar Sadat—who challenged Britain's imperial might. But once these rebels turned into rulers, their past "mis-
deeds" were largely forgotten by the easygoing British people. Some
even earned their affection and respect.

If Begin still stirs embers of hatred here, it is not—as he himself
may perhaps think—because he is a Jew. It is because, unlike so
many others, he did not emerge to lead his people once the British
yoke had been thrown off.

Thus, instead of being exposed to the healing processes of public
explanation and discussion, actions like the dynamiting of the King
David Hotel, in which about ninety people died, and the retaliatory hanging of two British sergeants have remained suppurating
wounds.

Even as late as 1972, when he had already been a member of the Knesset for nearly a quarter of a century, many members of the British Jewish community still viewed Begin as a terrorist. Immediately before a
scheduled three-day visit to London, all of the halls and caterers who
planned to host Begin fearfully canceled their events after a slew of bomb
threats and intimidations, some apparently from Labor supporters. The
Herut organizers of the event were left with no place to hold their formal
dinner. Finally, a certain Mrs. Lisser, a Holocaust survivor who owned a
restaurant, opened her doors for the event, and the group squeezed into
the restaurant to welcome Begin.

Outside the improvised hall, however, Mapam supporters joined with
some other groups, including some fascists, and demonstrated with signs
proclaiming BEGIN, ENEMY OF ZIONISM and GO HOME, TERRORIST.
The Jewish Agency's *shaliach* (representative in Britain) took a role in
leading the protests.[34]

With his characteristic memory and gratitude, Begin never forgot
Mrs. Lisser's gesture. When he returned to Britain in 1977 as prime minister to much pomp and circumstance, he made sure that she was invited
to the festivities.

Unlike in North America and Britain, however, Begin was rather

beloved in South Africa. South African Jews had developed a unique relationship with Israel, and many became lifelong Zionists after Jabotinsky
traveled to Johannesburg and Cape Town in 1930. Jabotinsky spent two
months in South Africa advocating for Revisionism, with great success.
By the time Begin himself began appearing in South Africa to raise money
for Herut, he was already widely feted as Jabotinsky's political heir. South
African Boers had their own historical resentments of the British; Begin's
fearless battle against the British no doubt contributed to their respect
for him.

Begin first visited South Africa in 1953, at the height of apartheid. A
member of the South African Betar, assigned as Begin's security guard
during his trip, later recalled with pride that the crowd of 4,000 people
who gathered to welcome Begin was the largest in the history of the local
airport. As soon as Begin landed, the crowd started singing "Hatikvah."[35]
Begin, characteristically, downplayed the massive turnout; he joked in
his speeches that they had come just to see if he really had horns.[36]

Begin's unique mix of religious tradition, secular practice, and unabashed Zionism appealed to the Jews of South Africa, who, though not
meticulously observant, were deeply respectful of the traditions of their
Eastern European ancestors; as citizens of a country that, like Israel, was
still figuring out its own identity, they felt a natural affinity for Israel that
some North Americans did not. Harry Hurwitz, one of the leaders of the
South African Jewish community, would become one of Begin's closest
friends and political allies, and would eventually write one of the first
Begin biographies. To this day, South African expatriates in Israel, the
United States, and Australia hold Begin in a regard that is markedly different from the sentiments of almost any other community.

In 1976 and 1977, Hart Hasten was telling his friends that Begin's time
was coming, and that he would win the next election. But Begin himself
was far from convinced, and many Israelis, including devoted members
of the Likud party, were equally dubious. Some, especially the more left-

wing members from the Liberal merger in 1973, were disappointed with Begin's performance, insisting that "with all due respect to Begin, he has to vacate his place as leader of the opposition after failing eight times to bring the opposition to victory."[37] The voices arguing that his political career ought to be behind him were gaining some traction.

But those voices dramatically underestimated the man that the British, the Soviets, and Ben-Gurion all thought they could break. And they underestimated the electorate's disgust with Labor, and its growing affection for someone they saw as a man of principle in a country increasingly devoid of such people.

In May 1977, Israelis went to the polls yet again. The sting of the Yom Kippur War still hung in the air, Labor had been discredited time and again, but Menachem Begin, present before the country had been created, was still running, committed to the same principles he had been advocating since he'd arrived in Palestine. It was the first Israeli election in which exit polls were conducted, and as informal results began trickling out, Israelis went into a state of shock. Even the newscaster Chaim Yavin, the iconic anchor of the evening TV news, had tears in his eyes, so great was the emotion. On May 17, 1977, after eight failed attempts, and following a debilitating heart attack in April that had caused him to be virtually absent from the election campaign, Menachem Begin and his party had won the largest number of seats in the Knesset. The Likud got forty-four seats, while voters gave the Alignment only thirty-two (a decrease by more than a third of its previous number). The Israeli historian Anita Shapira believes that Begin is the only leader in the history of democracies to have lost eight consecutive elections only to win the ninth.[38]

Menachem Begin had lived twenty-nine years before he arrived in Palestine. He spent nearly twenty-nine years in the political opposition. And now he was prime minister of the state that he had helped to create.

Wildly cheering crowds took to the streets. Mizrachi Jews, who had never had much to celebrate after one Laborite followed another, were virtually delirious with joy and with a sense that they suddenly mattered. The victory was dubbed the *Mahapach* or "Reversal," by Yavin. The word has rings of *mahapeicha*, too, the Hebrew word for "revolution." It was lost on few that this was Begin's second revolt. First he had toppled the British, and now he had ended the Labor bloc's seemingly interminable control of the government. Many Israelis, especially Mizrachi voters, took to the streets, chanting with jubilation "Begin! Begin!" It wasn't only Begin's day that had finally arrived; it was theirs, too.

Begin did not join the dancing in the streets. Instead, he donned a *kippah* and recited the *Shehechiyanu*. Israelis had never witnessed such an act by a high-ranking politician. Ben-Gurion had not even donned a *kippah* during the Declaration of the State in 1948.

Outside Israel, leaders were in shock. In the United Kingdom, Begin remained deeply unpopular. (Even Margaret Thatcher, who was generally positively inclined toward the Jewish state, would later describe Begin as the "most difficult man" with whom she had had to work.[39]) In the United States, too, the media gave Begin a tepid reception. On May 30, *Time* covered his election and wrote: "His first name means 'comforter.' Menachem Begin (rhymes with Fagin) has been anything but that to his numerous antagonists." In response to the reference to Dickens's anti-Semitic caricature of a Jewish criminal in *Oliver Twist*, Mayor Teddy Kollek of Jerusalem shot back, "*TIME* equals slime."[40] The *Time* article, entitled "Kind . . . Honest . . . Dangerous," portrayed Begin as a demagogue and a violent rebel, referring to his responsibility for Deir Yassin, the fatalities of the King David bombing, the two hanged British sergeants, the *Altalena*, and his three-month suspension from the Knesset during the reparations debate. It ended just as negatively as it started: "'Begin's private life is as clean as a pin,' says a Western diplomat. 'Everything they say about him is true. He's kind, honest and quite likable. But that doesn't mean he isn't dangerous.'"[41]

B ut in the aftermath of his election, Begin was thoroughly unconcerned with international reaction. He had things to say at home. When a reporter asked him, shortly after the results were announced, if there was anything in particular he wished to say, he said he wanted to thank Aliza. He then quoted from memory the verse from Jeremiah 2:2: "I recall with favor the devotion of your youth, your love as a bride; how you followed me in the wilderness, in a land not sown." But Begin slyly altered the last line, saying, "how you followed me in the wilderness, in a land sown with land mines."[42] In doing so, he spoke of love—his love for Aliza, hers for him, and in effect, his for the people who had just elected him. And he reflected on a life in which he'd constantly stared down danger; he had barely escaped the Nazis, had survived Soviet prison, had evaded arrest by the British and murder at the hands of Ben-Gurion's gunners the day that the *Altalena* ran aground off Tel Aviv's shore.

Begin wasted no time in reminding those who had elected him who he was. When he presented his government and its guiding principles for approval, Begin insisted, "The Jewish people has a historic right to the Land of Israel," he said. "It is our ancestral homeland, and that right is inalienable." Not long thereafter, he spoke to the Knesset for the first time as prime minister, to a chamber more packed with people than anyone could recall. Menachem Begin reminded his listeners of what it was that had always shaped him, and of the values for which he had been elected. He spoke of the ongoing link between the Jewish people and their land:

> It is the land that our ancestors loved, our only land. We cleaved to it for generations, we prayed for it and yearned for it. We loved it with all our hearts and with all our souls. We did not forget it for a single day as we wandered the Diaspora, and our sacred ancestors kept its name on their lips even as they were being dragged to their deaths by the murderous enemy.[43]

Israel had elected a prime minister unlike any it had had before. He was Israeli, yes, but first and foremost he was a Jew. Just hours after his election, in fact, when yet another reporter, in the midst of an exuberant crowd, shoved a microphone in front of Begin's face and asked him in what style he would be prime minister, Begin paused for a moment at the odd question, and then responded simply, "In the style of a good Jew."[44]

11

Give Those People a Haven

"You shall declare before the Lord your God: . . . 'I have given to the Levite, the stranger, the fatherless, and the widow, just as You commanded me.'" —*Deuteronomy 26:13*

In June 1977, shortly after Menachem Begin was elected prime minister, several dozen Vietnamese refugees were in danger of dying thousands of miles away from Israel. They had fled postwar Communist Vietnam in a leaky fishing boat and had been floating in the South China Sea for days with a dwindling supply of food and almost no water. Now, out of options, they were forced to ration their remaining water, with three teaspoons allowed for each child per day and none for the adults.[1]

As they bobbed helplessly in the sea, five ships had sailed past them, without a single one making even a minimal offer of help. Then an Israeli freighter, the *Yuvali*, en route to Taiwan, spotted them.[2] The captain, Meir Tadmor, knew that he did not have enough life rafts or jackets for them, but he brought them on board anyway.[3] The Israeli vessel, with its "visitors," stopped in Japan, Hong Kong, and Taiwan; each country not only declined to take the refugees in, but refused even to allow them ashore for medical treatment.

Tellingly, Begin's first official act as prime minister only a week after his inauguration was to grant the sixty-six Vietnamese asylum in Israel. He assured the group that "they will enjoy all hospitality"[4] and promised them help finding jobs and learning Hebrew. Many of these Vietnamese stayed in Israel—some have become restaurant owners, settling in Haifa and Tel Aviv, and their children have grown up speaking Hebrew.[5]

When Begin met with President Jimmy Carter in Washington in July 1977, Carter used the opportunity to publicly laud Begin for his rescue of the Vietnamese boat people:

> It was an act of compassion, an act of sensitivity and a recognition of him and his government about the importance of a home for people who were destitute and who would like to express their own individuality and freedom in a common way, again typifying the historic struggle of the people of Israel.[6]

In his response, Begin placed the episode in the larger context of Jewish experience and a distinctly Jewish universalism. He recalled the *St. Louis*, a ship with more than nine hundred Jews escaping Germany in 1939 that had been turned away by Cuba, the United States, and Canada and which was ultimately sent back to Europe, where many of the passengers perished in the Holocaust. "We have never forgotten the lot of our people, persecuted, humiliated, ultimately physically destroyed," Begin responded to Carter. "Therefore, it was natural that my first act as Prime Minister was to give those people a haven in the Land of Israel."[7]

It was, for Begin, an instinctive act that required little deliberation. Prior to Begin, Israel had not extended itself to non-Jewish refugees. Though in more recent years massive waves of Eritrean and south Sudanese refugees have arrived at Israel's borders after crossing through Egypt, no subsequent Israeli leader has spoken out on the issue with the moral and Jewish clarity that Begin exhibited. There was something about him that led the powerless to believe he cared for them, not as a matter of policy or political wisdom but as a matter of instinct. While visiting apartheid South Africa in the early 1950s, he refused to lecture in any hall that banned the entry of blacks,[8] and declined to be transported in a rickshaw pulled by a black man; it was, quite simply, a matter of *hadar*, but a universal *hadar* (in fact, Jabotinsky, the father of *hadar*, had also been an outspoken opponent of racism in the United States).[9] No man, he felt, should be pulled by another man. This was the Begin whom the *mizrachim* had elected en masse in 1977.

That same summer of 1977 found Begin dealing with yet another group of Jews he knew were desperate for help. A few short weeks after his inauguration, Begin met with Yitzhak Hofi, the head of the Mossad, and virtually demanded of him: "Bring me the Jews of Ethiopia."[10]

Theories abound about the origin of the Ethiopian Jews. What is virtually certain, however, is that these Jews made their way to Ethiopia, probably escaping some calamity in Judea, long before the appearance of rabbinic Judaism, the foundation of all contemporary forms of Jewish life. Entirely cut off from the massive changes that reshaped Jewish religion and civilization after the destruction of the Temple, they were in many ways a time capsule of Jewish life, living the tradition as no one else had for thousands of years.[11] Most people called them "Falashas," meaning "those without land" or "exiles,"[12] though the Ethiopian Jews referred to themselves as *Beta Yisrael*, "House of Israel." That was precisely how Begin saw them, as well.

Israel's 1950 Law of Return, which Robert Soblen had invoked in his attempt to gain asylum in the Jewish state, asserted that "every Jew has the right to immigrate to the country."[13] A 1970 amendment to the law defined *Jew* to mean a person born of a Jewish mother or someone who has converted to Judaism and is not a member of another religion. This led to an interesting question regarding Ethiopian Jews—were they Jewish, even if their culture and religion were essentially unrecognizable as Judaism in the modern era? It was the Sephardic chief rabbi who first ruled that these Ethiopians were Jews. In a historic ruling on February 9, 1973, Rabbi Ovadia Yosef said:

> I have therefore come to the conclusion that the Falashas are descendants of the Tribes of Israel, who went southward to Ethiopia, and there is no doubt that the above sages established that they [the Falashas] are of the Tribe of Dan . . . and [have] reached the conclusion on the basis of the most reliable witnesses and evidence . . . and have decided in my humble opinion, the Falashas are Jews.[14]

Rabbi Shlomo Goren, the Ashkenazi chief rabbi, was far less courageous. It was not until 1981 that any piece of his own writing even *suggested* that he approved their status as Jews, and this was after hundreds
of Ethiopian Jews had already entered the country and submitted to symbolic conversions. To Begin, however, for whom the Bible was a living and
defining document, the issue was clear: any people living by the Bible's
dictates, who had treasured their heritage as Jews for thousands of years,
was the responsibility of the Jewish state.

Begin, whose father had instructed him to brush his teeth on Yom Kippur because it was God he was speaking to, had no interest in the chief
rabbi's hairsplitting. He plowed ahead with his plan to save these people.
One of the Mossad agents involved in the operations was convinced that
he understood what compelled Begin to act: "Menachem Begin, who
reached the premiership after years in the political opposition wilderness,
not least because of the support of Sephardic Jews, saw himself committed to relocating the members of that remote [Ethiopian] community to
Israel, whatever the cost may be."[15]

The story had begun several years earlier. In 1966 and 1974, only a few
years before Begin's premiership, several desperate young Ethiopian Jews
traveled incognito into Israel on boats carrying meat from Ethiopia. The
establishment ignored them, and most were turned back by the Ministry of the Interior as soon as they arrived at the harbor of Eilat.[16] Even
the minister of foreign affairs, Abba Eban, was uninterested. The matter
received scant attention.

It was a political coup in Ethiopia in 1974 that caused the sands to
shift. The self-proclaimed "Lion of Judah," Emperor Haile Selassie, with
whom Israel had developed political ties, was overthrown by an army
officer, Mengistu Haile Mariam. Mengistu had a reputation for ruthless-
ness, with a track record that allegedly included political executions and
murders of young counterrevolutionaries. At Begin's instruction, Mossad
agents traveled to Ethiopia in the summer of 1977 and worked out a deal
with Mengistu: Israeli arms in exchange for Ethiopian Jews. The deal was
contingent upon its remaining entirely secret.

In August 1977, sixty-two Ethiopians came to Israel in an Israeli Air

Force Boeing 707 and were housed in an absorption center near the Sea of Galilee. In December, fifty-eight more arrived and were placed in Afula. These were merely the first of thousands who would arrive over the next ten years.

The operation that began in 1977 as a partnership of Begin, the Mossad, and Mengistu and that brought 120 Ethiopians to Israel was supposed to have been a long-term one with many flights. But in February 1978, Moshe Dayan, Begin's defense minister, spoke to a newspaper in Switzerland and reported that Israel was giving arms to Ethiopia.[17] Ethiopian officials promptly backed out of the deal.

Nonetheless, Begin and the Mossad officials kept working. Thousands of Ethiopian Jews had already undertaken the perilous trek on foot to Sudan, where they lived in crowded refugee camps, terrified of revealing their Jewish identity. Gad Shimron, a Mossad agent who was stationed in Khartoum during this period, estimated that there were one million mostly non-Jewish refugees in two of these camps.[18] The Mossad continued to identify the Jews, eventually using boats and airplanes to bring several thousand more Ethiopians to Israel.

In 1979, apparently amid concern among some Israeli and Diaspora leaders that he had abandoned the Ethiopian community, Begin hinted at his involvement in their rescue. In a national telecast on May 1, 1979, he said, "I am not at liberty to go into details, but I can tell you that we are working in order to bring them all to the land of Israel, and we shall persist in our efforts. We shall not rest, we shall not be silent until all the Jews—both in Syria and in Ethiopia—are with us in our land."

Interestingly, in that same speech, he spoke to Syrian Jews, as well, acknowledging that they, too, were waiting to be rescued by Israel: "I can tell you, my friends, that we have not forgotten these our brethren, some four thousand souls of an ancient Jewish community which made a prodigious contribution to Jewish knowledge and wisdom over the course of hundreds of generations and thousands of years. With just a few airplanes they can be taken out, brought to a safe [haven]."[19]

The world did not know it, but those Syrian Jews had long been on

Begin's mind, and they, though trapped in Damascus, somehow intuited the values at Begin's core. Indeed, around the same time that Begin was admitting the Vietnamese refugees soon after his election, he received a visit from a young Canadian law professor, Irwin Cotler. Cotler was on his way back from Syria, where he had met with Jews from the Damascus ghetto, created in 1967 during the Six-Day War. Cotler, who subsequently became Canada's minister of justice and attorney general, had a message for Begin. Cotler's request made its way to Ariela Ze'evi, who was then serving as legislative assistant to the just-elected Begin. An elderly man from the ghetto, whom Cotler had met, learned that Cotler was then heading to Israel. The man told Cotler: Give Begin a hug from us, and tell him that we know that if *he* had been prime minister in 1973, there would be no more Damascus ghetto, for we would all be living in Israel.

What that elderly Syrian Jew could not have known, but that Ariela Cotler (she subsequently married that young Canadian lawyer) did, was that Begin had actually tried to secure the freedom of Syrian Jews in 1973. She had been present toward the end of the Yom Kippur War when Begin urged Prime Minister Golda Meir to include the freedom of the Syrian Jews as part of the agreements with Syria. If Syria wanted Israel to move its tanks away from Damascus, Begin suggested that she insist, they would need to release the Syrian Jews. But Meir had no interest in taking on this additional complication; the Syrian Jews remained in the ghetto, waiting for rescue that never came (though in 1989, the Syrian government eased restrictions on Jewish emigration, with the stipulation that Jews who left Syria could not go to Israel).

Begin had never forgotten David Kroll, whose bones remained in the Soviet "frozen north." And though he had lost his battle with Golda Meir in 1973 about rescuing the Jews in Damascus, they were still very much on his mind. Perhaps because of that, and against many odds, he pushed ahead with the project to save Ethiopian Jewry. Between 1977 and 1984, some 8,000 of them had reached Israel via Sudan. In November 1984, Prime Minister Shimon Peres brought nearly 6,000 of these refugees to Israel in what was called Operation Moses. In 1991, under Prime Minister

Yitzhak Shamir, another effort was launched when Mengistu agreed to allow the Jews to be taken to Israel. That May, just after Mengistu was ousted, Operation Solomon airlifted 14,000 Jews from Ethiopia's besieged capital into Israel in twenty-four hours.

Though Operations Moses and Solomon took place under Peres and Shamir, respectively, it was Begin who had set the processes in motion. As Shimon Peres said in the Knesset in 1985, shortly after Operation Moses:

> The government of Israel has acted and will continue to act, within the range of its ability and even beyond it, in order to complete the mission which is so humane and so Jewish, until the last Ethiopian Jew reaches his homeland . . . This is also the right time to discharge a debt of honor to Menachem Begin, whose government invested efforts and resourcefulness to make possible the first, hidden trickles which have blazed a trail.[20]

When Begin died in 1992, the Ethiopian Jewish community mourned him with a profound sense of loss. Rahamim Elazar, who later became the first Israeli of Ethiopian descent to become an ambassador, understood Begin better than the Mossad agent who felt Begin's commitment to the weaker strata of Israeli society was connected to his seeking the country's highest office. It was about something much deeper, Elazar understood:

> It was Begin who broke down the walls. He believed that the place of the Ethiopian Jews is in Israel. He saw it as his destiny to bring the community here. He told his aides: "I want the Ethiopian Jews here." Before Begin, nobody wanted to hear from us. He didn't care about skin color. For him it was clear that all Jews should be in Israel. Begin was a warm Jew who loved the Jewish people.[21]

Elazar was right; at his core, Menachem Begin's central animating principle was the Jewish people. Ariela Cotler understood that, too; she saw nothing mysterious about the Syrians' confidence that Begin would have tried to rescue them had he been prime minister in 1973; "everyone . . . knew," she would later say, that for Begin, "*Am Yisrael* [the Jewish People] and *Eretz Yisrael* were *the* number one priority."

egin's commitment to "the helpless" was by no means limited to
Vietnamese refugees on the sea, the rescue of Ethiopian Jews, and
even a desire to do something about the Syrian Jewish ghetto. As early
as 1977, around the time he was asking the Mossad to "bring [him] the
Jews of Ethiopia," Begin also turned to Yitzhak Shamir, the Speaker of
the Knesset (who would succeed him as prime minister), for assistance on
yet another matter. This time, he told Shamir, he wanted to help Soviet
Jews.[22]

Unlike Ethiopian Jews, Soviet Jews of the 1970s were not a small group
stranded on the open sea or threatened by civil war in an impoverished
African country. They were a massive population of about 2.5 million,
many of whom had been highly successful until they lost their academic
and professional positions after petitioning for permission to immigrate
to Israel. The challenge with Soviet Jews revolved around legal niceties,
visa applications, and an ongoing struggle for freedom of speech. It was,
in many ways, exactly Begin's cup of tea. He was already sympathetic
to the plight of Jews in distress. He had training as a lawyer and—as in
the Robert Soblen case—a deep commitment to due process. And he was
intimately familiar with the horrors of being locked in the Soviet legal
and penal systems.

By the time Begin took office, the process of freeing Soviet Jews was
already well under way. Soviet Jewish pride had swelled in the aftermath
of the Six-Day War[23] (Soviet Jews knew well that the USSR had supported
Nasser, and lost), and increasing numbers of Soviet Jews sought to make
their way to Israel. Congressional pressure in the United States continued to mount on the USSR to permit them to emigrate. In 1970, approximately 4,200 Soviet Jews made their way to Israel; by 1971, the number
rose to 14,000, and by 1972 it had reached 30,000.[24] (In the 1990s, long after
Begin retired, one million Soviet Jews would come to Israel, constituting
a sixth of Israel's population, dramatically changing Israeli culture, politics, and society.)

Begin had been involved in the Soviet Jewry movement from the very beginning. At the first international conference on Soviet Jewry in Brussels in February 1971, he gave an impassioned speech in which he described Soviet Jews as the heirs of the Etzel fighters:

Against all this [government persecution], our brethren stand—young fighters overcoming the terror which is without comparison on earth. It is possible to say, without the slightest exaggeration, that in our day they are the bravest of all of those fighting for human freedom and dignity. In the name of those who fought in days gone by in *Eretz Israel*, may I be permitted to say to you from far and near: We bow our heads before you, our brothers, heroes of the revival.[25]

The speech was vintage Begin, not only for its historical richness and references, but because he avoided the use of the term *Israeli*. Indeed, the vast majority of Begin's speeches are remarkably devoid of reference to "Israelis"; rather it is Jews, "brothers," and "brethren" to whom he refers.[26] Jewish sovereignty was a tool, not an end in itself. The goal was Jewish thriving, *hadar*. For that to happen, Jews needed a state. Though Jews might live in Israel, or in Ethiopia or the USSR or elsewhere in the Diaspora, they were, no matter where they made their homes, one family.

But when he became prime minister, Begin found himself in a conundrum on the subject of Soviet Jews. What should Israel's policy be vis-à-vis those Jews who did not wish to go to Israel, but who, instead, preferred America or some other destination? When they had first begun to leave the Soviet Union, the plurality of Jews leaving the USSR had gone to Israel.[27] With time, though, and certainly by the late 1970s, the majority were settling in the United States instead.[28]

In Zionist circles at the time, the Soviet émigrés who had received invitations from the State of Israel for immigration (which were necessary if they were to receive an exit visa) but moved instead to other countries were dubbed *noshrim*, or "dropouts." But Jewish organizations such as the American Jewish Joint Distribution Committee (JDC), and particularly the Hebrew Immigrant Aid Society (HIAS), had a vested interest in allowing Soviet émigrés to head to the United States; this was the last great Jewish population move likely, they thought. Given that Jewish immigration to the United States had dwindled in the 1960s, the Soviet Jewish immigration provided them with a new focus, affording HIAS a new lease on life and restoring its relevance in an era in which many were wondering whether HIAS had a role to play anymore.[29] HIAS thus urged "freedom of choice" for Soviet Jews, arguing that they should receive aid regardless of which country of residence they chose.

But the issue of "freedom of choice" for the *noshrim* created a rift in Israeli society and politics. Many Israeli politicians felt that the emigrants should be encouraged to move to Israel, and thus attempted to impede financial compensation for the *noshrim* who did not make *aliyah*. In 1976, as the debate raged in Israel, Gallup reported that 46 percent of Israelis supported freedom of choice and 43 percent opposed it, a near-even split.[30]

The issue pitted Begin's obvious interests as leader of the Jewish state against his commitment to *hadar* and the dignity of each individual Jew. He tried to finesse the matter, but when push came to shove, simply refused to try to limit the émigrés' freedom of choice. In 1976, not wanting to sound like he was abandoning the classic Zionist position, he spoke to a crowd of thousands at a Manhattan synagogue and urged the implementation of a one-year "interim period" before cutting off aid to potential "dropouts." That year should be used to persuade those emigrants that it was in their best interests to make *aliyah*, he said.[31] In practice, though, despite significant internal political pressures, Begin's government resisted making any decisions to end "freedom of choice" or to cut off funding for *noshrim*. In April 1978, Begin spoke to the Coordinating Committee, a joint committee of the Israeli government and the Jewish Agency, and did not try to dissuade HIAS from assisting "dropouts." Israelis and Americans, he said, had no right to order Soviet Jews to come to Israel.[32]

To be sure, he still called on Soviet Jews to join the Zionist project. In May 1979, he said in a public address:

In my Independence Day message to the Jewish people wherever they may be, I called upon our brethren in the dispersions of the

Diaspora: Arise and come to Eretz Israel. The time has come, almost fifty thousand Jews will this year leave the Soviet Union, and unfortunately there exists the grave and negative "dropout" phenomenon. We shall try to put an end to it and call on all those leaving the Soviet Union for Eretz Israel to tell them: We are here. Let them come to Eretz Israel and not wander again to lands of the Diaspora.[33]

In November 1980, Begin publicly addressed the issue again and claimed that dropouts impeded immigration to Israel. Even then, however, he did not change the status quo; Jews moving from the USSR to the United States and to other places outside Israel still received HIAS funding.[34]

At one point in the saga, one of Begin's political advisors suggested that he ask President Carter to remove the "refugee" status of the Soviet Jews, based on the logic that they were not "stateless" because they could always become citizens of Israel. Begin refused. He had been born into a world in which Jews had no refuge. His family had fled Brisk, and later, many of them had been killed for lack of a place to go. He himself had suffered in the depths of a depraved and merciless Soviet prison system, and after his release, wandered across the Soviet Union on his way to Palestine, and once there, was forced to go into hiding. He was not about to replicate that horror for anyone else. *Hadar* demanded that Jews could live where they wished. He responded, "I will never ask a gentile not to allow a Jew to enter his country."[35]

H*adar* contributed to Begin's domestic agenda, no less. *"Ivri gam ben-oni ben-sar,"* the Betar anthem had insisted; every Jew, even if mired in poverty, was a prince. But not all Jews in Israel were living like princes, and Begin knew it. For the new Jewish immigrants to be completely at home and accepted in Israel, they needed to be self-sufficient, not reliant on transit camps and government welfare. Once elected, Begin initiated Project Renewal to address the problem of substandard housing and slum conditions, just as he had promised those voters living in transit camps during his election campaigns. He worked with various overseas Jewish organizations, particularly the Jewish Agency, to raise money for renewal of dozens of neighborhoods.

The original plan asked the overseas organizations to provide half of the funding, which was then estimated at between $100 million and $1.3 billion over three to five years. The project addressed several of Begin's commitments. It would support immigrants from Arab countries, who were overwhelmingly in need of aid, and give much-needed attention to those voters who had brought him into office (and who, presumably, he would need when he ran for reelection).[36] The project also addressed Begin's notion of a unified Jewish people, matching existing Israeli neighborhoods to Jewish communities abroad in an attempt to create a relationship between Diaspora Jews and the Jews of Israel.

By 1982, Project Renewal had done work in more than eighty neighborhoods; it built some 30,000 housing units and engaged in upgrades of physical infrastructure, roads, lighting, and sewage. It remains an ongoing project that to date has touched the lives of approximately half a million people.[37]

What motivated this concern for those less fortunate? From what wellspring flowed his desire to help Vietnamese boat people, Ethiopian Jews, and poor Jews already living in Israel? Begin was a politician with political interests, of course, but he was infinitely more than that. His comment to Carter that he had taken in the Vietnamese boat people because it was the Jewish thing to do was no mere rhetorical flourish. It may have made for good copy, but it was also undeniably true.

Undoubtedly, intimate acquaintance with anti-Semitism, statelessness, and exile reinforced his commitment to non-Jewish refugees in need. But for Begin, this commitment was most fundamentally simply part of being a Jew, a worldview he had internalized from the prophets of the Bible. He had inherited the Bible's unique Jewish particularism combined with a powerful sense of universal responsibility. That blend, he intuited, was simply what Jews were meant to live. Passionate concern for the welfare of the Jewish people did not have to come at the expense of compassion for human beings everywhere.

Begin, who spoke to his adoring crowds not as "Israelis" but as "Jews," was first and foremost just that—he was a person whose Jewish soul dictated virtually everything he said, every decision he took. Indeed, throughout the years of his premiership, both in style and in substance on a wide array of issues, it was his Jewishness that was most apparent. Begin was, and remains, the most Jewish prime minister that Israel has ever had.

Yehuda Avner, who had worked as a speechwriter and English-language secretary for Golda Meir and Levi Eshkol, would later recall Menachem Begin looking at his watch on the first Friday that Avner worked with him. "Yehuda, go home, it's almost Shabbat," the *kippah*-wearing Avner remembered Begin saying. "Finally," Avner said to himself, "I'm working for a Jew." Nor was Avner the only one who understood that. Avraham Shapira, of the ultra-Orthodox Agudat Yisrael party (which under Begin joined the government after being in the opposition since 1952), echoed Avner's sentiment: "For the first time we can see that we have a Jewish prime minister."

It wasn't only the Orthodox who took pleasure in Begin's Jewishness and appreciated how different he was from those who had come before. Rabbi Alexander Schindler, one of the leading American Reform rabbis and chairman of the Conference of Presidents of Major American Jewish Organizations, was equally taken with Begin's Jewish core. "I never heard Rabin speak Jewish," he said, "and I don't mean Yiddish."[38] Schindler and Begin became fast friends. From Reform to Orthodox, left to right, Begin's impish self-effacing nature, coupled with his deeply ingrained Jewish sensibilities, won over both hearts and minds.

All of Begin's predecessors had been Jewish, of course, but Begin was different. He had a finely honed appreciation for the rhythms and priorities of Jewish life and tradition, which had never yet been represented in the prime minister's office. The implications of that were clear during his years in office, both in style and in substance.

In 1981, for example, as Begin was beginning to form the coalition government after his successful reelection, seven rabbis from the Agudat Yisrael party barged into his office, contentiously demanding ministerial positions in the upcoming government. Begin listened calmly, but no progress was being made. At the first brief pause in the ruckus, Begin, with an impish smile, asked in Yiddish, a language he never used in public: "*Rabosai, hot mir schon gedavent mincheh?*" (Gentlemen, have you prayed the afternoon service?) They had not. The seven of them, along with Begin, his aide Yechiel Kadishai, and his friend Hart Hasten, constituted the requisite minyan. After their prayers, the men calmly continued their discussions; the next day, after Begin's prayer recess had cooled tempers and a compromise had been reached, the government was announced.[39]

When Avraham Shapira asked Begin to ground all El Al flights on Shabbat, Begin quickly agreed. The status quo, which had prevailed since a 1947 letter from David Ben-Gurion, then head of the Jewish Agency, to Agudat Israel, specified that the Sabbath would be a day of rest. Although other government-owned modes of transportation did not operate on Shabbat, El Al flew every day of the week. On May 3, 1982, Begin announced that El Al, Israel's national airline, would no longer fly on Shabbat.

As expected, pandemonium ensued. Some accused Begin of capitulating to the religious. Others argued that El Al could not remain solvent. But Begin, unfazed, defended the decision in terms not of politics or economics, but of the timeless values of the Jewish people:

The Shabbat, the day of rest, is one of the loftiest ideals in all of human civilization. The original idea was ours, the idea is all ours. We bequeathed it to all the nations, to all the regimes . . . Just one nation, a nation who searched for God and found Him, one small nation heard the voice, saw the voices: "Guard the Shabbat to make it holy—do not do any work, you and your son and your daughter and your male slave and your female slave and your ox and your donkey and the stranger in your gate, so that your male and female slaves may rest like you."

As for the claim that grounding planes on Shabbat would cause irreparable financial damage, Begin replied: "We cannot start calculating profits and losses with regards to an eternal value of *Am Yisrael*, for which our forefathers gave their lives—the Shabbat . . . One need not be a religious person to recognize this. If one is a proud Jew, one will accept it." The decision on El Al passed, 58–54.

Begin's critics continue to insist that El Al still struggles financially to no small degree due to his decision, and that the Israeli economy as a whole was in much worse condition when he left office than it was when he entered. But on this matter, he was single-minded. As far back as the reparations debate, Begin had sought to remind Israel of its Jewish soul, no matter what the cost. His ascent to power changed nothing about that; it remains, without question, one of the central qualities for which Israelis still remember him. He was, as Avner, Shapira, and Schindler understood, Israel's Jewish prime minister. And as Ethiopian, Syrian, and Russian Jews also came to understand, he became, no less, prime minister of the Jews.

Ironically, the magnitude of his commitment to those in need of assistance notwithstanding, none of this would be the theme by which Begin's first term would be remembered. What would truly color his first term, and indeed his life's legacy, was the news in the very first months of his administration that Anwar Sadat, president of the most powerful Arab nation in the region, wished to come to Israel.

Sadat wanted to address the Knesset; it was time to make peace.

12

A Time for War and a Time for Peace

> For everything there is a season . . .
> A time for weeping and a time for dancing . . .
> A time for loving and a time for hating,
> A time for war and a time for peace.
>
> —*Ecclesiastes 3*

Modern Egypt was born even later than Israel. King Farouk, an ineffective despot and incorrigible playboy, was overthrown in a military coup in 1952, and two years later, in 1954, Gamal Abdel Nasser seized power and declared himself president. Nasser had many hopes for Egypt, but chief among them was that it would be the instrument of Israel's destruction. Repeatedly, he promised not only the destruction of the Jewish state, but in the tradition of the anti-Semitism that had been at the core of Arab nationalism ever since Haj Amin al-Husseini, the Palestinian nationalist, had sought a partnership with Hitler, Nasser promised the deaths of the Jews who inhabited Israel: "We shall not enter Palestine with its soil covered in sand, we shall enter it with its soil saturated in blood."[1]

Despite the exterminationist rhetoric, in early 1956, the U.S. envoy Robert B. Anderson reported to Ben-Gurion that Nasser might be open to discussing peace with Israel, despite Nasser's worry that he would "make peace with Ben-Gurion in one meeting, but the next day he would be assassinated" by his own citizens.[2] Nasser understood well how deeply embedded in the Arab street was hatred both of Israel and of Jews.

So he never took the chance. Instead, in July 1956, he nationalized the Suez Canal. Ben-Gurion, who had ultimately come to realize that Jabotinsky was largely right when he understood that only force would convince the Arabs that Israel meant to survive, responded by capturing the Sinai Peninsula in the brief 1956 Sinai Campaign, but returned it to Egypt almost immediately due to massive American pressure. Nasser had lost, but he remained steadfastly committed to destroying the Jewish state, and within a decade, he had transformed Egypt into one of the most powerful military forces in the region. Then, in 1967, he precipitated the Six-Day War, in which he failed miserably once again.

Nasser tried to resign after the embarrassment of the June 1967 war, but Parliament refused to accept his resignation. He died in September 1970; five million people—considerably more than the entire population of Israel at that time—attended his funeral. He was replaced by Anwar el-Sadat, the son of a peasant, who had attended the Royal Military Academy, where he had been befriended by Nasser, who appointed him his vice president and presumed successor.

Sadat set out to complete what Nasser had tried, and failed equally miserably. In 1973, Egypt and Syria struck Israel on Yom Kippur. Publicly, Sadat told his nation that a great victory had been won. But he knew that the war had been a disaster; it was time, Sadat appears to have learned, for a radically different approach.

Four years after the Yom Kippur War, when Menachem Begin was elected prime minister of Israel, he made it clear that he was willing to negotiate with Egypt. In late August 1977, he visited Romania and asked President Nicolae Ceausescu for his help; given Ceausescu's close relationship with Sadat, Begin believed this avenue had a better chance of success than almost any other. He also sent Moshe Dayan to Morocco to secretly convene with King Hassan and express Israel's desire for peace talks with Egypt. When Sadat visited Romania shortly after Begin, Ceausescu said to him: "Begin wants a solution." Sadat replied, "Can an extremist like

Begin really want peace?" Ceausescu answered him, "Let me state categorically to you that he wants peace."³ He added, "Begin is a hard man
to negotiate with, but once he agrees to something he will implement it
to the last dot and comma. You can trust Begin."⁴

Perhaps knowing this, Sadat made his move on November 9, 1977, during a parliamentary address. Israel "will be stunned to hear me tell you
that I am ready to go to the ends of the earth, and even to their home, to
the Knesset itself, to argue with them, in order to prevent one Egyptian
soldier from being wounded."⁵

His Egyptian audience, which included PLO chairman Yasser Arafat,
was incredulous. In Israel, Begin—understanding that his message had
been received—was both receptive and wary. He told Yechiel Kadishai,
"We'll see how serious he is about this! We have to put Sadat to the test."⁶
In a November 11 radio broadcast aimed directly at the Egyptians, Begin
invited Sadat to Jerusalem, saying he hoped that the biblical model in
which "Egypt and Eretz Israel were allies; real friends and allies" could
be restored.⁷ But he also quoted from the fifth sura of the Koran to make
it clear that Israel had legitimate claims to its land: "Remember when
Moses said to his people, 'O my people, remember the goodness of Allah
towards you when He appointed prophets among you. O my people, enter
the Holy Land which Allah hath written down as yours.'"⁸

Following the radio address, Begin sent an official and cordial invitation to Sadat, unsure whether Sadat would even consider it. Two days
later, Sadat accepted.

Begin threw himself into the preparations, insisting that from the outset, Sadat must be made to understand the principles to which the Jewish
state was committed. He spoke to the Knesset about the importance of
having Sadat arrive late enough on a Saturday evening so that Shabbat
would not be violated:

President Sadat indicated he wished to come to us on Saturday evening. I decided that an appropriate hour would be eight o'clock,
well after the termination of the Shabbat. I decided on this hour in

order that there would be no Shabbat desecration. Also, I wanted the whole world to know that ours is a Jewish State which honors the Sabbath day. I read again those eternal biblical verses: *"Honor the Sabbath day to keep it holy,"* and was again deeply moved by their meaning. These words echo one of the most sanctified ideas in the history of mankind, and they remind us that once upon a time we were all slaves in Egypt. Mr. Speaker: We respect the Muslim day of rest—Friday. We respect the Christian day of rest—Sunday. We ask all nations to respect our day of rest—Shabbat. They will do so only if we respect it ourselves.[9]

The Knesset agreed, and preparations proceeded for Sadat's arrival on November 19. As Yehuda Avner would later recall:

Never had Ben-Gurion airport been more festooned as on that Saturday night—it was awash with light and color, hung with hundreds of flapping flags, Israeli and Egyptian. Rows of parading troops, their regimental ensigns aloft, framed the tarmac, and at one end was arranged a military band, its brass instruments flashing in the floodlight . . . A ramp was quickly rolled into position, and an expectant hush settled on the assembly. Even the air seemed to be holding its breath.[10]

As Sadat descended the steps of his plane, Begin met him at the bottom. The two men embraced, awkwardly for a moment, and then more comfortably. In the minutes that followed, Sadat met a veritable "who's who" of the Israeli leadership. He was introduced to Moshe Dayan and Yitzhak Rabin, who had led Israel's lightning victory in 1967, and to Golda Meir, who had ultimately defeated him in 1973. Rabin later recalled being immediately impressed with Sadat: "Here he was meeting all his former arch-enemies, one after another, in the space of seconds, and he nonetheless found a way to start off his visit by saying exactly the right thing to each and every one of them."[11]

The following day, after praying at the Al-Aqsa Mosque and visiting

Yad Vashem, Sadat delivered his momentous address in Arabic at the Knesset. It was the first time that an Arab leader spoke in the Israeli parliament. Sadat laid out five conditions for peace: Israel's complete return to the 1967 borders, independence for the Palestinians (a notion that he left entirely undefined), the right for all to live in peace and security, a commitment not to resort to arms in the future, and the end of belligerency in the Middle East.[12]

Not surprisingly, Begin's speech was laced with biblical references, and stressed the Jewish people's historical connection to the Land of Israel. He also repeated Israel's willingness since 1948 to engage in negotiations with Egypt among other Arab nations. Lastly, he offered a prayer "that the God of our common ancestors will grant us the requisite wisdom of heart in order to overcome the difficulties and obstacles, the calumnies and slanders." As he spoke, the Psalmist and the Prophet were brought to life in the Knesset chamber; Begin reminded his listeners: "The Psalmist of Israel said, 'Righteousness and peace have kissed' [Psalms 85:10], and, as the prophet Zechariah said, 'Love truth and peace' [Zechariah 8:19]."[13]

But it was one thing to love truth and peace, and another to negotiate it. The embrace at the bottom of the plane's stairs notwithstanding, Sadat and Begin were in many ways an emotional and political mismatch, and even with American mediation, negotiations quickly got bogged down and became acrimonious. Begin, the lawyer, understood that the devil was in the details and wished to proceed exceedingly carefully. Ceausescu had warned Sadat that Begin would be a tough negotiator, but trustworthy once a deal was reached; Sadat, however, was unprepared for the belabored give-and-take over so many details. Cyrus Vance, President Carter's secretary of state, also quickly lost patience with him. He later remarked that "unlike Sadat, Mr. Begin is a man of many words . . . Sadat sees things broadly, his eyes always on the horizon. He has no desire or willingness to get down to the nitty-gritty . . . Mr. Begin, on the other hand, can get lost in the small print; he's pedantic about semantics."[14] For Vance, Begin's inability to focus on the big picture was a page out of Jewish history; Begin, the Jew, was the legalistic Pharisee, while Sadat was the visionary.

One main substantive sticking point in the negotiations was the question of Palestinian autonomy. While Begin was, unhappily, willing to return the Sinai in exchange for peace, Sadat and Carter wanted to address the new Israeli settlements in the West Bank and Gaza Strip, the development of Palestinian autonomy, and the future status of Jerusalem. But those demands were nonstarters for Begin. His was still an era in which all Israeli prime ministers, of both the political left and the right, rejected out of hand the very notion of Palestinian statehood. Golda Meir, heir to Ben-Gurion's left-wing Labor Party, was famous for having said that there was "no such thing" as the Palestinian people.[15] And though it was not clear what Palestinian independence meant to the various parties, the mere notion of dividing Jerusalem and relinquishing its eastern half, captured in 1967 from Jordan—which had destroyed Jewish graves and synagogues and had prevented Jews from worshipping at their most sacred sites—was, for Begin, unthinkable. This was, after all, the man whose fighters had held out in Jerusalem long after Ben-Gurion had given up, the man who had insisted that some of the arms on the *Altalena* go to those desperate "Hebrew warriors" and the man who had suggested, even before the city was taken in the Six-Day War, that the chief rabbi prepare to blow the shofar at the Western Wall once Israel's soldiers reached it.

The issue was far deeper than the history of Begin's warriors who had been unable to hold on to Jerusalem, or of the paratroopers who had liberated the city in 1967; the issue was a religious one. Begin, Kadishai would insist years later, was absolutely unwilling to even discuss giving up one inch of the Land of Israel. The Sinai, though strategic, was not technically the Land of Israel; but Gaza, the West Bank, and Jerusalem were part of the Land of Israel, and Begin would not even discuss turning them over to anyone at all.[16]

Sadat and Carter had thus picked three issues on which Begin simply could not and would not compromise, and they had tacked them on to the

Egyptian-Israeli negotiations. In doing so, they demonstrated their utter misreading of Begin, and almost condemned the negotiations to failure.

N o less frustrating to Carter and Sadat was Begin's refusal to even discuss an end to the settlement project. But here, too, they simply did not understand Begin or Israel. Their frustration was in large measure a result of their failure to appreciate that the settlements were far more than a matter of policy for Israelis. Though the settlements would later become more of a right-left political issue in Israel, at that time, the mere subject still raised the question of whether or not Jews had a right to the Land of Israel. *Eretz Yisrael* was *Eretz Yisrael*. Either the Jews had a right to their ancestral homeland or they did not. For Begin, the belief that they did was axiomatic. Without that belief, what justification was there for the Zionist enterprise in the first place?

Then there was the psychological dimension of the mere notion of leaving the West Bank. Taking the West Bank in 1967 had also given Israel more defensible borders, and as a result, it gave Israelis a sense of being able to breathe more deeply. Ben-Gurion had said as early as 1948 that the Arab attack on Israel had abrogated the outlines of partition; even Abba Eban, a known dove, insisted that the pre–Six-Day War borders were indefensible, that they simply set up another massacre of Jews and that Israel would never return to them. "The June map is for us equivalent to insecurity and danger," he said. "I do not exaggerate when I say that it has for us something of a memory of Auschwitz."[17] Carter and Sadat seem to have had no appreciation for any of these issues: not for the fact that the settlements had been launched not by Likud, but by Labor governments, nor for the psychological implications of what they were asking of Begin, and of all Israel.

The American and Egyptian leaders also failed to understand Begin's ideological instincts. His heart had always been with the Gush Emunim, the religious-nationalist movement that spearheaded settlement growth. They were, after all, his ideological heirs. He had fought the British to make possible Jewish immigration and to achieve Jewish sovereignty, and the Gush Emunim pioneers, in turn, were moving to the desert to extend that sovereignty to portions of the ancestral homeland that Israel had captured in defensive wars, that had been part of the biblical boundaries of Israel and part, as well, of the original Mandate that Jews had been promised as a state. Thus, when Gush Emunim members had sought permission to build a settlement called Elon Moreh (one of the first) in 1974, Begin (who was not yet prime minister) did not object. When they were evicted from their original site and then from an alternative location at Sebastia, even the leftist prime minister Yitzhak Rabin agreed to a temporary relocation to the Kadum military base on the eastern side of Nablus. The settlers gained their traction under Labor governments, but Begin supported them wholeheartedly.

In May 1977, the day after his election as prime minister but before final results were announced, Begin visited the temporary Elon Moreh site with Ariel Sharon in order to attend a *hachnasat sefer torah*—a ceremony dedicating a new Torah scroll in the settlement's synagogue— and was treated to a hero's welcome. "He stood in the square between the mobile homes and took the velvet-covered scroll in one arm, putting the other around Ariel Sharon's shoulder . . . Before the ceremony, Begin made a statement to the crowd. 'Soon,' he said, 'there will be many more Elon Morehs.' "[18]

Reporters following the prime minister–elect queried whether Begin's firm commitment to the settlements implied a future annexation of the West Bank. They got a tongue-lashing in return:

> We don't use the word "annexation." You annex *foreign* land, not your own country. Besides, what was this term "West Bank"? From now on, the world must get used to the area's real—biblical—name, "Judea and Samaria" . . . is it so difficult for you to use these words?[19]

In the fall of 1977, Begin agreed to declare Elon Moreh a fully legal settlement, sparking controversy both within his cabinet and on the street. Leftist protesters, including the Peace Now movement, argued on behalf of the Palestinian landowners whose land the Israeli government had expropriated for Elon Moreh. Rallies were held in protest. Tellingly, though, when in July 1979 the Supreme Court deemed the expropriation of land illegal, Begin acquiesced. Reaffirming his undying belief in the rule of law, the man who had railed against Ben-Gurion's treatment of Robert Soblen said, simply but biblically, "There are judges in Jerusalem."[20] Elon Moreh was forced to move.

Thus, when it came to settlements, Begin was continually caught between his ideology on the one hand, and domestic politics and international pressure on the other. He both understood the explosiveness of the settlement project and, at the same time, believed in it wholeheartedly. As had the Labor prime ministers Golda Meir and Yitzhak Rabin who had preceded him, he allowed the number of settlements to grow. When he took office, there were approximately seventy-five existing settlements. By the time he left office that number had doubled.[21]

This, then, was the complex background to Sadat's visit to Israel and his demand for cessation of settlement growth. Carter pushed Begin to accede to Sadat's demands. But Begin insisted on moving deliberately. There were principles that had animated him his entire life, and he was not about to abandon them now, even for peace with Egypt.

Complicating matters, Begin already discerned that he was facing serious opposition in his own party. Desperately needing not to feel alone and seeking support in the face of those who were accusing him of selling out his principles in pursuit of a Nobel Prize, he decided to add Chaim Landau, his comrade from Etzel days, to the cabinet. But Shmuel Katz, who had been in the Etzel Paris office during the *Altalena* incident, furious at the mere idea that the Sinai might be returned, chose to compete for the spot that Begin had in mind for Landau. Begin tried to reason with Katz, urging him not to create a rift in "the fighting family," and to convince him that returning the Sinai was not, according to the Bible, tantamount to returning part of the Land of Israel. "What does this have to do with the Bible?" Katz asked in fury. "You can use it to prove almost any borders you want!"[22]

Katz refused to relent. Begin saw Katz's position at such a critical period as treasonous and—undoubtedly—an act of profound personal disloyalty; he never again spoke to Katz until Katz was a dying old man.

Cognizant that he was going to be assailed from all manner of sides, Begin moved with exceeding caution. But what to him seemed careful and responsible chess playing on the domestic front struck Sadat and Carter as foot-dragging. The relationships became increasingly fraught. At a joint summit in Ismailia on December 26, 1977, it became quite clear that the two sides faced "an unbridgeable abyss of misunderstanding and deadlock."[23]

Begin was willing to accept U.N. Resolution 242, which declared that "territories" (but not "all" territories, a distinction the Israelis had insisted on) taken by Israel during the 1967 war would be returned; he even offered Israeli citizenship and the right to vote to all Palestinians (a controversial and bold move in the eyes of many Israeli politicians). But he simply refused to accept a unilateral withdrawal of settlements from the West Bank, to which he referred by its biblical names, Judea and Samaria. The summit ended without as much as a joint communiqué.[24]

The poisoned relationship between Carter and Begin exacerbated the problem. Begin understood right away that he would never rival Sadat for Carter's affections. Brzezinski later noted that Sadat was Carter's "favorite person."[25] This was partially because of their shared rural background, but also because of what Carter perceived as Begin's stubbornness. "Where Sadat craved peace," one historian wrote, "it seemed to Carter, Begin craved land."[26] Sadat was quickly becoming the world's darling. He was anointed "Architect of a New Middle East" by *Time* (which, of course, had coined the famous phrase "Begin Rhymes with Fagin" upon Begin's election), and Sadat received the magazine's coveted "Man of the Year" title.[27]

The *Time* article celebrated Sadat's willingness to meet with Begin and referred to the Israeli premier as an "inverted *sabra*," a reference to the cactus fruit and a typical nickname for native Israelis. Unlike them, he was soft on the outside and tough on the inside. But *Time* also praised Begin's apparent determination to change the game in the Middle East:

> Retorts one supporter: "Begin is convinced that he can achieve the impossible. He is haunted by his heart problem [he has twice been hospitalized since the election with serious coronary attacks], which means that time is slipping away, and by how history will compare him with his greatest opponent—Ben-Gurion. He is trying to fight his way into Jewish history books as the leader who brought the peace Ben-Gurion never achieved." So far at least, Begin has maintained the peace momentum begun by Sadat; if he carries on, he will have assured his place not only in Jewish history but in world history.[28]

But it was not going to be easy. Carter's patience was running out, and everyone, including American Jews, understood that a breakthrough was critical. A few American Jews even worried about Begin's "*shtetl* Jew" appearance among better-dressed politicians, and sent "fashion police" to the prime minister's residence in order to tidy up his act. They

> came to his home, looked at his clothes and suggested that he make some changes to his wardrobe. While they were explaining the issue—and Begin was listening like a good student—Aliza went ballistic: "Forty years I have dressed you and you became the prime minister, why do you need all this?" she shouted. Begin looked at her patiently and said: "Alize'nka, if it is good for the Jewish people, what do you care?"[29]

But sartorial resplendence was no solution, and matters with Carter worsened. Following a meeting between Sadat and Carter in February 1978, Carter declared Israel's settlements in the Sinai illegal while simultaneously promising new fighter jets to Egypt. Intentionally or not, both Sadat and Carter were creating the impression that what animated them was simple hostility to Israel. Foreign Minister Moshe Dayan—who had served in the Haganah, became a leading member of the Labor Party, and was far from being a Revisionist—called the administration "anti-Israel" and said that Carter and the Americans "no longer could be honest brokers."[30] But Carter would not relent. Seated before Carter a month later, Begin was "shocked into silence"[31] as the president "ticked off the list of Egyptian-Israeli problem issues and faulted Begin on all of them: West Bank and Sinai settlements, West Bank sovereignty, [and] the principle of land for peace."[32] It felt like a personal blow to Begin, who believed that in his willingness to give up most of the Sinai, he had made sacrifices that were equal to those of the Egyptians. Disdainfully, Carter said to an ashen-faced Begin, "The likelihood that the peace talks can be resumed with Egypt is very remote." The stalemate, recounted Avner, was "absolute."[33]

Begin was depressed, and to those who knew him well, there were signs of physical decline. He had been hospitalized for heart issues in 1977, and in May 1978, he collapsed and was hospitalized again. His mounting physical health problems led a Hadassah Hospital physician to wonder about his mental health. "The problem is that he has to take conflicting medications—some dealing with his diabetes, other with heart problems—and as a result he's suffering from frequent and extreme ups and downs in mood swings," the doctor said.[34] Begin could rise to the occasion when needed, but it seemed that he could not sustain his energy or his focus. Having to make more weighty decisions than perhaps ever before, some observers doubted that he could fully shoulder the burden.

Yitzhak Navon, who had fought with the Haganah and eventually served as Israel's fifth president, recalled, "Begin was having difficulty functioning: He fell asleep in the middle of meetings, his head would droop, he wasn't focused."[35] Ezer Weizman, Begin's defense minister (he was a nephew of Chaim Weizmann, fought with the Irgun, later commanded the Israeli Air Force, and ultimately served as Israel's seventh president) noticed that "the prime minister seemed indifferent to what was going on around him, taking no part in the cabinet discussions . . . [He was] withdrawn within himself, his glassy eyes focused on some remote spot."[36] The combination of the exhausting negotiation process and his physical illness threatened to bring Begin down. Weizman, never Begin's strongest supporter, understood how much was at stake, and tried to bolster Begin's spirits: "Don't be down. Go out and meet the people . . . Sir, the people will replenish your strength."[37]

Carter had his own concerns. Fearful that the collapse of peace talks could send Egypt back into the orbit of the Soviet Union, he decided on a Hail Mary pass: an intense twelve-day summit in the secluded woods of Camp David. Seemingly a perfect setting for the summit, Camp David was guarded by U.S. marines and was isolated from the outside world and the press. Begin called it a "concentration camp deluxe."[38]

Prior to the summit, Carter told Begin how high he believed the stakes were. He told the prime minister that "peace in the Middle East was in his hands, that he had a unique opportunity to either bring it into being or kill it . . . an opportunity that may never come again."[39] But Begin's view of life was too deeply rooted in a Jewish historic consciousness to accept that sense of urgency. On Israeli television, he presented his rebuttal to Carter: "Our people lived thousands of years before Camp David, and will live thousands of years after Camp David . . . If we are told that this is the last chance to arrive at peace, we shall not agree: There are no 'last chances' in life."[40]

As he boarded the plane to the United States, Begin mentally girded himself for a challenging series of negotiations by calling to mind the words of his master and teacher, Ze'ev Jabotinsky: "The only way to achieve an agreement in the future is by utterly abandoning all attempts to achieve an agreement in the present."[41]

13

It Belongs to My People

When the Lord brought back the exiles of Zion, we were like
people who dream.
Then were our mouths filled with laughter, and our tongues with
songs of joy.
Then it was said among the nations, "The Lord has done great
things for them."

—*Psalm 126*

From the first day of the Camp David summit, on September 5, the
arguments were heated. Sadat demanded Israeli withdrawal from the
West Bank and Gaza in order to pave the way for a future Palestinian
state. To Begin, the request was ludicrous. The PLO had been founded in
Cairo with Egypt's support, had been sworn to Israel's destruction from
the very outset, and Sadat was demanding not only that Israel weaken
its buffer by giving back the Sinai to him, but that it create a state for
those who remained expressly committed to Israel's destruction. Sadat
also demanded financial compensation to the Egyptian government for
damages during and after the October War of 1973. Though he had apparently informed Carter in advance that he was willing to compromise on
all these issues, he felt he had to make a strong initial showing. (Ambassador Samuel Lewis later related that Sadat had also been warned by his
aides that if he compromised too readily, he might be killed.)

Begin rejected all of those demands, calling them "chutzpah!"[1] The
negotiations quickly descended into bitter acrimony. Carter wrote, "All

restraint was now gone. Their faces were flushed, and the niceties of diplomatic language and protocol were stripped away. They had almost forgotten I was there."[2] Within the first two days of the summit, Carter decided that there would be no more face-to-face meetings between Begin and Sadat at Camp David.

The Americans themselves were divided in their assessment of Begin. Sam Lewis felt that "Begin was not able personally to wrap himself around options and alternatives and possibilities and subtleties," but Cyrus Vance thought he was "one of the finest poker players" he had ever seen.[3] So determined was he to ensure that no detail was out of place that he stonewalled Carter to his breaking point. Subtleties in language, for example, the differences among "Palestinians," "Palestinian people," and "Palestinian Arabs," were the bricks on which Begin built his case. Carter, who undoubtedly did not understand the existential vulnerabilities Begin felt the president was pressuring him to accept, lost all regard for the Israeli leader. Begin is a psycho, he apparently told his wife.[4]

But what Begin was actually doing was carefully angling for a "compromise" that would ensure that the issue of Palestinian autonomy did not spin out of control. He was unwilling to give up any part of the Land of Israel, and was buttressed by Dayan, who believed that the West Bank was critical to Israel's security. What the parties slowly inched toward was an agreement in which the Palestinians would have a self-governing authority that would be elected for a period of five years. During that five-year period, a final-status agreement would be discussed—but the agreement was subject to the approval of all sides. That meant, in essence, that every side would have a veto. That arrangement both satisfied everyone in the short term and doomed any Palestinian prospects for real autonomy to failure. The Palestinians would demand Israeli withdrawal from the West Bank, and Israel would veto it; Israel would demand that it retain control over the West Bank, and the Arabs would veto it.

Negotiating carefully, Begin ensured that nothing beyond the limited autonomy he was willing to consider would develop. (To impose notions such as "statehood" on the Camp David discussion is an anachronism; the subject of statehood did not arise, and the conversation was far less defined than it would become in subsequent decades.) Begin would be satisfied with that stalemate, and intuited that Sadat would, as well. Sadat would get both peace and the Sinai, and would be able to claim that he had tried to secure at least something for the Palestinians. Indeed, Aryeh Naor, who was cabinet secretary under Begin and was present at Camp David, believed that Sadat gave up on nothing that mattered to him. He "couldn't care less" about the Palestinians, Naor insisted; as the leader of the most populous Arab nation, he simply had to be able to claim that he'd done his utmost to make the Palestinian case.[5]

But even so, the haggling was intense and acrimonious. Shabbat was around the corner, with no agreement in sight. Begin insisted there be a Shabbat meal. Agreement or no agreement, Jewish life went on. Challah, wine, gefilte fish, and skullcaps were all brought in from Washington. Both the Americans and the Egyptians were invited to participate, but the Egyptians declined.[6] At dinner, Begin recited *kiddush*. Beset from all sides, he drew strength from the core that had always defined him—he was a Jew, a link in a sacred chain.

Carter, who made no attempt to hide his disdain for Begin, went to Ezer Weizman, Moshe Dayan, and Aharon Barak (then Israel's attorney general, and later President of the Supreme Court) directly. But that was a tactical error of no small proportions, for in doing so, he estranged Begin from the process, giving the aging man the impression that no one was interested in speaking with him. Several times in the second week, Begin attempted to extricate himself from the entire ordeal and return home. The heightened tension, as his body continued to fail him, was too much to bear.

Curiously, the president of the United States also seemed unable to grasp the challenges that a democratically elected leader such as Begin would face in selling peace to the citizens of Israel. Sadat, of course, had no democracy with which he had to deal; but Carter, who knew well the challenges of governing a democracy, seems to have had no awareness or concern for the political challenges that any deal Begin agreed to would face in the Knesset.

Nor did Carter come to understand Begin any better, even as the negotiations proceeded. His public protestations of Christian piety notwithstanding, Carter had none of the biblical sensibilities or knowledge that were central to who Begin was. When Begin told Brzezinski, "My right eye will fall out, my right hand will fall off before I ever agree to the dismantling of a single Jewish settlement," few grasped the biblical allusion to "If I forget thee, O Jerusalem" and the attachment that Jews had felt to their ancestral home for thousands of years.[7] Without an appreciation of the ways in which thousands of years of Jewish history had deeply shaped Begin, the way he read Bible and his sense of Jewish vulnerability, there was no way that Carter could begin to understand him.

Even more bewildering to Carter was Begin's resolute refusal to even discuss the subject of dividing Jerusalem. When the topic was broached, Begin related to Carter the story of Rabbi Amnon of Mainz, the eleventh-century Jewish scholar who was pressured by the archbishop of Mainz to convert to Christianity. Rabbi Amnon asked the archbishop for three days during which to consider, but immediately regretted having done anything at all that might be interpreted as his even considering such an unthinkable act. When he did not appear before the archbishop on the third day, he was dragged in by guards. Rabbi Amnon, when accused that he had broken his pledge to appear after three days, admitted his guilt and asked that his tongue be cut out, since it was with his tongue that he had expressed doubt of his everlasting commitment to Judaism. But the archbishop ruled that instead of his tongue, Rabbi Amnon's hands and feet should be cut off. Dying, Rabbi Amnon asked that he be brought into the synagogue, as it was Rosh Hashanah. There, in his last moments, he recited a prayer called the *U-Netaneh Tokef,* which became one of the central prayers of the High Holiday liturgy. And then he died.

Begin's point was clear. Rabbi Amnon sinned by even suggesting that he would consider conversion. Begin was not going to pretend for a moment that Jerusalem was up for discussion. He had struggled to procure the *Altalena*'s arms for his fighters defending the city in 1948, the Jordanians had desecrated it after his fighters could not hold on, and Israel had recaptured it in 1967 through the sheer grit and bravery of its young sons.

This point, at least, Carter understood. Begin was making it clear that he would not make Rabbi Amnon's mistake; when it came to Jerusalem, there was nothing to talk about. Carter shared the story with Sadat, and the issue of Jerusalem was dropped.

But there was nothing Begin could do to get the Sinai settlements off the table. Though Sadat insisted that they be dismantled, Begin hoped that they could be preserved. He actually proposed that the Jewish settlers be permitted to stay in their settlements, lightly armed, even after the Sinai was returned to Egypt. Whether the areas the settlements covered would be Israeli or Egyptian was never discussed; as Kadishai himself acknowledged, on that issue Begin was "living a fantasy."[8]

Many observers felt then, and still believe, that one of Begin's concerns was that an agreement to dismantle the Sinai settlements would later be used as a precedent for the West Bank. The settlements would also be one of the critical political battles he would have to face upon coming home. Undoubtedly, moving Jews out of their homes was also deeply painful for Begin. But Sadat was not going to be moved on this issue, and everyone on the Israeli team understood that if a deal were to be reached, Begin was going to have to back down. It was Ariel Sharon who apparently convinced Begin that leaving the Sinai would not set a precedent for having to evacuate the West Bank and that the political battles ahead could be managed. The two men, who were linked by Begin's father's friendship with Sharon's grandfather in Brisk and whose most complex collaboration was still to come, partnered in moving the proposal forward. Begin agreed to dismantle the Sinai settlements and dislodge their inhabitants, if the Knesset approved.

Little by little, despite the manifold challenges, progress was made. In the end, Begin sacrificed the Sinai but kept the West Bank, and the Egyptian president got the Sinai back by selling out Palestinian hopes for sovereignty.

Both Begin and Sadat had moved significantly from their opening positions. At the signing ceremony on September 17, Sadat thanked Carter for his commitment, but failed to mention either Menachem Begin or the State of Israel. But Begin complimented Sadat profusely, frequently referring to him as a friend. "In Jewish teachings," Begin lectured the small audience, "there is a tradition that the greatest achievement of a human being is to turn his enemy into a friend, and this we do in reciprocity."[9]

Even Jimmy Carter grudgingly thanked Begin for the political distance he had traveled:

> This was a remarkable demonstration of courage, political courage, on the part of Prime Minister Begin, who had to go against his own previous commitments over a lifetime [and] against his own closest friends and allies who sustained and protected him during his revolutionary days.[10]

An agreement in hand, Begin returned to Israel more popular than ever before. The renewed popularity and momentum in the peace process seemed to revive Begin; suddenly, he was not failing, but was leading the charge once again.

But many of his former Etzel comrades were devastated, and in the Knesset, divisions ran deep. It took a full seven hours of heated deliberation to convince his cabinet to sign off on the Camp David agreement and to bring it to the Knesset. In the seventeen-hour marathon Knesset session that followed, Begin defended his position passionately, reminding his listeners both of the imperative of peace and of the enduring vulnerability of the Jewish people and how Israel would be perceived if they turned the deal down.

On September 28, 1978, at roughly three o'clock in the morning, the Knesset voted 84 "yes," 19 "no," and 17 abstentions in favor of the Camp David agreement. The man the British had once called Terrorist No. 1 had made peace with Israel's most powerful enemy.

Menachem Begin was nominated for the Nobel Peace Prize. But the Nobel Committee argued heatedly over whether Begin was deserving of the award, given his involvement in Deir Yassin.[11] Significantly, no one mentioned that Sadat had attacked Israel on Yom Kippur, Judaism's holiest day. And years later, Yasser Arafat—the inveterate murderer of innocent Israelis—would be awarded the prize with less resistance raised than in Begin's case. Several European newspapers argued that Begin's prize should be given to Carter instead.

But Aase Lionaes, chairman of the Nobel Committee, stated in her address, "Never has the Peace Prize expressed a greater or more audacious hope—a hope of peace for the people of Egypt, for the people of Israel, and for all the peoples of the strife-torn and war-ravaged Middle East."[12] The Nobel Committee decided to give the peace prize to both Begin and Sadat. Sadat, though, understanding that in not having achieved anything for the Palestinians he had sullied his reputation in the Arab world, did not attend the Nobel ceremony on December 10, 1978. He sent his son-in-law instead.

In Israel, too, old party animosities endured. Golda Meir, who was close to death, remarked that Begin should have received an Oscar instead of a Nobel. Heir to Ben-Gurion's Labor Party, she and Begin had long had a cordial relationship, but she had also inherited the Old Man's instinctive resentment of Begin.[13] She died while he was in Oslo receiving the prize.

While Sadat refused to attend the Nobel ceremony, Begin used his speech there to restate one of his life's most fundamental commitments. A passionate, profound, and unrelenting commitment to the Jewish people did not have to come at the expense of caring about humanity at large. In fact, Zionism was but the Jewish expression of a universal yearning. He would have been utterly bewildered by those who, several decades after his death, felt that they had to abandon Zionism for the sake of their universal commitments.

Begin began by setting the Jewish context of what was unfolding: "I have come from the Land of Israel, the land of Zion and Jerusalem, and here I stand in humility and with pride as a son of the Jewish people, as one of the generation of the Holocaust and Redemption."

And then he continued with a reminder of the Jewish commitment to peace:

The ancient Jewish people gave the world the vision of eternal peace, of universal disarmament, of abolishing the teaching and learning of war. Two Prophets, Yeshayahu Ben Amotz [Isaiah] and Micha HaMorashti [Micah], having foreseen the spiritual unity of man under God—with His word coming forth from Jerusalem—gave the nations of the world the following vision expressed in identical terms: "And they shall beat their swords into ploughshares and their spears into pruning hooks. Nation shall not lift up sword against nation; neither shall they learn war anymore."[14]

Then, however, fully conscious that many of those watching the ceremony felt they were listening to a terrorist, he intentionally echoed Thomas Jefferson, reminding the world that Israel was but a more recent, and certainly the most watched, example of the universal quest for human freedom:

At such a time, unheard of since the first generation, the hour struck to rise and fight—for the dignity of man, for survival, for liberty, for every value of the human image a man has been endowed with by his Creator, for every known inalienable right he stands for and lives for. Indeed, there are days when to fight for a cause so absolutely just is the highest human command. Norway has known such days, and so have we. Only in honoring that command comes the regeneration of the concept of peace. You rise, you struggle, you make sacrifices to achieve and guarantee the prospect and hope of living in peace—for you and your people, for your children and their children.

Begin then moved away from Jeffersonian universalism and returned to the distinct history and unique needs of the Jewish people. He spoke of the eradication of Jewish life in Europe and of the Jews' subsequent striving to build a state of their own. Invoking his mentor and father figure, Jabotinsky, he told his international audience that the story of Israel was not war or peace, but rather, peace through strength.

Let it, however, be declared and known, stressed, and noted that fighters for freedom hate war. My friends and I learned this precept from Ze'ev Jabotinsky through his own example, and through the one he set for us from Giuseppe Garibaldi. Our brothers in spirit, wherever they dwell, learned it from their masters and teachers. This is our common maxim and belief—that if through your efforts and sacrifices you win liberty and with it the prospect of peace, then work for peace because there is no mission in life more sacred.

And so reborn Israel always strove for peace, yearned for it, made endless endeavors to achieve it. My colleagues and I have gone in the footsteps of our predecessors since the very first day we were called by our people to care for their future. We went any place, we looked for any avenue, we made any effort to bring about negotiations between Israel and its neighbors.[15]

Finally, as a last trope to emphasize the centrality of Jewish peoplehood in his life's work, he reminded his audience that he accepted the prize not as Menachem Begin the man, but as the representative of the Jews, a people still struggling to heal:

> Allow me, now, to turn to you, Madame President of the Nobel Peace Prize Committee and to all its members, and say, Thank you. I thank you for the great distinction. It does not, however, belong to me; it belongs to my people—the ancient people and renascent nation that came back in love and devotion to the land of its ancestors after centuries of homelessness and persecution. This prestigious recognition is due to this people because they suffered so much, because they lost so many, because they love peace and want it with all their hearts for themselves and for their neighbors. On their behalf, I humbly accept the award and in their name I thank you from the bottom of my heart.[16]

The Nobel Prize had been awarded (Begin donated all the prize money to a foundation for disadvantaged students), but the deal was not fully done. There were still numerous details to be negotiated. Carter made a trip to Jerusalem to try to bolster Begin, but if anything, it convinced him that Begin's domestic support was waning and that time was running out. Desperate, he convinced Sadat to drop a few demands (such as

Sadat's late—and transparently malicious—demand to place Egyptian liaison officers in Gaza and the West Bank, ostensibly to assist the populations there in preparing for autonomy),[17] and the sides inched slowly to agreement.

The peace treaty signing was scheduled for March 26, 1979, sixteen months after Sadat's visit to Israel. Begin suggested that the signing take place in Jerusalem, but Sadat refused. The historic event was held on the South Lawn of the White House before an audience of 1,600 people. Sadat declared that a "new chapter . . . in the history of coexistence among nations" was beginning, and once again, he failed to mention Begin's name in the address. And as he had at Oslo, Begin complimented Sadat for the "civil courage" he displayed in the face of adversity and hostility both domestically and in the Arab world.

Yehuda Avner, who attended the ceremony, described Begin's closing: "Begin felt into his pocket and took out a black silk yarmulke, which he placed on his head, and in a gesture pregnant of symbolism, recited in the original Hebrew the whole of the Psalm of David . . . without rendering it into English."[18]

Those listening may not have appreciated the symbolism. Psalm 126 is one of the few Psalms that many Jews know by heart, as it is recited as a preamble to the "Grace after Meals." What even many Jews might not have known, however, was that Psalm 126 had also been seriously considered by the Fourth Zionist Congress in 1900 as a candidate for the Zionist anthem.[19] "Hatikvah" won out, but among knowledgeable Zionists, Psalm 126 was no less a paean to the modern State of Israel than it was to the ancient Jewish dream of returning to the homeland.

This, then, is what Begin chose to read only in Hebrew, the language in which Jews had been reciting it for millennia:

A song of ascents. When the Lord brought back the exiles of Zion we were like people who dream. Then were our mouths filled with laughter, and our tongues with songs of joy. Then it was said among the nations, "The Lord has done great things for them." The Lord did do great things for us and we rejoiced. Bring back our exiles,

Lord, like streams in dry land. May those who sowed in tears, reap in joy. May one who goes out weeping, carrying a bag of seed, come back with songs of joy, carrying his sheaves.[20]

Ten days after signing the peace treaty, Begin visited Egypt, taking veterans of the Etzel, Haganah, and Lechi with him. His stay included a tour of the pyramids and visits to synagogues in Cairo and Alexandria. On a subsequent trip a month later, a very moving moment unfolded at a ceremony in El Arish. There, disabled Israeli and Egyptian veterans were gathered in "a gesture of chivalrous reconciliation."[21] Avner relates the tension of the ceremony:

Close to where I was standing, an Israeli in his thirties, blind, bent low to embrace a whimpering child. The child was eight or nine, with big eyes as black as his curly hair. Their resemblance was striking.

"Kach oti eleihem" [Take me to them], whispered the father, but the child looked up at his father pleadingly. *"Ani m'fached meihem"* [I'm scared of them], he sniveled. Gently, the father nudged the child forward and, timidly, the boy led the father into the no-man's land. At his very first step, an Egyptian officer in a wheelchair, legless, began rolling himself toward them. They met in the middle and the officer placed the blind man's palm into his own, and shook it. Instantly, the tension eased. A Jew began to clap; he was joined by an Arab. The sprinkling of claps quickly swelled into a burst of boisterous applause as the two groups moved toward each other, melting into a huddle of embraces, handshakes, and backslapping. With laughter and tears, the maimed soldiers of the 1948 war, the 1956 Sinai War, the 1967 Six-Day War, the 1970 Attrition War, and the 1973 Yom Kippur War fell on one another, calling out "Shalom!" "Salaam!" "Peace!"

The dream had seemingly become reality. Fouad Ajami, professor of international studies at Johns Hopkins University, explained, "There can be no big Arab-Israeli war without Egypt . . . With Egypt leaving the Arab-Israeli wars, the age of the Arab-Israeli wars came to an end."[22]

Decades later, Egypt was once again in turmoil, and the fate of the Israeli-Egyptian peace treaty was still in question. Begin, it was clear, had a view of history in general and of Jewish history in particular that with time made him seem not only wise, but prescient.

If Begin was right to be nervous about the long-term viability of the accord he had signed, Sadat apparently underestimated the foes of peace. His willingness to make peace with Israel made him the most reviled leader in the Arab world. The Arab League ostracized and expelled Egypt, closing its headquarters in Cairo. Egyptian students studying abroad were expelled from other Arab states. Attitudes toward Sadat only worsened when Israel passed the 1980 Jerusalem Law, which stated that all of Jerusalem was Israel's capital and was interpreted as Israel's annexation of East Jerusalem.

On October 6, 1981, Anwar Sadat was assassinated at an annual parade commemorating the Egyptian crossing of the Suez Canal during the October War. Begin was distraught. "God knows what this will do to the peace treaty," he said.[23] His grief was personal, too. He would later recall:

> Our families became very close. We were drawn to one another—our wives, our children. His family became like my own. And when Anwar was assassinated we grieved, oh how we grieved. I said to Jehan [Sadat's wife], and to Anwar's sons and daughter, I said, and I meant every word of what I said, that his death was a loss to the world, to the Middle East, to Egypt, to Israel, and to my wife and to myself personally.[24]

He flew to Cairo to attend the funeral, with a delegation that included Yitzhak Shamir, Yosef Burg (one of the most impressive leaders of the religious Zionist faction, and minister of the interior under Begin), and Ariel Sharon. Because the funeral took place on a Saturday, Begin and the rest of the delegation chose to walk several miles to the cemetery from the special accommodations the Egyptians had provided, so as not to violate the Sabbath.

For their part, the Egyptians had to ensure that the Israelis did not share the same space as the few Arab representatives that chose to attend. To the Arab world, the Israeli delegation was still no less toxic than it had ever been.

Half a year later, in November 1981, with Sadat dead and Begin recuperating from a broken pelvis, Begin fulfilled Israel's obligation to remove the Sinai settlements. That was, without doubt, the most painful sacrifice that he made in order to close the deal with Sadat. A man who had fought his entire life to restore Jewish life in the Jewish people's ancestral homeland was now enforcing its dismantling.

As early as the signing of the Camp David Accords in 1978, Jewish residents of the Sinai had protested the Knesset's decision to withdraw. The largest standoff took place at Yamit, a smallish secular town near the border with Gaza, in April 1982. Though the government was successful in persuading many of the residents to relocate in exchange for compensation, the members of Gush Emunim refused to leave.[25] In the end, Israeli soldiers were ordered to forcibly remove the protesters. Though there were no significant injuries, the sight of Israeli citizens fighting Israeli soldiers on rooftops, smoke billowing from a building as Jews extricated other Jews from their homes, cast a pall over the country.

For Begin, the irony had to have been beyond painful. The man who had insisted "Civil War—Never!" after the *Altalena* was, unwittingly, leading Jew to battle Jew. It would not be the last time that the settler movement, to which Begin was so soulfully committed, would lead to sparks of violence between Israeli troops and Israeli citizens who loved the land no less than did Menachem Begin.

It was, for Begin, a defining period. Decades earlier, he had called for armed revolt against the British, and now he had made peace with Egypt; he had gone from the underground to the Oslo stage to receive the Nobel Prize. He had, it seemed, entirely recast his legacy.

In a Knesset speech in April 1982, he dreamed aloud of a long-lasting, biblical peace:

But I have always wished that our people would be granted a period of history, a generation or two. "And the Land was at peace for forty years" [Judges 3:11]. Maybe eighty years, like every other people has been granted. And we would rest from wars, and there would be no grief, and there would be no sadness, and there would be no sorrow and bereavement among our people. That was our wish.

And this time we have signed a peace treaty with the largest and strongest of the Arab states. The population of all the neighbors around us does not reach even half the population of Egypt. There is reason to hope that Egypt has left the vicious circle of war against Israel for a very long time. Perhaps someday it will be written: "And the Land was at peace for forty years—and perhaps even for twice that long." No one can say that with confidence. No one can define the time. But this was our aspiration.[26]

The man whom people had thought the least likely to do so had now brought peace to the land he had once helped set ablaze in his bid to drive out the British. The "terrorist" had become the statesman, and the statesman the peacemaker. The man who declared the revolt had ushered in, it seemed for the moment, the beginning of the end of war.

But Menachem Begin had been born into a world at war, had lain down between the armies of the Czar and the Kaiser. He had fled the Nazis, suffered under the Soviets, fought the British, and defended Israel against multiple armies. It was, perhaps, an aspiration too great that the Middle East might now be at peace. And indeed, not long after he spoke to the Knesset of peace "for a very long time," he had no choice but to attack again, to preserve the state on which his entire people's future depended.

14

Crazy Like a Fox

And the sun stood still and the moon halted, while a nation
wreaked judgment on its foes.   —*Joshua 10:13*

I t was about three in the afternoon on the eve of the Jewish holiday of
Shavu'ot, on June 7, 1981, when Yehuda Avner, Begin's English speechwriter and one of his closest advisors, was suddenly summoned to the
Begin residence. General Ephraim Poran, Begin's military secretary,
offered Avner no explanation as he told him to hurry over, despite the
fact that Jerusalem was settling into holiday mode and that religious Jews
like Avner would soon be heading to synagogue for services and then, as
customary, staying awake all night to study Torah.

Avner, who lived not far from the prime minister, half walked, half
ran to the residence. When he was ushered in, he found himself alone
with Begin and Poran. Begin, normally the gentleman who always had
time for social graces, greeted Avner almost perfunctorily and said,
"Freuke [Poran's nickname] will fill you in." With that, the prime minister returned his gaze to the binder of papers he had been reading.

Freuke told Avner that eight Israeli jets were about to take off for
Iraq in order to destroy the nuclear reactor at Osirak. Begin wanted
Avner to prepare communiqués for three possible scenarios: complete
success, partial success, and utter failure. He also told Avner that
Yechiel Kadishai had invited all the cabinet members to the residence
for 5:00 p.m. Each member of the cabinet had been invited individu-

ally; each thought he had been summoned to a private meeting with the prime minister.

Begin was still lost in his binder, filled with the Mossad's assessment of Saddam Hussein's personality—convincing himself one last time, Avner surmised, that the risky operation was utterly unavoidable—when the red telephone on the desk rang. All three men jumped, and Freuke answered. Begin's eyes bored into him, Avner recalled. Freuke listened, and made a few staccato replies. As soon as he hung up, he reported that the army's chief of staff, General Rafael Eitan, had just briefed the pilots, telling them that if they failed, the State of Israel might not survive. The planes were now taking off.

"*Hashem yishmor aleichem*"—May God protect them—Yehuda Avner recounts Begin saying, "with an air of consecration." Begin walked to and fro across the room, his lips moving silently. Avner, who had never seen Begin pacing that way, assumed the prime minister was reciting Psalms. The Polish boy who had grown up in a Bible-loving home and had studied in a yeshiva still knew Psalms by heart.

Begin prayed while Freuke and Avner waited in agonizing, purposeful silence. Eventually, Begin spoke. He knew that his decision to bomb Osirak with Israeli elections looming might be read as an effort to influence the outcome of his race against Shimon Peres, who was leading in the polls. But no matter, he insisted to Freuke and Avner. The reactor needed to be destroyed now, because it would soon go hot, meaning that any later attack would unleash radiation. It needed to be destroyed now because Peres, who had called the possibility of such a strike "stupid and reckless," might win.[1] Begin was certain that Peres, though instrumental in securing Israel's own nuclear capability from the French years earlier, was not made of what it would take to launch the attack and protect the Jewish people from a maniacal tyrant. So before he lost power, Begin was doing it himself.

Again, the phone rang. The planes had been in the air for about forty minutes. Again, Freuke answered, and again Begin and Avner waited in steely silence. Freuke put down the receiver. "The planes are now over the target."

Begin's lips moved once more in silent prayer.

Moments later, the phone rang again; Freuke answered, listened, then hung up. It was the chief of staff, he said. Direct hits. All targets completely destroyed. The planes were on their way home. "Thank God we have young men like these as pilots," Begin muttered, his religiosity and Zionism melding as they had ever since his Betar days in Brisk.

Begin asked Avner to get Sam Lewis, the American ambassador to Israel, on the phone. Lewis, like virtually everyone else in the country, was at home in those preholiday hours. Begin informed him of what had just occurred; Lewis was astounded. Avner, who took careful notes of the conversation, recalls that Begin asked Lewis to brief President Reagan, in response to which Lewis asked delicately, "Are you sure there's nothing else you want me to convey to the president?" as if Lewis knew that the president's response was going to be negative in the extreme.

At 5:00, the members of the cabinet gathered at the prime minister's residence. Upon seeing one another, they realized that they were there for some purpose other than what they had initially assumed. Within minutes they were all in the know. Begin asked Avner to read the draft communiqué to the group assembled. Yosef Burg, minister of the interior and religious affairs, whispered to Avner that the hour was late, and he needed to get to the synagogue where he was scheduled to teach. No communiqué was needed, Burg insisted; the Iraqis were not going to admit the attack, so there was time before the world would find out. It was Shavu'ot; Jews had matters to attend to. And so, without approving that communiqué or any other, the group dispersed. As the sun set, an unknowing Israel settled into the holiday celebration.

The attack on Osirak,[2] codenamed "Operation Opera," had been long in the planning. Saddam Hussein had been building the facility, less than twenty kilometers from Baghdad, with the technical assistance of the French government, since 1974. Israeli intelligence, based on information it had gathered in both Iraq and France, believed that the Iraqis would have the ability to create the level of enriched uranium required for a nuclear bomb within five to seven years.

Saddam, indeed, did nothing to keep his enterprise a secret. In 1975, he shared with a Lebanese magazine his intention to construct the first Arab nuclear arms program. The memory of the Holocaust still cast its shadow over Israeli society; when Saddam threatened to "drown" the Jewish state "with rivers of blood,"[3] he virtually invited an Israeli response.

Israel's leaders had long feared they would face a scenario like this. Addressing the subject before the Knesset in 1963, long before he was elected prime minister, Begin's position had been uncompromising and unrelenting: "Don't even ask whether unconventional weapons are a greater threat to our future than conventional weapons—in my mind, there is no doubt regarding the answer. The greatest and gravest threat we can anticipate: to our future, our security, our existence, is from unconventional weapons."[4]

When he was finally elected, just as concerns about the Iraqi program began to deepen, Begin knew that it was up to him to block Saddam's developing genocidal capability. He began to insist that action be taken against what he called "the bloodiest and most irresponsible of all Arab regimes, with the exception of Kaddafi in Libya."[5] He had grown up knowing well what it meant to live or die at the whim of others, and insisted, "No nation can live on borrowed time."[6] At the end of August 1978, the prime minister began the first of dozens of secret cabinet meetings to determine the appropriate course of action.[7]

Several months later, in the dead of night on April 6, 1979, several core reactors waiting to be shipped to Iraq from the docks of La Seyne-sur-Mer (near Toulon) were detonated and severely damaged. Someone claiming to be a member of the "French Ecological Group" phoned *Le Monde* and assumed responsibility for the detonation; but the group was apparently fictitious and the French assumed it to be the work of "Mideast Agents" or, in simpler terms, the Mossad.[8] A year later, in June 1980, the Egyptian nuclear scientist Yahya El Mashad, who had been contracted to work for the Iraqis, was killed. That, too, was suspected as a Mossad hit.

But these hits merely slowed the construction of Osirak, and only temporarily. Work on the reactor continued to progress. By October 1980, Begin won standby approval from his cabinet for a military operation on the condition that an "inner committee" consisting of the prime minister, Foreign Minister Yitzhak Shamir, and Chief of Staff Eitan signed off.[9]

This "inner committee" invited a series of intelligence and military officials to make presentations regarding a possible military strike. Deep differences of opinion quickly emerged. Some of the experts argued that, at best, a strike on the reactor would set back Iraq's nuclear program only by several years. Some worried that the strike would tempt the Egyptians to pull out of the newly signed peace treaty. Still others feared that an attack would ruin relations with France, which had taken the most active role in building the Osirak plant, and "remained unmoved by . . . dramatic descriptions of the Holocaust"[10] that Israeli officials presented.

More disconcerting to many, however, was the potential impact a strike might have on relations with the United States. Even as late as 1980, the State Department continued to claim that there was "no hard evidence that Iraq has decided to acquire nuclear explosives."[11] Ronald Reagan, interested in protecting his broader interests in the Arab Middle East, might well condemn and isolate Israel following an attack.

But Begin remained undeterred and his committee secretly devised their strategy. Operation Opera called for two squadrons of Israeli fighters that would take off from the Etzion base in the Sinai Peninsula (which had not yet been returned to Egypt) and fly across Jordanian and Saudi Arabian airspace on their way to Iraq. The reactor would be bombed prior to its completion specifically to eliminate the risk of nuclear contamination and thus to diminish any justification for a counterattack.

It sounded simple, but Begin and his team knew that the operation was treacherously dangerous. The pilots would be flying more than 1,200 miles across enemy territory, dangerously low and close to the ground to avoid radar. The mission clearly meant risking the pilots' lives; yet failure, as far as Begin was concerned, meant risking the future of the Jewish people. Making reference to the then well-known novel *The Clock Overhead* by the Auschwitz survivor Yechiel De-Nur, who went by the pen name "Ka-Tzetnik" (the name used by Germans to denote "concentration camp prisoner"), Begin said in one meeting, "A giant clock hangs above our head, and it is ticking."[12]

Shimon Peres, head of the political opposition and the primary challenger to Begin in the looming elections, questioned the wisdom of a preemptive strike from the very outset. Begin met with him in December 1980 to inform him that such an operation was being considered, but Peres remained unconvinced of its necessity, and Begin did not share with Peres the details of Operation Opera. Peres apparently found out that the plan was actually scheduled only through Dr. Uzi Even, a member of Israel's Atomic Energy Committee who was invited to several of the secret meetings. After details about the operation were leaked to him, Peres sent a direct letter to the prime minister voicing his vehement objection to the planned operation:

> At the end of December 1980, you [Begin] called me into your office in Jerusalem and told me about a certain extremely serious matter. You did not solicit my response and I myself (despite my instinctive feeling) did not respond under the given circumstances. I feel this morning, however, that it is my supreme civic duty to advise you, after serious consideration, and in weighing the national interest, to desist from this thing. I speak as a man of experience. The deadlines reported by us (and I well understand our people's anxiety) are not realistic. Materials can be changed for other materials. And what is meant to prevent [disaster] can become a catalyst [for disaster]. Israel would then be like a thistle in the desert. I am not alone in saying this, and certainly not at the present time under the given circumstances.[13]

Just as Moshe Dayan had scuttled the deal with Ethiopia's Mengistu by leaking the information about the arms deal, Peres's letter forced Begin to delay the strike. The fact that Peres knew about the attack meant that information had been leaked, and Begin refused to either risk the operation or the lives of the pilots. As he would later explain to Max Fisher, a leading philanthropist and American Jewish communal leader, he was consumed by the risks of failure and, at the same time, the risks of not risking it:

> . . . for months I had sleepless nights. Day after day I asked myself: to do or not to do? What would become of our children if I did nothing? And what would become of our pilots if I did something? I couldn't share my anxiety with anyone. My wife would ask me why I was so disturbed, and I couldn't tell her. Nor could I tell my son, whom I trust implicitly. I had to carry the responsibility and the burden alone.[14]

It was not only Begin who kept silent. Everyone involved—from the inner committee to the Air Force grounds crews—was expected to keep the operation an absolute secret. Yitzhak Shamir's son, Yair, who had been an Air Force pilot and, in 1981, responsible for the IAF's test-flight program, was involved in planning the attack. He recalled years later that his father, who was part of Begin's inner committee, would call him in the period before the attack, asking about refueling, how far planes could fly, and the like. The younger Shamir knew that his father must have been aware that plans for an attack were being formulated. Yitzhak could not inform Yair, however, because he'd been sworn to secrecy; the son, at the same time, could not tell his father that he, too, was working on the very same plans. Father and son kept everything from each other; the blanket of secrecy was impenetrable.[15]

Begin may have had his sleepless nights, but at his core, he had no doubt as to what had to be done. On several occasions he warned Samuel Lewis that "either the U.S. does something to stop this reactor or we shall have to."[16] He did not relish what he suspected might be the world's reaction; but his own life story convinced him that inaction was infinitely more dangerous. "Better condemnation without a reactor than a reactor without condemnation," he said.[17]

On June 7, 1981, the pilots took off from the Sinai Desert and streaked east toward Iraq.

The F-16 pilots selected for the mission were among Israel's best. Months of intensive practice had preceded the attack. Three pilots, including the son of Chief of Staff Eitan, perished during trial runs: two collided in midair, and another died in a training mishap.[18] Led by Ze'ev Raz, the squadron included Amos Yadlin, who retired as a major general and would later become the head of the IDF Military Intelligence Directorate, Amir Nachumi, Yiftach Spector, Relik Shapir, Chagai Katz, Dobbi Yaffe, and Ilan Ramon. Ramon, later Israel's first astronaut (who was aboard the space shuttle *Columbia* mission that disintegrated upon reentry into Earth's atmosphere on February 1, 2003), was not only the youngest of the pilots, but was flying his first mission. Like several of the others, he was the son and grandson of Holocaust survivors; Ze'ev Raz was named after a grandfather who perished, while Aviam Sella, one of the attack's chief planners, was also descended from victims of the Holocaust. Ramon, still unmarried, was assigned to pilot the eighth and final plane, the riskiest position in the squadron, since if he were killed, no woman would be left widowed.[19]

But none of the pilots died. The attack was a glorious moment for Israel's military and it fit Menachem Begin's worldview perfectly. The Jewish people would not survive without military power and a willingness to use it. And though planned in a spirit of self-reliant pragmatism, Begin saw in the success of the operation the hand of God. Speaking to the American Jewish leader Fisher, Begin said that while he was no mystic, he did believe in *Elokei Yisrael*, the God of Israel.

> How else to account for our success in accomplishing the virtually impossible? Every conceivable type of enemy weaponry was arrayed against our pilots when they flew in and out of Baghdad. They had to face anti-aircraft guns, ground-to-air missiles, fighter planes—all there to defend Osirak—yet not one touched us. Only by the grace of God could we have succeeded in that mission.[20]

The rest of the world, however, saw something very different. International reaction was immediate, and unremittingly critical. The French, of course, were incensed, but even in the United States Begin encountered a blanket of criticism. Two days after the strike, *The New York Times* published an editorial lambasting it as "an act of inexcusable and short-sighted aggression."[21] With a hint at Begin's past, the paper declared that the prime minister "embraces the code of his weakest enemies, the code of terror. He justifies aggression by his profound sense of victimhood."[22] Joseph Kraft of the *Los Angeles Times* likened the attacks to Arafat's terrorism, insisting that "Americans need not be afraid to point out that the Palestinian leader, Yasser Arafat, looks no more prone to terrorist tactics than does Menachem Begin."[23]

In response to Operation Opera, a unanimous United Nations Security Council passed Resolution 487, which depicted the attack as a "clear violation of the Charter of the United Nations and the norms of international conduct."[24] The United States supported the resolution, since Saddam was a critical ally against Iran. However, the United States agreed to the resolution only after convincing Iraq to accept a revised version that would not levy international sanctions upon Israel. This was largely due to Reagan's ambivalence about the strike. On the one hand, the operation's use of American-made weaponry for what was perceived as a nondefensive strike obliged the United States to impound four F-16 jets already purchased by Israel. But Reagan, on the other hand, was also sympathetic to Begin's position. In his diary entry on June 9, 1981, Reagan wrote:

> Under the law I have no choice but to ask Congress to investigate and see if there has been a violation of the law regarding use of American-produced planes for offensive purposes. Frankly, if Congress should decide that, I'll grant a Presidential waiver. Iraq is technically still at war with Israel and I believe they were preparing to build an atom bomb.[25]

Years later, when the United States went to war against Iraq during Operation Desert Storm, American officials would essentially recant. In June 1991, Secretary of Defense Dick Cheney presented to David Ivri, who had been commander of the IAF at the time of Operation Opera, a satellite photograph of the Osirak reactor remnants. On it, Cheney wrote:

> For General David Ivri, with thanks and appreciation for the outstanding job he did on the Iraqi Nuclear Program in 1981, which made our job much easier in Desert Storm!
> Dick Cheney, U.S. Sec. Def.[26]

As Begin had foreseen, the attack was assailed inside Israel as well. Shimon Peres, who had delayed the attack in May when he wrote his letter to Begin, now accused Begin of timing the strike in order to affect the results of the upcoming elections, less than a month away. At an Alignment gathering, Peres fumed: "What reason would Begin need to publish that our Air Force blew it [the nuclear reactor] up? Only for elections!"[27]

Begin's blistering response was immediate, derisive, and fueled by rage. Characteristically, he spoke not about Israelis, but about Jews:

> Saddam Hussein, that bloody tyrant who murdered his best friends with his own hands in order to take control of Iraq, prepared for our children the poison of radioactivity that will be released from atom bombs, and he would have dropped them without mercy on Tel Aviv, Petach Tikvah, and on Jerusalem, and on Haifa in order to wipe out the Jewish people in its land.
>
> The Ma'arakh [Alignment] party trumpeted since the beginnings the accusation that we undertook the operation against the nuclear reactor in Iraq because of the elections. Shame on you! You should be embarrassed! How dare you! [My fellow] Jews, you have known me for forty years . . . Would I, for the sake of elections, send young Jewish men toward certain death, or into captivity, which is

worse than death because these barbarians would subject our boys to excruciating torture? Would I send our boys?[28]

Israelis, it would soon be clear, believed Begin.

I t no doubt helped Begin's cause that the peace treaty with Egypt survived the attack on Iraq. No Arab armies responded. If anything, Israel's show of strength probably quelled whatever residual hopes Arab leaders or generals might have had of attacking the Jewish state once again. The reactor was gone, the peace treaty survived, and everyone understood that even Reagan was not as incensed as he had pretended.

Begin was a hero again, and he knew it. As the elections grew closer, he had no compunctions about milking his renewed popularity for everything it was worth. Just days prior to the elections, he addressed a large crowd assembled in Kings of Israel Square (the future site of Yitzhak Rabin's assassination) in Tel Aviv, and rejoiced in language that could have been lifted from one of the biblical books of the prophets:

> The nuclear reactor has been destroyed, it is no more! There will be none in the future! The Children of Israel shall live! And they will build for themselves homes, and the Jewish people will live in the Land of Israel, for generations and generations, and there will be no horror. These were acts of salvation, for the sake of our nation, and most important, for the sake of our children . . .[29]

A new era had dawned, Begin insisted:

> We have changed the methods by which we defend. In the days of the Labor government, there was [a policy of] retaliation. We are not discrediting it. We have changed this method. There will no longer be retaliation. There will be preventative initiative. We are going out to meet them, penetrating their bases, and delivering justice upon them. We will not wait until they come to us.

It was the principle that would be known as the Begin Doctrine, which would endure long after Begin himself had exited the political arena, and which held that Israel would not countenance any of its mortal enemies seeking to develop or acquire a nuclear weapon.[30] The doctrine was reasserted in 2007 when Prime Minister Ehud Olmert destroyed the nuclear reactor that Syria was building near the Euphrates River and was powerfully invoked, and some thirty years after Begin destroyed Osirak, when Benjamin Netanyahu insisted that if the international community did not prevent Mahmoud Ahmadinejad's Iran from going nuclear, Israel would do it alone.

Having staved off what he perceived as the greatest threat to the Jewish people since the Holocaust, Begin won the elections of June 30, 1981. He had won more than a second term, however; he had made it clear once again that though the days of the revolt were long since over, there was no work more sacred, no principle to which he was more deeply committed, than defending the Jewish people and their future.

In August 1981, two months after the attack, former president Richard Nixon met Anwar Sadat in the United States. Nixon was no longer in power, but his proclivity for strongly held opinions was more than intact. Nixon opined to Sadat that Begin had acted irresponsibly and erratically in his destruction of the Iraqi nuclear reactor at Osirak.

But Sadat, it seems, understood Begin and the danger of the Middle East better than Nixon did. "Yes," Sadat responded, "he is crazy. He is also probably crazy like a fox."[31]

15

Nobody's Cowering Jew

Jacob said to Simeon and Levi, "You have brought trouble on me, making me despised among the inhabitants of the land."

— *Genesis 34:30*

The man who had once hidden for four years while being hunted as Britain's "Terrorist No. 1" had, it seemed, redeemed his reputation indelibly. He had made peace with Egypt, had been awarded the Nobel Peace Prize, and, with the stunning destruction of the nuclear reactor at Osirak, had removed the stigma that he could not effectively manage military operations. In the process, he also established a policy of preemption that enshrined what in the Six-Day War had been born of expediency. He had not only managed to battle back from a series of physical ailments, but he had come into his own. A new legacy for Menachem Begin was beginning to take shape.

The threats to Israel's existence, however, had not passed. Begin had lived a life in which one menace had given way to another, and his second term would be no exception. Now, though Iraq had been neutralized, he had to address the Palestinian issue. For Begin, it was one thing to make peace with a country that only six years earlier had tried to destroy the Jewish state; it would be another thing altogether to permit the *creation* of a state that he believed would, by definition, forever seek to destroy Israel.

Palestinian nationalism had been born in revolt against Israel, and the Palestine Liberation Organization in those years had no interest in negotiating with the Jewish state. Its genocidal charter openly called for Israel's destruction; *Mein Kampf* was required reading at Fatah training camps (Fatah was the largest faction of the PLO).[1] For that reason, and because he lived in an era long before the Palestinian cause was universally recognized as it is today, Begin simply refused to engage the question of Palestinian autonomy or statehood.

> I hereby announce, in the name of the government and I hope in that
> of the majority of the members of the Knesset, that we will under
> no circumstances agree to a Palestinian state, we shall not permit
> its establishment. We will carry out our obligations—nothing else.
> I am certain that as those tempered by experience we will know to
> stand up—hopefully united—to pressure in this fateful question,
> and we shall prevail.[2]

Israel had sufficient mortal enemies, he was convinced, among the Arab nation-states that already existed, perhaps with the exception of Egypt. He was not going to allow the emergence of yet another country hell-bent on erasing the Jewish state.

But Yasser Arafat and his PLO were becoming a much more stubborn problem for Israel than Begin might have imagined that they would be. More than a decade earlier, Jordan's Hashemite king Hussein saw the growing PLO presence in his kingdom as a threat to his rule. When the PLO began launching international terror attacks from within Jordan, Hussein took action. In September 1970 (in an operation the PLO dubbed "Black September"), Jordan killed several thousand members of the PLO and then expelled the organization in 1971. Arafat relocated and had begun using Lebanon as his new base of activities against Israel. Lebanon's increasingly bitter civil war between the entrenched Maronite Christians and the country's Muslim populations (Sunni and Shiite, plus some Druze) made Lebanon a perfect launching pad for terrorist activity.

Initially, the Palestinian leadership had opted for high-profile terrorist attacks that would bring the Palestinians to the attention of the international community. The murder of the Israeli athletes at the 1972 Munich Olympic Games and the June 1976 hijacking of Air France Flight 139 (which triggered Israel's "Operation Thunderbolt," the famous raid on Entebbe) were two of the most prominent examples. Then, however, Arafat and the PLO had begun to fire rockets on Israeli towns from their new bases in southern Lebanon. Now the goal was different; Arafat's hope was to bring Israeli daily life to a grinding halt through systematic shelling and cross-border assaults. PLO rocket fire into northern Israel became relentless; for Israel's citizens, bomb shelters were becoming a regular part of life, and a sense of siege took over. And the PLO's presence just across Israel's border continued to grow. By 1982, more than 15,000 Palestinian guerrillas were operating in southern Lebanon, from Beirut down to the area increasingly called "Fatah-land."[3]

Begin's initial response was to send planes over Lebanese airspace to eliminate PLO artillery, but the PLO's resilience made it painfully clear to Israelis—both the leadership and the citizens—how difficult it was even for an Air Force like Israel's to locate and destroy single pieces of artillery.[4] As the Palestinian barrage continued unchecked, Begin understood that he had two choices. He could either launch a military operation designed to push the PLO away from Israel's border, or he could order the construction of large civilian shelters to which Israelis could run whenever the PLO decided to strike.

The man who had spent his youth singing the Betar anthem—with its stress on "dignity" and the notion that every Jew was a prince—and who had been forced underground as the British hunted him, was not about to consign the citizens of his country to a life in bomb shelters. Begin visited the northern city of Kiryat Shmona, was shown the devastation that the rockets were causing, and promised the residents that soon "there will not be a single Katyusha in Kiryat Shmona."[5]

Public pressure on the government to do something had intensified after the Coastal Road massacre on March 11, 1978, when an eleven-man Palestinian terror cell infiltrated Israel from the sea, hijacked a bus en route to Tel Aviv, and, in the course of a brutal firefight with Israeli security forces, killed thirty-eight Israelis and injured seventy-one. *Time* called it "the worst terrorist attack in Israel's history."[6]

The attack and the Jewish vulnerability it highlighted unleashed the old Begin, the man defiantly committed to protecting the lives of Jews and determined to fight back against those who acted on their hatred of the Jewish people. He first approved sending IDF troops into Lebanon with the goal of driving the PLO across the Litani River on March 15, just days after the terrorist attack, some twenty kilometers from the border. "Gone forever," he thundered to the Knesset, "are the days when Jewish blood could be shed with impunity. We shall sever the arm of iniquity!"[7]

"Operation Litani" was successful, forcing a hasty PLO retreat to Beirut. Israeli troops returned home within a week. But Begin understood that the quiet would be short-lived and that a more permanent solution would be required. Indeed, PLO activities resumed shortly after Israeli troops withdrew. As Chaim Herzog (Israel's sixth president) would later say, "War was unavoidable. No sovereign state can live for long with a loaded gun held to its temple."[8]

Thomas Friedman, who was working as the *New York Times* correspondent in Beirut from 1982 to 1984, argues in his book *From Beirut to Jerusalem* that the escalation to war was "only the latest round in Israel's long struggle for survival against its eternal enemy, the Palestinians, as represented by the PLO." But this was too narrow a reading of Begin's worldview. For Begin, the PLO was simply another enemy in his perennial battle against *anti-Semitism*. He made this clear in his interactions with Ronald Reagan, who had earlier had mixed feelings about the raid on Osirak, and who fiercely opposed any military intervention in Lebanon.[9]

Frustrated by the American president's doubts, Begin wrote to him directly: "The purpose of the enemy is to kill—to kill Jews. Is there a nation in the world that would tolerate such a situation?"[10] Even if it caused a rift in U.S.-Israeli relations, Begin argued, he was willing to pay whatever price it took in order to defend the Jewish people in the face of escalating violence and neighboring unrest. He hoped that Reagan would see Israel's predicament through the historical prism though which he,

Begin, saw everything: "My generation, dear Ron, swore on the altar of God that whoever proclaims his intent to destroy the Jewish State or the Jewish People, or both, seals his fate, so that what happened from Berlin . . . will never happen again."[11]

Reagan continued to pressure Begin, but to no avail. Addressing an American audience on NBC TV during an April 1982 visit to the United States, Begin declared:

> If they attack us again, we shall hit them; because we will not allow—in our generation of the Holocaust and redemption—Jewish blood to be shed again, while those responsible for its shedding enjoy impunity and even luxury. It happened in the Holocaust. It will never happen again.[12]

Begin did promise Reagan that if Israel had to invade, it could accomplish its goals within forty kilometers of the border, and would go no farther.

Beyond the American president, however, Begin also had to deal with his new cabinet, many of whose members were resistant to a protracted Israeli operation. The National Religious Party head, Dr. Yosef Burg, was particularly concerned. But Begin was uncowed, even with the formidable Burg. In a meeting with Burg, Begin beseeched him:

> We will be nobody's cowering Jew. We won't wait for the Americans or the United Nations to save us. Those days are over. We have to defend ourselves. Without readiness for self-sacrifice, there will be another Auschwitz. And if we have to pay a price for the sake of our self-defense, then we will have to pay it. Yes, war means bloodshed, bereavement, orphans—and that is a terrible thing to contemplate. But when an imperative arises to protect our people from being bled, as they are being bled now in Galilee, how can any one of us doubt what we have to do?[13]

While some members of his cabinet continued to resist, worried that the operation was unnecessary, Begin received wholehearted support from his defense minister, Ariel Sharon. Sharon had already become a polarizing figure in Israeli politics. In his short time as minister of agriculture, he had authorized the development of sixty-four settlements in the West Bank and Gaza Strip. He had also presided over the completion of fifty-four towns and fifty-six *kibbutzim* and *moshavim* (Jewish communal villages) in the Galilee,[14] some of which were now under PLO fire. For Sharon, the emerging conflict with the PLO was thus both strategic and personal.

Despite their differences, Begin respected Sharon's abilities as a soldier. Begin, in fact, had an abiding awe for Jewish soldiers in general, and he referred to Sharon as "the most fearsome fighting Jew" since the time of Judah Maccabee.[15] If he was "the horseman," Begin also said, Sharon was his "prize stallion" (albeit one with an unbridled, indomitable character).[16]

Just as the Coastal Road attack had unleashed Begin's first foray into Lebanon, an attack by a Palestinian splinter terror group on Ambassador Shlomo Argov in London on June 3, 1982 (almost a year to the date after the Osirak attack), contributed to the second. Though shot in the head, Argov did not die. He remained in a coma for three months; after he regained consciousness, Argov was returned to Israel, where he remained a permanent patient in a rehabilitation hospital, blinded for life. (He died in 2003, at the age of seventy-three, having been hospitalized for twenty-one years.)

Begin had had enough of Jews being attacked, both in Israel and abroad. He called a cabinet meeting, and instructed Sharon and the IDF chief of staff, Rafael Eitan, to present "Operation Peace for Galilee"—a plan drawn up by the IDF that would establish a buffer zone deep enough into southern Lebanon to prevent further shelling and which would punish the PLO. Despite the fact that this plan conformed to the forty-kilometer limit that Begin had promised Israel would abide by, cabinet members were concerned by the operation's length, scale, lack of international support, and public reception. Sharon promised the cabinet, however, that the IDF would not go near Beirut. Fourteen ministers voted in favor of the operation, two abstained, and no one was opposed.

Israel's plan was risky for yet another reason—it depended on the political survival and cooperation of Bashir Gemayel, the head of Lebanon's Christian Phalangist party. Lebanon at the time was mired in a civil war among Maronite Christians, Sunnis, Shiites, and Druze, all vying for power in a rapidly disintegrating country. It was this chaos that Arafat and the PLO had exploited as they turned southern Lebanon into their base of activity and a launching pad for terrorist activity.

Decades earlier, Jabotinsky had remarked that when two ships are sailing in opposite directions, each buffeted by the same storm, which ship would reach its destination was all a matter of the captain's skill. Storms could be destructive, but they could also be opportunities.[7] Like his nemesis, Arafat, Begin saw in the Lebanese civil war a potential opportunity. Along with others in his cabinet, he hoped that in return for supporting the Christian Gemayel and his men in their ongoing conflict with Lebanon's Muslims, Israel might even be rewarded with a peace treaty. If Gemayel could assert his power over Lebanon, Israelis would live quieter lives. But that meant staking the success of Operation Peace for Galilee on one major element—Gemayel's success—over which Israel had virtually no control.

The operation was launched on June 6, 1982, just days after the Argov attack (and almost precisely fifteen years to the date after the start of the Six-Day War), with little fanfare. The expectation was that the operation would take several days, and initially, sophisticated coordination between aerial strikes and ground movements allowed the IDF to achieve its opening goals quickly. But almost as soon as the operation began, Sharon began to tell Begin that more extensive goals for the operation were becoming necessary.

Even since his Etzel days, Begin's style of leadership had been to concern himself with broader strategy, and to leave the detailed planning to others. This had been the case with the King David bombing, the *Altalena*, and Deir Yassin, and it was no less true in Lebanon. If anything, due to his declining physical condition, Begin seemed even less able to master the details of the operation than he had been when he was

Begin carrying a newly written Torah scroll at a ceremony in the West Bank settlement of Kedumim, May 19, 1977 (*Corbis/Bettmann*)

Begin playing chess with Zbigniew Brzezinski at Camp David, September 1978 (*Courtesy Jimmy Carter Library*)

(Left to right) Brzezinski, President Jimmy Carter, and Begin in conversation at Camp David, September 1978 (*Courtesy Jimmy Carter Library*)

Above: Begin and Egyptian president Anwar El-Sadat share a happy moment in Alexandria, Egypt, 1979. (*Moshe Milner/Government Press Office, State of Israel*)

Left: Begin and Sadat in Beersheba, 1979 (*Yaacov Saar/Government Press Office, State of Israel*)

Below: Begin (third from left) and cabinet ministers Yosef Burg (wearing hat), Ariel Sharon, and Yitzchak Shamir walk to Sadat's funeral in Cairo on Shabbat, October 10, 1981. (*Chanania Herman/Government Press Office, State of Israel*)

Begin and Defense Minister Ariel Sharon tour the Beaufort fortress after its capture in the Lebanon War, 1982. (*Jabotinsky Institute Archives/IDF Spokesperson's Unit*)

Protesters outside the prime minister's residence in Jerusalem during the 1983 Lebanon War. The sign to the left of the protesters lists the latest number of soldiers killed during the war. (*Zoom 77*)

Begin helps his beloved Aliza with her shoe, 1978. (Yediot Ahronoth/*David Rubinger*)

Begin in the Knesset, unshaven during the mourning period for Aliza, November 1982 (*Isaac Harari*)

Called as a witness before the Kahan Commission, Begin sits between cabinet secretary Dan Meridor (to his left) and his personal aide Yechiel Kadishai (to his right), November 1982. (*Government Press Office, State of Israel*)

Defense Minister Ariel Sharon looks on as Begin joins the Knesset vote to remove him from office in the aftermath of the Lebanon War, February 1983. (*Agence France-Presse*)

Begin in a wheelchair in the Knesset, after breaking his hip, December 1981 (*Chanania Herman/Government Press Office, State of Israel*)

Begin and Aliza with their children and grandchildren, 1982 (*Yediot Ahronoth/ David Rubinger*)

(Handwritten Hebrew text from Begin's will)

"...בבוא היום, הואל נא לקרוא באוזניהם של יקירי נפשי, ידידים וחברים, את בקשתי זו: אני
מבקש לקבור אותי בהר-הזיתים, ליד מאיר פיישטיין ומשה ברזני...והריני מודה לך, ולכל מי
שיעשה לקיום הבקשה..."
קטע מצוואתו של מנחם בגין שנתנה למזכירו הנאמן יחיאל קדישאי

The paragraph in Begin's will, addressed to Yechiel Kadishai, indicating where he wished to be buried (*Menachem Begin Heritage Center*)

(Far right and far left) Menachem and Aliza Begin's graves, just behind the graves of Begin's Irgun comrades Meir Feinstein (near right) and Moshe Barazani (near left) on the Mount of Olives, Jerusalem (*Eli Spector*) younger. Indeed, according to one source, when Sharon began to press for a wider assault deeper into Lebanon, Begin "limited his operational involvement to pressing the defense minister to avoid casualties."[18]

For all intents and purposes, Begin's long-standing hands-off approach granted Sharon, who the cabinet believed would be tethered to a short leash, almost complete control over the operation. And Sharon wasted no time in beginning to suggest that the operation's initial parameters were simply insufficient. "As long as the terrorist command centers are in Beirut," he explained through the IDF Spokesperson's Unit, "it will be difficult to believe that the IDF's goals have been executed to their fullest."[19] Within the first few days, Syrian forces were beginning to engage Israeli troops, and the conflict was widening. Israeli forces crossed the forty-kilometer line and pushed hard toward Beirut.

Yehiel Kadishai, ever loyal to Begin's memory and legacy, explains matters differently. He has insisted that Sharon, too, was originally committed to the forty-kilometer limit, but that once Israeli troops entered Lebanon, he quickly realized that Arafat had much more than clusters of terrorists at his disposal. While Arafat lacked heavy military equipment, he had well-trained and organized soldiers; the PLO, in essence, had an army. The threat was greater than either Begin or Sharon had assumed prior to the invasion, Kadishai asserted.[20] Both Begin and Sharon began to worry that Arafat's armed troops might cross the border and seize the several-kilometer-long area between Lebanon and the Israeli town of Nahariyah, declaring a Palestinian state on the small parcel of land. That area was outside the borders given to Israel in the November 1947 United Nations General Assembly vote, Kadishai pointed out, so that if Arafat took it he could have said that he was merely taking back what Israel had grabbed in the War of Independence.

How likely is it that Israeli intelligence did not know of these armed units? How plausible is it that Arafat could have crossed the border without being repelled by Israel's massive military superiority? Kadishai's loyalty to Begin is legendary; to what extent that colors his recollection and shapes his narrative is difficult to know. But Kadishai insists that

Begin knew precisely what Sharon was doing. Indeed, when Kadishai told Begin that there were those who believed that Sharon was manipulating the prime minister, Begin turned to him and said, staccato-like, "Yechiel, *Mit-kad-mim*—We're pushing forward."

But most observers, including Aryeh Naor, believe that Sharon simply manipulated and outfoxed Begin.[21] Begin and Sharon were in very different phases of their careers. Begin had never been particularly robust, and had long had a series of ailments. Already in 1969, at the age of fifty-six, he had been diagnosed with diabetes; subsequently, he would be rushed to the hospital on numerous occasions. In the spring of 1977, he suffered first a severe case of food poisoning, then a heart attack from which he recuperated for two weeks in the intensive care unit of Ichilov Hospital in Tel Aviv. He was so weak afterward that he could barely hold a pen. In October 1977, Begin was again in the hospital for an inflammation of the heart membrane, a condition that caused him to be reliant on an array of medications for the rest of his life. Even then, he was keenly aware of his decline; during peace negotiations with Egypt, as the idea of West Bank sovereignty after a five-year period was raised, Begin had remarked to Cyrus Vance that "by that time, I may not be around."[22] Now, during the war, the physical decline continued and Begin was increasingly frail.

Ariel Sharon, on the other hand, was fifteen years Begin's junior, and his political career was just getting under way. Always healthy, even robust, he was the picture of health. Even in a much-reproduced photograph of him during the Yom Kippur War, with his head bandaged from a wound, he appeared vigorous and a commanding presence.

Sharon thus had both a clearer personal agenda for the war and greater capacity to carry it out. At this stage, at least, he was by far the wilier of the two. Ambassador Samuel Lewis would later assert that Sharon put an end to the intelligence division's reporting to the prime minister on a daily basis, which left Begin "intellectually dependent on Sharon, alone, for military information and advice."[23]

But this period of Begin's premiership is still fiercely contended, and not everyone agrees. Alexander Haig, Reagan's secretary of state from

1981 to 1982, said that he "didn't find any evident tension [between Begin and Sharon] . . . I know some people say Sharon didn't tell Begin what was going on in Lebanon. I have a hard time buying that."²⁴ Ned Temko, however, one of Begin's earlier biographers, believes that Sharon told Begin what he wanted the prime minister to know, and withheld the information he did not wish Begin to have. Naor shared that assessment, and asserts that were Begin not committed to the forty-kilometer line, he would never have promised Reagan that Israel would stop there; Sharon, however—Naor believes—intended, from the very outset, a much deeper invasion.

When Israeli tanks approached the outskirts of East Beirut on June 13, Begin initially denied U.S. Special Envoy Philip Habib's accusations that the tanks were there. Habib must have assumed that Begin was lying, and yelled at him: "Your tanks are already in Baabda! Our ambassador in Beirut has already reported the presence of Israeli tanks next to the presidential palace!"

At that moment, Sharon called. Begin related Habib's accusations, and Sharon replied matter-of-factly, "So we'll move the tanks."²⁵

Begin should have sensed that Sharon was toying with him, but apparently didn't. And as Begin was being outmaneuvered by Sharon, the soldiers in the field were being drawn into a battle infinitely more complex than that which had been designed up front. The casualty count began to rise and the Israeli public began to wonder whether the entire operation had gone wrong. Large protests were held right outside Begin's window.

Begin, though, continued to defend the operation and the casualties that were being inflicted on the civilian Arab population, invoking repeatedly the images and memories of World War II and the Holocaust, equating the PLO with the Nazis. (He said nothing about the danger of a PLO incursion into Israel.) But the analogies had worn thin. The once-powerful and convincing Begin Jewish history–Holocaust lexicon was no longer convincing a people who had tired of war and saw no need for this one. One much-discussed letter, written to Begin by a bereaved father and then publicized across the country, gave powerful expression not only to the war's cost, but to the deepening divide between Begin and the Israeli public, which had not long before ushered him into a second term. It could have been lost on very few that it was now Begin's accusers who invoked the Jewish tradition and the unbroken chain of Jewish history:

> I, remnant of a rabbinical family, only son of my father, a Zionist and Socialist who died a hero's death in the Warsaw ghetto, survived the Holocaust and settled in our country and served in the army and married and had a son. Now my beloved son is dead because of your war.
>
> Thus you have discontinued a Jewish chain of age-old suffering generations which no persecutor had succeeded in severing. The history of our ancient, wise and racked people will judge you . . . Let my sorrow haunt you when you sleep and when you awaken, and let my grief be the Mark of Cain upon your forehead forever![26]

As the historian Howard Sachar put it, "Never before had a war been debated in purely Jewish—in contrast to Israeli—terms."[27]

Casualties continued to mount. Yehuda Avner, Begin's close friend, advisor, and English speechwriter, wrote in his memoirs that "whenever the newest casualty figures were brought to Begin's attention . . . his heart broke silently and a dull throb of grief possessed his spirit."[28] By the time Begin went to visit Reagan in late June, Beirut was under siege, and 216 Israeli soldiers had been killed. A thousand more had been wounded.

Reagan was worried, and began to distance himself from Begin. Speaking at a joint news conference with the American president on June 21, 1982, Begin sought to convince the American public directly:

> We don't covet even one inch of Lebanese territory, and shall willingly withdraw our troops and bring them back home as soon as possible—as soon as arrangements are made that never again will our citizens—men, women, and children—be attacked, maimed, and killed by the Soviet Union and its satellites.[29]

Whatever impact Begin's protestations may or may not have had on the American public, they were utterly lost on the president. Reagan was entirely unmoved by Begin's frequent reminders that the PLO was being armed with Soviet weapons or his claim that Israel's fight against Arafat was a critical link in the Cold War. Begin had assumed that their mutual disdain for the Soviets would convince Reagan to support Israel, but was met with only "an unfathomable remoteness" from the American president.[30] Under relentless pressure, Begin departed Washington with the Americans expecting that all foreign forces—most notably, Israel's—would soon withdraw from Lebanon.

But Arafat refused to leave Beirut, and with each passing day became more adept at using the Western media for his purposes. He appeared on television regularly, showing pictures of maimed Palestinian children and still-smoldering Palestinian homes. "The siege of Beirut transformed him, in the eyes of millions of viewers worldwide, into the heroic leader of the Palestinian people."[31] As Israel's siege of Beirut dragged into August, the Jewish state's image—as well as that of its prime minister—suffered. Begin had invaded Lebanon to rid Israel's north of the Palestinian threat. What was happening, however, was that for the first time the world was taking seriously the plight of the Palestinians. It was a shift in public opinion that Israel would never succeed in reversing.

Nonetheless, whatever media gains they may have scored, Arafat and the PLO were no match for Israel's massive firepower. Israel's Air Force began relentless bombing of Palestinian refugee camps in southwest Beirut, since they were home to significant PLO positions. International condemnation was both immediate and scathing, but the military tactic worked. By August 12, Arafat had agreed to leave Lebanon.

Arafat had been forced out of Jordan in 1971, and now, as a result of Begin's operation, was being evicted from Lebanon. Between August 21 and 30, some 9,000 PLO fighters (and another 6,000 Syrian troops) were escorted out of the city. Arafat, in the company of some of his fighters, set sail for Tunisia.[32] Out of the jaws of impending disaster, it seemed, Sharon (and perhaps Begin) had snatched a victory. With Arafat gone, the citizens of Israel's north had reasonable hopes of some quiet. Begin had long called the war a *milchemet haztalah*, a war of self-preservation, and never veered from that claim.[33] In August 1982, at least, there was reason to believe the war had accomplished his objective; he was even optimistic that Bashir Gemayel, president-elect of the Lebanese parliament, would sign a historic peace treaty with Israel.

From its outset, though, nothing about the Lebanese operation had gone as expected, and its end was no exception. On September 14, 1982, less than a month after Arafat's departure from Beirut, a Syrian operative bombed the Phalangist headquarters in Beirut. Twenty-seven people were killed, among them Bashir Gemayel. Israel had lost its "Great Lebanese Hope" for peace, and its only ally in the war-torn country.

Suddenly, Begin's entire strategy was crumbling.

Fearful that the Christians would exact revenge in the name of their fallen leader, Begin instructed Sharon to take up strategic positions in West Beirut itself. But Sharon and Chief of Staff Eitan went even further. Sharon saw an opportunity to capture the overcrowded Palestinian refugee camps on the southwest edge of the city, which were home to PLO fighters who had not departed Lebanon, before international forces arrived. This would be his opportunity to wipe out the terrorist threat, once and for all.

At a cabinet meeting the following day, Sharon disclosed his plan to secure Sabra (he did not mention a second camp, Shatila), emphasizing that the Phalangists—who were seeking revenge for Gemayel's death— "would be left to operate 'with their own methods,' and that the Israelis would do no fighting in Beirut."[34] On the evening of September 16, IDF divisions secured the perimeters of both Sabra and Shatila. Under Israeli watch, Phalangist forces entered the camps.

Two nights later, on the second evening of Rosh Hashanah, the Jewish New Year, Menachem Begin turned on the radio to listen to the BBC. Just as had been the case when he listened to the BBC in the aftermath of the King David bombing and when the *Altalena* had been approaching Israel's shores, he learned from the British broadcasters, and not from his own men, how terribly awry his plans had gone.

Unbeknownst to Begin, the previous days had been days of vicious fighting. When the Christian Phalangists had first entered the camps on

September 16, they were initially met with fierce resistance from PLO fighters. But the Christians quickly overwhelmed them, and then began to open fire on civilians. For three days, the Phalangists indiscriminately massacred Palestinians, along with many Lebanese Shiites. When the killing was over, there were "groups of young men in their twenties and thirties who had been lined up against walls, tied by their hands and feet, and then mowed down gangland-style with fusillades of machine-gun fire."[35] At least eight hundred civilians were killed.[36]

The following evening, which was the first night of Rosh Hashanah, Sharon received calls from Chief of Staff Eitan, the situation officer at the defense ministry, and an Israeli television journalist, all of whom reported that the Phalangists had attacked civilians but had since been ordered to leave the camps. "They went too far," Eitan remarked.[37] Sharon said nothing to the prime minister.

It was only the next evening, when listening to the BBC, that Begin learned what had happened. The following morning, on his way to High Holiday prayer services, Begin processed the event with Yehuda Avner. He clearly had no sense of the gravity of what had happened, not only in human terms, but to Israel's reputation, and his. Speaking Yiddish, his deep-seated Polish Jewish roots still defining him, he asked Avner:

> *Host du gehert aza meisa?* [Have you heard of such a thing?] Christians massacre Muslims and the goyim blame the Jews . . . predictably, the foreign media are blaming us . . . This is why we have to stand up to these people and never be apologetic. We have to constantly remind them how their papers didn't say a single word while six million of our brethren were being slaughtered. Never once did they make an effort to pressure their governments to come to the rescue of even a single Jewish child. So I'm not at all surprised at this innate bias . . . goyim kill goyim and they hang the Jews.[38]

But many Israelis were not buying the "goyim kill goyim and they hang the Jews" line. A horrific massacre had taken place at Sabra and Shatila, and given the IDF's role, Israel could not shirk all responsibility.

As the prime minister worshipped inside Jerusalem's Great Synagogue, a crowd gathered to demonstrate against him as he exited. Though fore-warned by his concerned security detail, Begin refused to avoid his crit-ics. "I will not slink out of the synagogue. I will leave the way I came, through the front door, demonstration or no demonstration." Yehuda Avner recounted those fateful hours:

> As the prime minister emerged into the synagogue's forecourt, a horde of demonstrators tried to crush in upon him. Spittle, clenched fists, and cries of "Murderer!" assaulted the sanctity of the day as anxious policemen and guards pushed, kicked, and elbowed the bay-ing crowd, cutting a channel through the crush to form a close cordon around us, while swarms of reporters recorded the pandemonium.[39]

Some of those in the crowd were holding signs that read BEIRUT—DEIR YASSIN and BEGIN—CHILD KILLER.[40]

It had been a disastrous few days. Hundreds of men, women, and chil-dren had been killed under Israel's neglectful watch. Begin had lost his Lebanese partner for peace, the Nobel Peace Prize winner had lost the moral high ground and was being accused of genocide, and public opin-ion, both domestic and global, was eroding everywhere. It would have been astounding if Begin—who had once been called the "Butcher of Deir Yassin"—did not relive some of the memories of having been so loathed forty years earlier.

Many leaders in Begin's position would have decided that it was time to throw Ariel Sharon under the bus. After all, it was Sharon who permit-ted the Phalangist troops to enter Sabra and Shatila. It was Sharon who failed to notify him after the first reports of the slaughter had reached his ears, keeping him in the dark. But Begin had always been cut from a dif-ferent cloth when it came to taking personal responsibility, and even now, late in his career and beset from every direction, he remained steadfast. Sitting with an old Etzel comrade, Yehuda Lapidot, the same day that he faced the mob outside the Great Synagogue, Begin made clear that the responsibility was his, and he would do nothing to shirk it. "As a member of a government one must take responsibility, whether one knows about it or not. They [my peers in the government] must act as I did, with Deir Yassin."[41]

But this was not a crisis that could be "managed." Egypt, with whom Begin had signed a peace treaty not long before, recalled its ambassador. On September 26, hundreds of thousands protested in Tel Aviv against the government, demanding a judicial inquiry into the massacre, calling for the resignations of both "Sharon the Murderer" and "Begin the Murderer."[42] Resistant at first, Begin quickly realized that this was no tempest in a teapot; he was embroiled in a deep national crisis. He acquiesced two days later and established the Kahan Commission to determine whether Israel was responsible for the massacre.

Once defiant, the premier now appeared resigned to his fate. U.S. Ambassador Sam Lewis later recalled: "You could see he found no pleasure of any sort in the job. Everything seemed to come apart."[43]

As the Lebanon imbroglio deepened, Begin's long-failing health deteriorated even further. Years earlier, in July 1979, he had suffered a stroke and was hospitalized again in November 1981 after a fall in the bathtub in which he broke his pelvis. He was confined to a wheelchair for weeks, even when he had to address the Knesset, and throughout the war walked slowly and hesitantly with a cane.

But the greatest blow was yet to come.

Aliza, too, had long been ill. She had had asthma ever since he'd known her; indeed, while Begin was in the Soviet prison and wondering if Aliza had also been jailed, he asked himself, "How would she, ill as she was, fare here in jail, without her medicines?"[44]

By the summer of 1982, Aliza was occasionally reliant on a respirator and a wheelchair. On October 4, she was hospitalized at Hadassah Hospital with severe pneumonia, intubated and unable to speak. She wrote notes in order to communicate. Begin understood that she was failing, and weighed submitting his resignation. He wrote to Sam Lewis, "I must devote myself to *her*, in whatever time she has left."[45]

Begin was scheduled to go to the United States for fund-raising events and a meeting with Reagan; he seriously considered canceling in order to stay at Aliza's hospital bedside. But she insisted that he go: "Don't worry; everything will be fine; you have to go."[46]

On November 13, a Shabbat, Begin was in Los Angeles for the General Assembly of the Council of Jewish Federations. Benny, who was in Israel, called Kadishai in Los Angeles to inform him that Aliza had died—at that point, it was early in the morning in Israel on November 14.[47] Begin was too frail to be told without his cardiologist (with whom he traveled) in attendance, but the doctor had gone to synagogue. It was several hours before he returned, was apprised of what was happened, and, together with Kadishai, made his way to Begin's hotel room.[48]

Begin burst into tears. *Lama azavti otah? Lama azavti otah?* "Why did I leave her? Why did I leave her?" he wailed.[49] He flew home that same day, spending the entire flight in the bedroom on the plane,[50] speaking to no one, occasionally puncturing the silence with mournful moans.[51]

The next day, on the long-hallowed Mount of Olives of which the prophets had spoken, overlooking both the Old City of Jerusalem and the New, Menachem buried Aliza.

He had lost his parents, his brother, his comrades. Throughout it all, the one constant presence—in Poland, Russia, Palestine, and then Israel—had been Aliza. Their lives together had been a great and resilient love story, and now it was over. The woman he had thanked on the night of his election for following him into the wilderness had now left him in the wilderness, and he was utterly alone.

The Kahan Commission, chaired by the Supreme Court president, Yitzhak Kahan, who was joined by the Supreme Court justice Aharon Barak and Major-General Yona Efrat, began its work. Begin was called to testify. Frail, hunched over, but still defiant, he sat before the panel and was asked his name. *Menachem ben Ze'ev Dov ve-Chasia Begin*, he replied, "Menachem, the son of Ze'ev Dov and Chasia Begin." It was the traditional Jewish way of giving one's name: to the end, Begin wanted the world to know that was what he was. He was a Jew.

Begin, loyal to the end, tried to give Sharon cover without lying. When the commission asked him whether Sharon had erred in not keeping him fully apprised of what was happening in the field, a frail and defiant Begin simply answered, "No."[52]

After four months of deliberations, the commission announced its findings. It determined that while no Israelis were directly responsible for the massacre at Sabra and Shatila, Ariel Sharon, above all others, bore "personal responsibility" for the affair:

> It is impossible to justify the Defense Minister's disregard of the danger of a massacre . . . His involvement in the war was deep, and the connection with the Phalangists was under his constant care. If in fact the Defense Minister, when he decided that the Phalangists would enter the camps without the IDF's taking part in the operation, did not think that the decision could bring about the very disaster that in fact occurred, the only possible explanation for this is that he disregarded any apprehensions about what was to be expected.[53]

The commission stated, "If necessary, that the Prime Minister consider whether he should exercise his authority under Section 21(A)(a) of the Basic Law: The Government, according to which 'the Prime Minister may, after informing the Cabinet of his intention to do so, remove the minister from office.' "[54]

As for Begin's role in the affair, the commission's language almost seemed to suggest that the job was now too much for the prime minister. "We find no reason to exempt the Prime Minister from responsibility for having not evinced . . . any interest in the Phalangists' actions in the camps . . . The Prime Minister's lack of involvement in the entire matter casts on him a certain degree of responsibility."[55]

The protests in front of Begin's home, which had begun in the first weeks of the war, swelled. One antiwar group kept a sign outside the prime minister's residence with the number of soldiers who had been killed in the war. Begin refused to even consider shutting the protests down. "It is their democratic right," he said, still the man who had railed against Ben-Gurion's treatment of Robert Soblen.[56]

The Israeli political right had long felt that Begin had betrayed them by returning the Sinai. Now the left assailed him. Peace Now, which had been established a few years earlier to support relinquishing the Sinai to Egypt, held frequent marches and rallies protesting the war. Counter-demonstrations quickly emerged. As the cabinet convened on February 8, 1983, to discuss the findings of the Kahan Commission, Israel's leadership found itself surrounded by the public battle on the street, much as the Knesset had when it convened to discuss German reparations.

As the cabinet was meeting, a mentally ill man named Yona Avrushmi threw a grenade into the crowd of Peace Now demonstrators outside, killing thirty-three-year-old Emil Grunzweig, an employee of the Van Leer Foundation in Jerusalem. Yosef Burg, who was participating in the cabinet meeting, did not know then that his son, Avrum, had also been injured. Begin was beside himself: "God forbid we should go the way of heinous violence. God forbid."[57] He had prevented civil war twice in his lifetime; now, it seemed, matters everywhere were spinning out of control.

Despite his desire to be loyal to Sharon, Begin never doubted that the cabinet had to accept the findings of the Kahan Commission. Indeed, if he had seemed indecisive during much of the war, the aging man's moral compass was plainly visible once again; if he had been too silent as Sharon had manipulated him, now he led, and he did so with clarity. "We can only accept the recommendations," he insisted. "That's the rule. We accepted the recommendations when we appointed the commission. Those are the rules. To the best of my understanding, there is no other way."[58] The cabinet voted in favor of accepting the Kahan Commission's recommendations, 16–1.

Embittered, Sharon agreed to step down as defense minister, but remained in the government as a minister without a portfolio.

Begin's respect for the rule of law had left him no choice but to accept the Kahan Commission's conclusion, but he remained, in his now very quiet way, unrepentant. In a letter to Senator Alan Cranston, Begin argued:

The whole campaign of blaming Israel for the massacre, of placing moral responsibility on Israel, seems to me, an old man who has seen so much in his lifetime, to be almost unbelievable, fantastic, and utterly despicable . . . The first horrific truth is that Arabs murdered Arabs. The second truth is that Israeli soldiers stopped the carnage. And the third truth is that if the current libelous campaign against Israel should go on without a reaction of outrage by decent men—yes, outrage—then within a matter of weeks or months everyone everywhere will have gotten the impression that it was an Israeli military unit which perpetrated the horrible killings.[59]

Several motions of no-confidence followed in the Knesset, but Begin easily defeated them all. Though he could not stem the tide of increasing criticism, he tried, continuing his tradition of relying on the Book of Books and his belief that, in the end, Jews needed to be able to rely on one another in a world that would forever be hostile to them:

I will repeat myself again: It never occurred to us, not for a second, neither to those who knew nor to those who did not know about the decision to allow the Phalangists into the camps, that such a horror would occur in the camps in Beirut. And so yes, we can say that "our hands have not spilt this blood"[60] and there is no need to vilify the Jewish people . . . and there is no need to give the gentiles an opening through which to slander us [Cf. Ez. 16:63 and 29:21].[61]

But most people understood that matters were far more complicated. As Aryeh Naor put it, the Phalangists were told to go into the camp, to arrest terrorists, and to use force if anyone resisted. But, as Naor (whose dislike for Sharon is well-known) mused, "Have you ever heard of an Arab army fighting that way? When did they not kill everyone they could?" It was inevitable, Naor still believes, that there would be a bloodbath.[62]

Did Begin blame Sharon for what had happened? Did he believe that he was responsible for allowing the war to spin out of control? Did he ever assemble, even for himself, a unified, coherent explanation of what had transpired? We cannot be certain. He left no personal account like *White Nights* or *The Revolt* about this period of his life. All we know is that it was more than he could bear.

The erupting Israeli fury did not subside. Begin had once brought peace with Egypt, without a bullet being fired. Then he had attacked Osirak, and every pilot had returned home safely. But the war in Lebanon had taken 657 Israeli lives, just short of the number killed in the Six-Day War. Hundreds of civilians had been massacred under Israel's watch. And Israel's reputation in the international world had been terribly damaged.

The Lebanon War was the first war that Israelis had fought that they were not entirely certain was necessary. Israelis had long suffered mightily at the hands of their enemies, but they had been buoyed by the belief that their military ventures had been forced on them, that they had not taken unnecessary risks with their sons' lives, and then when they had fought, they had done so honorably. All those assumptions now cracked, and a period of grave self-doubt, from which Israel has never fully recovered, was unleashed.

Menachem Begin never wavered in his belief that the Lebanon War was a war of self-preservation. More prophetic than practical, never the calculating risk manager that Peres always was, he operated on instinct, and on the belief that his most central obligation was the protection of the Jewish people. And even with all that went wrong, he may well have been right. Without question, the dangers of allowing Arafat and the PLO to root themselves in southern Lebanon, and of abandoning northern Israel to the ongoing dread of Palestinian attacks, could have changed the dynamic of life in the Galilee and of Israeli self-perception altogether. Having moved from fighting standing armies to fighting terrorists, no matter how potent their firepower, Israel was the first country to confront the murkiness that now has the entire Western world in its grip.

It would be decades, however, before the Western world would confront head-on the strategic, tactical, and moral conundrums that invariably come with fighting terrorists. At that time, Israelis simply felt alone, confused, and even betrayed. It was an era of shattered assumptions about security, about trust in the government not to treat the lives of Israeli young men cheaply, and about Israel's very morality.

Most Israelis had no alternative but to soldier on. Soldiering on, however, was simply more than Menachem Begin could manage.

16

I Cannot Go On

And Moses spoke these things to all Israel. He said to them: . . . "I am no longer able to lead you."   —*Deuteronomy 31:1–2*[1]

With Aliza gone, Begin was alone. Then in February came the Kahan Commission's report. When he read the report, he said to Yechiel Kadishai, simply: "I should resign."

Shortly after the report was issued, Sharon told Begin that when Sharon had been preparing to join the Haganah, his father had said to him, "Never, ever turn a Jew in." Sharon had never violated his father's command, he said, "Yet you turned me in." Begin was shaken; years later, Sharon—fully aware that he had been a key factor in Begin's political demise—wrote with no regret that he believed that his comment had been too painful for the prime minister to bear.[2]

Begin's physical condition worsened. His sight was impaired from a stroke that he had suffered earlier that year, he had lost weight, and his medication left him disoriented.[3] He came to the Knesset less often. Nahum Barnea, one of Israel's most widely read columnists, wrote that Begin was a "disconnected zombie." Batya Eldad, a friend of Aliza's, told Benny's wife that Begin looked to her like someone who simply wanted to die.[4]

Begin's daughter, Leah, a socially timid woman, had never married (a subject that had caused Aliza much distress), and she moved into the Balfour Street home with her father. Daily, the two of them watched movies together; Leah selected the titles, without her father ever objecting to any of her choices.

He rarely gave public appearances or granted interviews. In May 1983, he postponed a meeting with Ronald Reagan, and by June he still was not up for the president's visit. He told Kadishai that there was no way he could meet Reagan: "Look at my collar," he said, "I can fit two fingers between my throat and my collar. Can I go to Reagan in my condition?" He called the president directly to tell him that the reason for the cancellation was strictly personal.[5]

By the summer, Begin was avoiding cabinet meetings and was so weak that he could barely take off his own shoes. When he celebrated his seventieth birthday on August 19, 1983, Kadishai remembered that Begin had said to him on several occasions that he planned to retire at age seventy.[6] Kadishai expected him to resign then, but Begin apparently wanted no festivities surrounding his resignation. The birthday celebrations meant that he would have to wait.

On August 27, though, German flags were flown at the prime minister's office building; Helmut Kohl, the new German chancellor, was visiting. For Begin, whose parents and brother had been killed by the Germans, and who had railed against German reparations because he believed that the Germans should forever bear their guilt, the fluttering of German flags in the Jewish capital was simply too much for a man whose reservoirs of strength were depleted. As prime minister, he would have to shake Kohl's hand. The next day, on August 28, as Kadishai arrived at Begin's office, Begin said to him, "It's good you came. I want to let you know that today I'm announcing that I'm resigning my position."[7] Kadishai had wanted him to stay on, but he both understood and had intuited that the decision was coming; there was nothing for him to say.

At the cabinet meeting, Begin explained that his reasons were "personal." "I can no longer fulfill this role," he said. The ministers, who did not have Kadishai's intuitive understanding of Begin, were—despite his obvious decline—still stunned. The notion that Menachem Begin would give up the fight seemed utterly inconceivable. They begged him to reconsider. "The people love you," one said.[8]

Begin's response was simple: *ani lo yachol yoter*, he said. "I cannot go on."[9] It was eerily reminiscent of Ze'ev Jabotinsky's final words before his death in 1940: "I am so tired."

Begin did not deliver his resignation notice to President Chaim Herzog as protocol called for. He had a rash on his face and did not want to leave the house in that condition. It was the first time a resigning prime minister sent a messenger to deliver his resignation letter to the president.[10] Dan Meridor, a Likud MK, a Begin protégé, and future minister of justice, minister of finance, and deputy prime minister, delivered it for him.

The next day was Erev Yom Kippur, the beginning of the holiest day of the year. Begin had observed Yom Kippur even in Soviet prison, but that night, he did not attend synagogue.[11]

Yitzhak Shamir replaced Begin as interim prime minister. During the days of the British Mandate, Shamir had been at the helm of the Lechi, the most militant of the three Jewish organizations operating in Palestine. Begin received numerous phone calls requesting that he give his public blessing to Shamir. "I'm not a king, and I have no heirs," he insisted. Pressed, he repeated what he'd said earlier, "I cannot go on."[12]

Shamir himself had begged Begin not to resign. "We followed you through fire and water; revoke your decision," Shamir urged. To that plea, too, Begin replied, "I cannot go on."[13]

On the first anniversary of Aliza's death, in November 1983, Begin, still suffering from his rash, chose not to join the rest of his family when they visited her grave on the Mount of Olives. In December, he and Leah moved out of the prime minister's residence and into an apartment on Shlomo Tzemach Street, a quiet side street near Mount Herzl overlooking the Jerusalem Forest.[14]

He refused almost all who asked to come and see him. His circle of visitors was limited to family, Kadishai, and Dan Meridor, who came on Friday afternoons for coffee. Kadishai visited every day, bringing him mail and the day's papers.

After undergoing successful prostate surgery at the end of 1984, Begin began attending physiotherapy sessions and put on some weight. For a while, he expanded his social circle and began hosting several couples on Saturday evenings. Harry Hurwitz, a close friend who also wrote a biography of Begin, and Hart Hasten, an American Jewish philanthropist and longtime friend who had been with him in Los Angeles when Aliza had died, and their wives were among those periodically included. These weekly get-togethers assiduously avoided discussion of current events.

The reasons for Begin's retreat into solitude have never been adequately explained. Those who were close to him tend to honor him by still refusing to speculate, at least aloud. Perhaps the wounds of what he had weathered and the betrayals he had had to endure were still too raw for him to venture, even in speech, back into the world of politics, and seclusion was the only way to avoid it.[15] Kadishai has suggested that Begin recalled that Ben-Gurion had been called out of retirement and back to the premiership, and that Begin wished to avoid that.[16] Anita Shapira, one of Israel's most respected historians, has written that retreating into silence was part of the core ethic of early Israeli society. Though she does not mention Begin in her excursus on silence, her insights might apply to him no less than to others. There was, she insists,

> an ethos of self-restraint, of biting one's lip, and stubborn adherence to the national purpose . . . The ethos of biting one's lip and restraining oneself in expressions of mourning shaped the behavioral culture of two generations, the generation of the Founding Fathers and the generation that fought in 1948. This was a decision of the Jews of the Land of Israel against the demonstration of emotions and in favor of internalizing them.[17]

Had Begin also internalized this ethic after half a century in Israel? Whatever the reason, he refused to emerge.

From 1984 onward, Begin attended every annual memorial ceremony for Aliza—but he left the house only for those ceremonies on the Mount of Olives and for hospital visits.[18] The press began to refer to him as "the prisoner of Zemach Street"; an article in *The Washington Post* reported that at a ten-year anniversary marking Sadat's visit to Israel, Begin was not present, and that Israelis tended to refer to both him and Sadat in the past tense.[19] Thomas Friedman, who consistently criticized, even condemned, Begin's role in the Lebanon War, saw his exile as a self-imposed sentence: "For all intents and purposes Menachem Begin seemed to have tried himself, found himself guilty, and locked himself in jail."[20] But Friedman, so relentlessly critical of Begin, seems not to have considered the simple possibility that now it was Begin, not Ben-Gurion, who was the Old Man, and he just couldn't go on.

Begin did make one unexpected public statement. In March 1982, he had appointed the Bechor Commission to investigate the murder of Haim Arlosoroff fifty years earlier. In June 1985, the commission released its report, exonerating the three Revisionists (including Begin's childhood friend Avraham Stavsky, who had perished aboard the *Altalena*) accused of the murder. "At least their families can now read that they were completely innocent. Justice has been done and this is a good day for Israel," said Begin.[21] He still believed in exacting history, and was still committed to truth as a fundamental value. As the sun was setting on his own life, he'd attended to Stavsky's reputation.

Israel, in the meantime, was going through turbulent times. The IDF was still mired in Lebanon, and whatever tenuous cease-fire had prevailed there was by now dissolved; the stock market tumbled. Some observers went so far as to say that Begin was a captain who had once again abandoned the ship.[22]

His days were spent in pajamas and a robe, reading every major Israeli newspaper, as well as *The Times* of London, *Le Monde*, *Time*, and *Newsweek*.[23] He read Jehan Sadat's autobiography and books by Bob Woodward and William Safire.[24]

Before his resignation, Begin had announced his desire to write an autobiography upon retirement, entitled *From Holocaust to Rebirth*, which would cover his life and the history of Israel. Some, including Begin himself, thought that his seclusion would allow him time to write the memoir.[25] Charles Hill, a senior Foreign Service advisor during the Lebanon

War who had extensive contact with Begin, heard him reflect on the book, and recalls that it was to have a much larger scope. It was to be, Hill recalled, "a vast work, a multivolume work on Jewishness, statehood, and the human condition in world affairs," on the scale of Gibbon's work on the decline and fall of the Roman Empire.[26] Begin never undertook the project, but he had lived what he could not write. His life, which began between the armies of the Czar and the Kaiser, was coming to its close with the Jewish people reborn, a Jewish state renewed, and a new Jewish sense of self in the world—he had been responsible for those changes no less than anyone, anywhere.

By the late 1980s, Begin was allowing certain diplomats to meet with him at home and began granting rare interviews. He reacted to only two political events: Operation Moses, which brought thousands of Ethiopian Jews to Israel (he was ecstatic), and the signing of the London Agreement—which proposed a Jordanian-Palestinian confederation in the territories and a peace treaty with Israel and the Jordanians in 1987 (he was utterly opposed).[27] What he still had no interest in, however, was feuding publicly with Ariel Sharon. Sharon had filed his libel suit against *Time* in 1984, and had continued to press his version of what had happened in the Lebanon War. Five years after the war, in August 1987, Sharon gave a four-hour-long speech at Tel Aviv University in which he proclaimed his innocence and insisted that he had done nothing without the approval of the cabinet. The speech unleashed a public outcry, opening the wounds of the war, which had just begun to heal. One Israeli journalist noted that "although you can get the Israelis out of Lebanon, you cannot get Lebanon out of the Israelis."[28]

In 1988, Benny Begin, enraged at Sharon's misleading the Israeli public after having misled his father, and disappointed by his father's silence, published articles in *Yediot Ahronoth* and in *Ma'ariv*, defending his father. The elder Begin was pleased, but when Benny chose to run for a seat on the Likud list, his father did not assist the campaign. Did Begin not want to see his son take the same personal risks as he had in the world of politics? Did he believe it was the wrong choice for Benny? No one knows.

Begin's children almost never speak about their father in public; the code of silence that Begin adopted for himself has survived him.

When Jimmy Carter returned to Israel on a visit, Begin refused to see him.

In 1990, Begin broke his hip again, and his health deteriorated dramatically. He underwent surgery and was transferred to Ichilov Hospital in Tel Aviv for rehabilitation. Though unable to stand, he did gain some weight, and ultimately became more and more sociable with the young physical therapist who attended him; periodically, Begin the perfectionist actually corrected the therapist's colloquial but technically incorrect Hebrew.[29]

In January 1991, he was still hospitalized when Iraq fired missiles at Israel during the Persian Gulf War. In light of the limited impact of Saddam Hussein's missile strikes, one hundred MKs signed a letter of appreciation for Begin's fateful decision to bomb Osirak back in 1981. Begin was released from the hospital in March, and on his way down the stairs, in front of television reporters and photographers, he forgot to hold on to the rail on his left side. When his doctor reminded him to use the railing, he grinned. "I never lean to the left," he said.[30] As he thanked his doctors, he kissed the hands of all of the nurses. Even in his decline, the impish grin, the sense of humor, and the European gentleman were still in evidence.

But he refused to come out of seclusion. The man who had begun his years in Palestine by hiding underground spent the last years of his life hiding once again. Perhaps, without Aliza, he simply couldn't go on. Perhaps it was the physical decline of a man who had run out of strength. Or was it, perhaps, a symbolic silence, a return to the underground, where loyalty had been paramount, after he'd been misled by Sharon and castigated by Kahan? Did a return to the shadows, and to silence, afford him a purity of purpose that the world of politics had denied him? No one knows. Perhaps Begin himself did not know.

Begin and Leah moved to Tel Aviv, close to the hospital where he continued to receive treatment. Finally, Begin granted a interview to Israel's Channel 1 in the spring, in honor of the fiftieth anniversary of the death of Jabotinsky, his "master and teacher." In July he was interviewed again. With renewed rigor, he defended his tenure as commander of the Etzel. Asked what his most difficult decision as Etzel commander had been, he replied that it was the hanging of the two British sergeants. He defended the decision, however, noting that after the Etzel hanged the sergeants, the British never again hanged anyone in *Eretz Yisrael*. He referred, as well, to his relationship with Ben-Gurion. They had been "rivals, not only politically, but there were times that we even became friends."[31]

He continued to see Kadishai and Meridor, and he reconnected with old friends, Yochanan Bader among them. They had met in Poland (it was Bader who had persuaded Begin to join the Polish Army, which got him to Palestine), and for years, as David Ben-Gurion refused to utter Begin's name in the Knesset, he referred to him as "the man sitting next to MK Bader." Kadishai mediated the visit. Bader was almost completely deaf, and Begin was too weak to raise his voice. So Kadishai passed notes back and forth, and later recalled that more than anything, the two seemed simply to enjoy each other's company, preferring simply to sit together, even when they had exhausted their conversation.[32]

In early March 1992, Begin suffered a serious heart attack and was rushed to Ichilov Hospital. Two books were found at his bedside: *Where the Buck Stops: The Personal and Private Writings of Harry S. Truman* and Seymour Hersh's *The Price of Power: Kissinger in the White House*.[33] He died a few days later, on March 9, at the age of seventy-nine, in the very early hours of the morning.

He left the briefest of wills, in the form of a note to Kadishai. It read, in its entirety:

My dear Yehiel, When the day comes, I request you to read to my dear ones, to my friends and comrades, this request: I ask to be buried on the Mount of Olives next to Meir Feinstein and Moshe Barazani. I thank you and all those who will carry out my request. With love, Menachem

Feinstein and Barazani, one Ashkenazi and the other Iraqi, were the two underground fighters (one Etzel and one Lechi) who, rather than allow themselves to be hanged by the British, had embraced and detonated a smuggled hand grenade between them, singing *Adon Olam*. It was next to them, not near Ze'ev Jabotinsky, Levi Eshkol, Golda Meir, and the notables in the national cemetery on Mount Herzl, that Begin wished to be buried.

Begin had actually written his brief will prior to Aliza's death. With his request in mind, Aliza was buried on the Mount of Olives so that he would be buried next to her. Interred next to Aliza, Feinstein, and Barazani, Menachem Begin would lie forever with his family; he would return to the woman he had adored and to the "fighting family" he had loved so deeply in his early years in Palestine. And he would, as his very last act, integrate the Etzel a bit more into the mainstream of Israel's historical narrative.

The report of his death led the morning news broadcasts. The funeral was scheduled for 4:00 p.m. the very same day. By his request, there was no military guard, and no lying in state.[34] Just hours after the announcement, some 75,000 mourners lined the streets of a sunny but chilly Jerusalem to join the procession.

The masses flooded the streets near the Mount of Olives. Traffic ground to a halt. There was room at the grave only for family, a few government officials, and Begin's closest associates. With traffic snarled, many people walked miles to get as close as they could.[35] The mourners were a cross-section of Israel: young and old, Ashkenazi and Sephardi, religious and secular, public officials and ordinary citizens of the country he had helped to found.

There was no casket. Instead, in traditional Jewish fashion, Menachem Begin's body was wrapped in a white shroud and covered by a tallit (prayer shawl). The men who had been the Etzel's senior command, now old and barely recognizable as the strapping young fighters who had executed the daring attacks on the British that Begin had ordered years earlier, carried the wooden stretcher with his body from the bottom of the hill up the gravel path to the gravesite on the Mount of Olives. Ya'akov Meridor, who had assumed command of the Etzel after Raziel was killed and had then convinced Begin to take the helm, walked alongside. Yitzhak Shamir was there, as were Yitzhak Rabin, Dan Meridor, and other leading government officials. Present also, of course, were members of Begin's family: Benny and his wife, Chasia and her husband, Leah, and Begin's grandchildren.

Benny recited Kaddish, and Kadishai spoke the words of *El Malei Rachamim*. And then, in full view of the Old City of Jerusalem, which he had desperately tried to arm and to protect, with the New City just beyond it, the tallit was removed and Menachem Begin's body was lowered into the rocky ground of the Mount of Olives.

Begin had asked that there be no eulogies, no ceremony beyond what Jewish tradition mandated. But after the grave was filled with sacks of earth from the holy city of Safed—the city in which a number of Etzel men who had been hanged by the British were buried—the old men, veterans of the Etzel, began to sing the anthem that had shaped their lives, and which had changed the course of Jewish history.

> From the pit of decay and dust
> Will arise to us a generation
> Proud, generous, and fierce
> Fallen Betar
> Yodfat and Masada
> Risen again in strength and dignity [*hadar*]
>
> Dignity [*Hadar*]
> A Jew, though in poverty, is of royal strain
> Slave or refugee—the son of a king
> Crowned with the diadem of David
> In the open or in concealment
> Remember the crown
> Symbol of pride and fortitude [*tagar*]

Fortitude [*Tagar*]
In the face of every obstacle
In times of ascent, and of setbacks
A fire may still be lit
With the flame of revolt
For silence is dirt
Sacrifice blood and spirit
For the hidden glory

To die or to conquer the mountain
Yodfat, Masada, Betar.

EPILOGUE

Two Revolutions and a Looming Question

But the people would not listen to Samuel's warning. "No," they said. "We must have a king over us, that we may be like all other nations." —*I Samuel 8:19*

On July 6, 1958, a decade after Israel's independence and speaking in honor of America's birth, Menachem Begin made reference to the American Revolution in justification of the Zionist enterprise. Ever conscious of the ultimate sacrifice made by the men from the Etzel and Lechi who had been hanged by the British, he declared:

One hundred and eighty-two years ago, thirteen North American colonies under the repressive regime of George III rebelled, and in the process of their uprising declared their independence and the belief in human freedom. In their war, the colonists made enormous sacrifices amid many moments of heroism. Americans justifiably call this war—against a foreign regime—the War of Independence.

For the American people, there was one who fought for freedom who was eventually hanged at the gallows. His name was Nathan Hale. He was caught by the British, found guilty of espionage, and taken out to be executed via hanging. Before his death he uttered the following words: "I only regret that I have but one life to give for my country." From then onward, all Americans have bowed their heads in respect to that man.[1]

It was far from the only time Begin invoked the American Revolution. In an article commemorating the thirty-fifth anniversary of Ze'ev Jabotinsky's death, he combined two passages from Thomas Jefferson's letters—one to James Madison and another to William Stephens Smith. "I hold it that a little rebellion now and then is a good thing, and as necessary in the political world as storms in the physical," Begin quoted Jefferson, adding the American revolutionary's sobering observation that "the tree of liberty must be refreshed from time to time with the blood of patriots and tyrants."[2]

It was natural that Begin thought about the Zionist revolution in light of what American revolutionary patriots had wrought 175 years earlier. After all, the American and Zionist revolutions shared much in common. Both were fueled by a people's desire for freedom after long periods of oppression in which religion had played a central role in their persecution. Both were designed to force the British to leave the territory in question so that they (the American colonialists and the Zionists) could establish their own, sovereign countries—in Israel's case on the very ground where a sovereign Jewish nation had stood centuries before. Both produced admirable democracies. And both were violent revolutions.

Most interesting, perhaps, is the fact that these two revolutions were among the few that did not unleash a torrent of bloodletting when the revolution was over. As Joseph Ellis, the lyrical historian of early America, notes, "With the American revolution, as with all revolutions, different factions came together in common cause to overthrow the reigning regime, then discovered in the aftermath of their triumph that they had fundamentally different and politically incompatible notions of what they intended."[3] But then Ellis notes that America's was different from most revolutions, pointing to "the French, Russian, and Chinese revolutions, as well as the multiple movements for national independence in Africa, Asia, and Latin America." In these, Ellis observes, "the leadership class of the successful revolution proceeded to decimate itself in bloody reprisals that frequently assumed genocidal proportions."[4] That did not happen in the United States, and it did not happen in Israel, either.

The similarities between the revolutions are remarkable.

Not surprisingly, American Jewish leaders had long seen the Zionist movement through the lens of the American Revolution. In 1902, the project of settling Jews in Palestine evoked for Richard Gottheil, president of the Federation of American Zionists, an image of "the Puritans [who] fled from persecution." The Zionist pioneers "are building the new Judea even as the Puritans built a new England three hundred years ago," opined Bernard Rosenblatt in 1907. "Hederah and her sister colonies are . . . the Jamestown and the Plymouth of the new House of Israel."[5] Justice Louis D. Brandeis spoke of "the Jewish Pilgrim Fathers" in Palestine working in "the Colonies," in a region that most closely resembled "a miniature California." "A revolutionary war is going on in Palestine," wrote Ben Hecht, the fiery playwright. "The few survivors [of the Holocaust] . . . are making history in the same way as the Maquis, the Partisans, the Irish rebels, and the American revolutionists." An American brigade who volunteered to join the Irgun was named the "George Washington Legion."[6]

The comparison with the American Revolution has been made in other surprising ways. Yair Shamir, today Israel's minister of agriculture, the son of Yitzhak Shamir, Begin's successor and the onetime head of the Lechi, said to me once as we were discussing the two revolutions, "Ben-Gurion was a Loyalist."[7] His comment was a reference to the British citizens in the colonies who did not wish to rebel against the Crown, who would have been content to remain under the dominion of the king.

To call Ben-Gurion a "Loyalist" is an extraordinary claim; Ben-Gurion, after all, did explicitly seek an independent Jewish state. But Shamir's comment is telling. It is a reminder that in the minds of many of that period, Ben-Gurion—for all his greatness—needed the Etzel to remind him that it wasn't enough to *want* a Jewish state; one had to actually *do* something in order to achieve it. Yes, Ben-Gurion had accepted partition and declared statehood at precisely the right moment. Without him, Israel might not be. But getting the British to leave was more Begin's accomplishment than Ben-Gurion's, and to the children of the Etzel and Lechi fighters, Ben-Gurion's conduct of the *yishuv* still seems too tentative and too accommodating.

Given that need to *do* something to achieve independence, the ongoing comparison of the American and Zionist revolutions—whether by Begin, Shamir, or many others—poses a looming, if unstated, question. Why do even Jewish Americans bow their heads in respect to Nathan Hale, but wince in shame at the mention of Feinstein, Barazani, and the other Hebrew freedom fighters who sought precisely what it was that Nathan Hale died for? Why is George Washington, who conducted a violent, fierce, and bloody campaign against the British, a hero, while for many, Begin remains a villain or, at the very least, a Jewish leader with a compromised background?

Some of the difference has to do with time. We have photographs of the two hanged British sergeants and of the shattered King David Hotel. We know the names of the sergeants and of the victims in the hotel attack. But the names of the British young men who died at the hands of America's revolutionaries are largely unknown by now. The passage of time and the absence of details have allowed the heroic story of American's freedom fighters to endure, while the pain and suffering of those whom they fought has gradually faded into oblivion. The leaders and fighters of the Zionist revolution have been afforded no such luxury.

The fighters of the Zionist revolution have also had the misfortune of another inequality. Native Americans are not the object of the world's sympathies. Early Americans killed or moved entire tribes, yet the American revolution is now seldom assailed for its treatment of Native Americans as vehemently as is the Israeli revolution for its conflict with Arabs. The Palestinians have been infinitely more successful in their quest for international support, and the reputation of Israel's revolutionaries— despite their similarity to those in America two centuries earlier—has borne the brunt of the international community's displeasure.

But Begin's reputation was also scarred by David Ben-Gurion's refusal to acknowledge his own participation in some of the events for which Begin is vilified. Ben-Gurion consistently denied having had anything to do with operations that did not go as planned, while Begin stood ready to take responsibility. The Haganah's David Shaltiel had approved the Deir Yassin operation, but when it went awry, and many innocent people died, Ben-Gurion painted Begin as a violent thug. The Haganah was deeply involved in the approval and planning of the King David bombing (for Ben-Gurion had come to see that Begin was right, that the British would need to be dislodged), but when civilians were killed because the British refused to heed the Etzel's warnings to leave the building, Ben-Gurion assailed Begin as if the "Old Man" and his men had known nothing of the plan.

Nor did Ben-Gurion acknowledge his debt to Begin's worldview. David Ben-Gurion was one of the greatest Jewish leaders ever to have lived, and the Jewish state might well not have come to be were it not for him. But his greatness notwithstanding, he was unfair to Menachem Begin— consistently and mercilessly. His dishonesty about his own role in these operations and his refusal ever to acknowledge that it was the combination of the approaches of Ben-Gurion and Begin that led to the departure of the British and to the creation of the Jewish state, are ugly blemishes on a largely extraordinary record.

David Ben-Gurion was not alone, of course. Menachem Begin is, in many ways, still the victim of campaigns waged against him by Diaspora Jews. When, on the eve of Begin's planned 1948 trip to the United States, Albert Einstein and Hannah Arendt joined some two dozen other prominent American Jews in writing to *The New York Times* to protest his visit, they could probably not have imagined the long-term damage they would do not only to Begin's reputation, but to the causes for which he stood. Their claim that "240 men, women, and children" had been killed was utterly false. Begin denied it, but no one believed him. Decades later, Palestinian historians would corroborate his claims.

"Within the Jewish community," Einstein and Arendt wrote, the Etzel has "preached an admixture of ultranationalism, religious mysticism, and racial superiority." American Jews believed them. But that characterization of Begin was utterly false. Unless believing in God makes one a religious mystic, Begin was far from any such thing. The Menachem Begin whom they accused of "racial superiority" was the same Begin who argued for the end of military rule over Israel's Arabs,[8] who welcomed the Vietnamese boat people, who gave up the Sinai to make peace with Egypt.

That Albert Einstein and Hannah Arendt, both immigrants to America who had found in the United States freedom that they would never have been afforded in their native Germany, could not—or would not—see the similarities between the two revolutions is astounding. They saw the colonists as harbingers of freedom who created the world's greatest democracy, a land of unlimited opportunity for those who came to its shores, but Begin and the Etzel as "terrorists" worthy only of shame and denigration.

Why?

Part of the problem was that Begin's Jewish worldview was, in many ways, infinitely more sophisticated than that of his detractors. He understood that life is a messy enterprise, and that great things cannot be accomplished in the pristine conditions of the laboratory. Were he alive today, he would be perplexed by those American Jews who are despondent about the conditions of Arabs living under Israeli rule but who rarely so much as mention the horrific conditions of Native Americans, whom those very same heroic American colonists cheated, deported, and murdered. He would in no way have condoned the treatment of Native Americans, of course; he was far too great a humanist for that. Indeed, he might well have identified with them, considering himself native to Israel. What would have saddened him beyond measure was the Jewish people's ability to be so intolerant of the messiness of life in its own unfolding history, yet so understanding of that messiness in the actions of others.

Another factor was Begin's uniquely nuanced view of Jewish life. His was a Judaism in which, as he stressed at the Nobel Prize ceremony, one

could harbor both deeply humanist convictions and a passionate alle-
giance to one's own people. A particularism that comes at the expense
of broader humanism is inevitably narrow, and will likely become ugly,
he would have said. But a commitment to humanity at large that does
not put one's own people first and center, Begin believed and made clear
time and again, is a human life devoid of identity. He understood that to
love all of humanity equally is to love no one intensively. Such unabashed
yet nuanced particularism, even tribalism, was and remains difficult for
many contemporary Jews, who see in Western universalist culture an
ethos utterly at odds with the peoplehood that has always been central
to Jewish life.[9]

Beyond the tribalism, Begin's reputation has suffered because even
while survivors of the Holocaust are still alive, many contemporary
Jews want to move beyond it and to usher in a new era in which human-
kind forswears the use of force. Begin's association with force is a critical
dimension of the complexity of who he was. That one man could be so
emblematically associated with both peace-making and war-making is
difficult for many to fathom today.

To be sure, some of the lengths to which Begin and the Etzel went raise
painful ethical questions. It is impossible to read about the results of the
Deir Yassin battle (despite our knowledge that the heavy outcome was
never planned), the hanging of the sergeants, or the horrific human toll in
the King David Hotel without pausing to reflect on the great loss of life,
without at least wondering—if only momentarily—whether there might
not have been another way. Dozens of British soldiers were killed in the
Zionist campaign for independence; in the annals of Zionist history, they
were the enemy. To their families, of course, they were simply innocent
young men doing a job that their country had demanded of them. The toll
was heavy, and it was painful.

Begin himself was emphatic and clear that ends do not always justify
means. Toward the end of *White Nights*, he wrote with a syncopation that
remains eerily evocative of his oratory, "The end justifies the means?—If
you are faced with tyranny, do not hesitate to say: Yes! Every end justifies

the means?—No! The end justifies all the means?—No! Every end justifies all the means?—No, never!"[10]

Yes, he would say were he alive today, some of the means were extreme.
But Jews were dying in Europe. And no one did anything to help them.
Not Churchill. Not FDR. Not even American Jews, for the most part.
The British had sealed the shores of Palestine. The United States sealed
its own shores. Yet American Jewish life continued apace without huge
disruptions; American Jews did not mass around Capitol Hill or the
White House time and again, exerting pressure until FDR dropped at
least one bomb on one track to one camp. As thousands upon thousands
of Polish Jews went up smokestacks at Auschwitz, American Jews celebrated Bar Mitzvahs almost as if nothing was awry. The world knew,
Begin understood, but still reacted with silence. There were ships filled
with Jews, roaming the globe, searching for a place to drop anchor, but no
one would have them.

Someone needed to carve out a home for those Jews whom no one else
would have. Someone needed to stand up for the Jews that even Jews had
abandoned. Menachem Begin had survived his flight from the Nazis. He
had endured Soviet prison. He had made it to Palestine as a Jew in the
Free Polish Army. How on earth, he would have asked, could anyone not
believe that something had to be *done* to make one small space for the
Jews?

When Thomas Friedman wrote, "What made Begin . . . dangerous was
that his fantasies about power were combined with a self-perception of
being a victim . . . Begin always reminded me of Bernhard Goetz, the
white Manhattanite who shot four black youths he thought were about
to mug him on the New York subway . . . [Begin] was Bernhard Goetz
with an F-15,"[11] he failed to understand that the issue was not "fantasy."
Begin was opposed to fantasy: Why should Jews buy into some fantasy
that they had no power, when they finally did? Why should they imagine
that they could not once again become victims, when others were clearly
plotting their destruction? How was destroying Osirak, when Saddam
had explicitly stated that he was going to destroy Israel, indicative of a
fantasy or of a power fetish?

Begin's legacy is that he would not be still and could not be silenced. He said that he hoped to be remembered for having prevented civil war; but no less important, his life is a reminder of the obligations that Jews have to one another and of the responsibility they have for their own safety.

Thankfully, Einstein, Arendt, and Friedman were not the only perspectives voiced about Begin, even during his life. Abba Hillel Silver, the American Reform rabbi and Zionist leader, had said, "The Irgun will go down in history as a factor without which the State of Israel would not have come into being."[12]

Silver was right. Jewish sovereignty did not happen by chance, nor simply through negotiation. It came about through determination, grit, courage, and blood. It was wrought not only by Ben-Gurion and those he invited to that memorable afternoon in Tel Aviv when he declared independence, but also, to paraphrase Moses, by "those standing there that day, and those not standing there that day."[13]

Despite the animosity that divided them almost all their working lives, Ben-Gurion and Begin were both necessary elements of the creation of a Jewish state. Without either one, Israel might well not have come into being.

Menachem Begin's life was a study in the possibilities of "both/and," rather than "either/or." Born into war, he never gave up the hope for peace. Forced into hiding upon declaring the revolt, his greatest moments were in public, in front of adoring crowds. Animated and energized by the citizens who rallied behind him, he spent the last decade of his life out of their sight, as if hiding from them. Hunted by the British as "Terrorist No. 1," he was awarded the Nobel Peace Prize. He made peace with Egypt, but attacked Iraq and invaded Lebanon. Capable of great emotional highs, he was also dogged by periods of great lows. Willing to use force to expel the British, he was also among the chief protectors of the rule of law in the Jewish state. Fiercely and uniquely devoted to the Jews, he gave refuge to Vietnamese boat people and urged the end of military rule over Israel's Arabs. Having avoided civil war over the *Altalena*, he threatened it with reparations and brought Israel to the brink of it, once again, when he ordered the evacuation of Yamit. By no means punctiliously observant, he both loved and honored Jewish tradition. As Minister Dan Meridor put it, "He spoke Jewish."[4] Among much else, Begin taught the Jews that love of their tradition was by no means exclusively the province of the ritually observant, that the religious-secular distinction in Israeli life could be rendered meaningless by people with a profound knowledge of and love for Jewish texts and rituals.

And yet, despite this "both/and" life, there was also one unwavering constant, a guiding principle that shaped everything. Begin's was a life of selfless devotion to his people, the Jewish people. It was a life in which determination eradicated fear, hope overcame despondency, love overcame hate, and devotion to both Jews and human beings everywhere coexisted with ease and grace. It was, more than anything, a life of great loyalty—to the people into which he was born, to the woman he loved from the moment he met her, and to the state that he helped create.

That is a legacy infinitely greater than most are able to bequeath. In an era in which many are increasingly dubious about the legitimacy of love for a specific people or devotion to its ancestral homeland, the life and commitments of Menachem Begin urge us to look again at what he did and what he stood for, and to imagine—if we dare—the glory of a Jewish people recommitted to the principles that shaped his very being.

CHRONOLOGY

1913 *August 16* Menachem is born to Ze'ev Dov and Chasia Begin, in Brisk (Brest-Litovsk), Russia, now in Belarus. He is the youngest of three children.

1915 Begin family flees Brisk during World War I

1919 Begin family returns to Brisk, now part of Poland

1929 Joins Betar, youth movement of Revisionist Zionism

Appointed commander of the Betar group in Brisk

1929(?) Hears Ze'ev Jabotinsky speak for the first time in Brisk

1931 *June* Graduates from local Polish high school

Enrolls in Warsaw law school

1935 Completes law school

1938 *September* Over Jabotinsky's objections, revises the Betar oath to stress armed defense as well as preemptive conquest

1939 Appointed commissioner of Betar Poland

May Marries Aliza Arnold, both wearing their Betar uniforms

September 1 World War II; Germany invades Poland; Menachem and Aliza Begin flee Warsaw with the goal of Palestine but are forced to settle in Vilna, Lithuania

1940 *September* Arrested by Soviet NKVD

Aliza travels to Palestine and waits for Menachem

1941 *March* Sentenced to eight years in Siberian labor camp for Zionism

June / July Menachem's father, Ze'ev Dov, and brother, Herzl, killed by the Nazis

September (?) Released from prison

1942 *Winter* Joins Anders's Army of Free Polish Forces

May Arrives in Palestine with the Free Polish Army; reunites with Aliza

October (?) Begin's mother, Chasia, is killed by Nazis

1943 *December 1* Assumes command of the Irgun Zva'i Leumi (Etzel)

March 1 First child, Binyamin Ze'ev Begin, is born

1944 *February* Declares revolt on Great Britain

Assumes alias and goes underground after attacks on British

November 6 Assassination of Lord Moyne by the Lechi; *Saison* begins

1945 *October* The Haganah, Etzel, and Lechi launch Hebrew Resistance Movement against British Empire

1946 *May 2* Daughter Chasia, named after Menachem's mother, is born

July 22 King David Hotel bombing

1947 *July 11* Kidnapping and execution of two British sergeants

November 29 United Nations vote on the Partition Plan to create Jewish and Arab states; Jews accept, Arabs reject

1948 *February 22* Daughter Leah is born

April 9 Etzel is involved in killing of numerous civilians in Deir Yassin

April 24 Etzel attacks Jaffa in last major battle; Begin leaves the underground

May 14 David Ben-Gurion declares Israeli independence

June 15 Founds Herut party, enters political opposition where he will remain for twenty-nine years

June 22 Sinking of the *Altalena*

1949 *January 25* First elections, Herut wins fourteen seats in the Knesset

1952 *January* Knesset debates reparations from Germany; Begin is banned from Knesset for three months

1962 Robert Soblen affair

1967 *June 5* Knesset approves Begin's merger into unity government

June 6–12 Six-Day War; Begin advocates for conquest of East Jerusalem

1970 *August 6* Resigns from National Unity Government

1973 *September 12* Forms Likud party

1977 *May 12* Likud wins elections; Begin is elected prime minister

June Grants Vietnamese refugees asylum in Israel

August The first group of Ethiopian Jewish refugees secretly brought to Israel

November 19 President Anwar Sadat of Egypt visits Jerusalem

1978 *September 5–17* Camp David Peace Accords signed with Jimmy Carter

December 10 Awarded Nobel Peace Prize with Anwar Sadat

1979 *March 26* Peace treaty with Egypt signed

1981 *June 7* Israel destroys Iraqi nuclear reactor at Osirak

June 30 Likud wins elections; Begin is elected to second term as prime minister

1982 *June 5* Operation Peace for the Galilee (beginning of Lebanon War)

September 16–18 Sabra and Shatila massacre

November 14 Aliza dies in Jerusalem while Menachem is in Los Angeles

1983 *February* Kahan Commission issues report on Sabra and Shatila

September 15 Resigns as prime minister and retires from public life

1992 *March 3* Suffers serious heart attack, hospitalized in Tel Aviv

March 9 Dies at age seventy-nine; buried later that day on Mount of Olives

MENACHEM BEGIN'S GRADUAL RISE IN THE KNESSET

Number of Seats in the Knesset

	1949	1951	1955	1959	1961	1965	1969	1974	1977	1981
Begin Bloc	14	8	15	17	17	26	26	39	43	48
Labor Bloc	69	67	68	71	63	67	60	51	32	47
Other	12	7	5	6	24	10	14	14	16	13
Religious Parties	16	15	17	18	16	17	18	15	13	10
Centrist Parties	7	20	13	8	0	0	2	0	15	2
Arab Parties	2	3	2	0	0	0	0	1	1	0

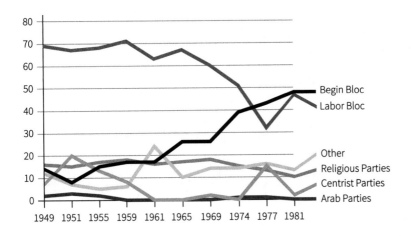

FOR FURTHER READING

Biographies of Menachem Begin

Avner, Yehuda. *The Prime Ministers* (Jerusalem: Toby Press, 2010).

Grosbard, Ofer. *Menachem Begin: The Absent Leader* (Glilot, Israel: Strategic Research and Policy Center National Defense College, IDF, 2007).

Hurwitz, Zvi Harry. *Begin: His Life, Words and Deeds* (Jerusalem: Gefen Publishing House, 2004).

Shilon, Avi. *Menachem Begin: A Life*. Trans. Danielle Zilberberg and Yoram Sharett (New Haven, Conn.: Yale University Press, 2012).

Silver, Eric. *Begin: A Biography* (London: Weidenfeld and Nicolson, 1984).

Temko, Ned. *To Win or to Die: A Personal Portrait of Menachem Begin* (New York: William Morrow, 1987).

The History of Israel

Gilbert, Martin. *Israel: A History* (New York: William Morrow, 1998).

Sachar, Howard M. *A History of Israel from the Rise of Zionism to Our Time* (1976; repr. New York: Alfred A. Knopf, 2007).

Shapira, Anita. *Israel: A History*. Trans. Anthony Berris (Waltham, Mass.: Brandeis University Press, 2012).

Introduction and Chapters 1 and 2

Hertzberg, Arthur. *The Zionist Idea: A Historical Analysis and Reader* (Philadelphia: Jewish Publication Society, 1997).

Jabotinsky, Vladimir (Ze'ev). "The Iron Wall" (1923). Trans. Jabotinsky Institute in Israel. Courtesy of the Jabotinsky Institute in Israel, online: http://www.jabotinsky.org/multimedia/upl_doc/doc_191207_49117.pdf. Accessed February 24, 2013.

Katz, Shmuel. *Lone Wolf: A Biography of Vladimir (Ze'ev) Jabotinsky, Vols. 1 and 2* (New York: Barricade Books, 1996).

Peres, Shimon, with David Landau. *Ben-Gurion: A Political Life* (New York: Random House, 2011).

For Further Reading

Chapter 3

Begin, Menachem. *White Nights*. Trans. Katie Kaplan (1957; repr. Bnei Brak, Israel: Steimatzky, 2008).

Sharansky, Natan. *Fear No Evil: The Classic Memoir of One Man's Triumph over a Police State*. Trans. Stefani Hoffman (New York: Random House, 1998).

Chapter 4

Begin, Menachem. *The Revolt*. Trans. Samuel Katz (1951; repr. Bnei Brak, Israel: Steimatzky, 2007).

Berkman, Ted. *Cast a Giant Shadow: The Story of Mickey Marcus Who Died to Save Jerusalem* (New York: Doubleday, 1962).

Clarke, Thurston. *By Blood and Fire: The Attack on the King David Hotel* (London: Hutchinson, 1981).

Collins, Larry, and Dominique Lapierre. *O Jerusalem!* (New York: Simon and Schuster, 1972).

Heller, Joseph. *The Stern Gang: Ideology, Politics, and Terror 1940–1949*. (London: Frank Cass, 1995).

Koestler, Arthur. *Promise and Fulfillment: Palestine 1917–1949*. (New York: Macmillan, 1949).

Chapter 5

Bowyer Bell, John. *Terror out of Zion: The Fight for Israeli Independence*. (1977; repr. New Brunswick, N.J.: Transaction, 2009).

Medoff, Rafael. *Militant Zionism in America: The Rise and Fall of the Jabotinsky Movement in the United States 1926–1948* (Tuscaloosa: Alabama University Press, 2002).

Morris, Benny. *1948: A History of the First Arab-Israeli War* (New Haven, Conn.: Yale University Press, 2008).

Segev, Tom. *One Palestine—Complete*. Trans. Haim Watzman (New York: Henry Holt, 1999).

Uris, Leon. *Exodus* (New York: Bantam Books, 1959).

Chapter 6

Auerbach, Jerold S. *Brothers at War: Israel and the Tragedy of the Altalena* (New Orleans: Quid Pro Books, 2011).

Katz, Shmuel. *Days of Fire* (Tel Aviv: Steimatzky, 1968).

Chapter 7

Arendt, Hannah. *Eichmann in Jerusalem: A Report on the Banality of Evil* (1963; repr. New York: Penguin Books, 2006).

Lipstadt, Deborah E. *The Eichmann Trial* (New York: Random House, 2011).

Chapter 8

Oren, Michael. *Power, Faith, and Fantasy: America in the Middle East, 1776 to the Present* (New York: W. W. Norton, 2007).

Chapter 9

Meir, Golda. *My Life* (New York: Dell, 1975).

Oren, Michael. *Six Days of War* (New York: Oxford University Press, 2002).

Rabinovich, Abraham. *The Yom Kippur War* (New York: Schocken Books, 2004).

Chapter 10

Beckerman, Gal. *When They Come for Us, We'll Be Gone: The Epic Struggle to Save Soviet Jewry* (New York: Houghton Mifflin Harcourt, 2010).

Shimron, Gad. *Mossad Exodus: The Daring Undercover Rescue of the Lost Jewish Tribe* (Jerusalem: Gefen Publishing House, 2007).

Chapter 11

Carter, Jimmy. *Keeping Faith: Memoirs of a President* (Toronto: Bantam Books, 1982).

El-Sadat, Anwar. *In Search of Identity: An Autobiography* (New York: Harper and Row, 1978).

Gorenberg, Gershom. *The Accidental Empire: Israel and the Birth of the Settlements, 1967–1977* (New York: Times Books, 2006).

Hurwitz, Harry, and Yisrael Medad, eds. *Peace in the Making: The Menachem Begin–Anwar El-Sadat Personal Correspondence* (Jerusalem: Gefen Publishing House, 2011).

Weizman, Ezer. *The Battle for Peace* (New York: Bantam Books, 1981).

Chapter 12

Bar-Joseph, Uri, Michael Handel, and Amos Perlmutter. *Two Minutes over Baghdad* (London: Frank Cass, 2003).

For Further Reading

Nakdimon, Shelomoh. *First Strike: The Exclusive Story of How Israel Foiled Iraq's Attempt to Get the Bomb* (New York: Summit Books, 1987).

Wisse, Ruth R. *Jews and Power* (New York: Schocken Books, 2007).

Chapter 13

Bloom, Gadi, and Nir Hefez. *Ariel Sharon: A Life* (New York: Random House, 2006).

Friedman, Thomas. *From Beirut to Jerusalem* (New York: Farrar, Straus and Giroux, 1989).

Sharon, Ariel. *Warrior* (New York: Simon and Schuster, 2001).

ACKNOWLEDGMENTS

In writing this book, I have been assisted and encouraged by a wide array of colleagues, students, and friends; it is a pleasure to have an opportunity to thank them.

Shalem College is an extraordinarily rich intellectual environment. I am grateful to our entire Board of Directors for their support and friendship, and for providing the intellectual home that enables all of us at Shalem College to do our work in the company of such challenging and stimulating colleagues. To David Messer, chairman of our board and friend ever since I joined Shalem, particular thanks for his warmth and loyalty. Many of my colleagues at Shalem, too numerous to name individually, have enriched this project, and I am grateful to them all. Particular thanks, however, are due to Dr. Daniel Polisar, executive vice president and provost at Shalem College, who embraced this project immediately upon hearing about it and made it possible for me to take the time necessary to complete it. Without Dan's encouragement and support, I simply could not have written this book. Dan also read a late draft of the manuscript, pointing out dozens of places that could be improved or made more accurate; this book is significantly more precise than it would have been without him. It would be hard to imagine a better colleague, and I am more grateful for his friendship than I can adequately express.

To Seth Goldstein, for his friendship and warmth, his ongoing support, and his efforts to make it possible for me to balance time for this project with other Shalem responsibilities, and to Ido Hevroni, for his participation in a particularly important brainstorming process, my thanks as well. Erica Halivni gave generously of her time and great talent as we designed materials for the preparation of the manuscript. Yair Shamir, who was chairman of the board of directors at Shalem as I was writing this book, and is now minister of agriculture in the Israeli government, is both a loyal and devoted friend as well as a voracious reader of history; my conversations with him about this project were of great value, and I'm grateful for his time and generosity of spirit.

I have been very fortunate to have Richard Pine, of Inkwell Management, as my literary agent for almost a quarter of a century. My writing career would have been very different and far less satisfying without Richard, and I remain deeply grateful that our paths crossed, almost accidentally, so long ago.

It was Carolyn Hessel, executive director of the Jewish Book Council and, no less important, a leading figure in the American Jewish writing world, who first urged me to consider writing a book for the prestigious Nextbook series. A muse, goad, and extraordinary friend, she has taken me (among many others) under her wing and has

Acknowledgments

shown me kindness and thoughtfulness that I never earned, but for which I'm deeply grateful.

Jonathan Rosen is a supremely insightful and gifted editor. It was his idea that I write about Menachem Begin, and his intelligence, prodigious knowledge, and passionate voice have done much to make this book significantly better than it would have been without him. For his depth, wisdom, and friendship, I'm very grateful.

Altie Karper, editorial director of Random House's Schocken imprint, befriended this project from the outset and has been consistently warm, encouraging, and helpful.

Talia Harcsztark (Barnard College) and Bina Peltz (Princeton University), who were Shalem interns during the summer of 2012, joined the project in its nascent stage. I had scarcely started my research on this volume when they arrived at Shalem; but they embraced the project with energy and enthusiasm, not allowing its early amorphousness to stand in their way. It was they who got the research off the ground, and I made use of the work that they did throughout the process of writing this book.

And now for the Dream Team. Because of our desire to complete this book during Menachem Begin's centennial year, Daniel Polisar insisted that I find myself a staff of researchers to assist me. Neither of us could have imagined, however, how fortunate I would be to find the three simply extraordinary research assistants with whom I worked on this biography. I crossed paths with Caroline Hughes, Gabriel Mitchell, and Shira Petrack serendipitously, each in an entirely different way. They are all extraordinarily bright, talented researchers, able writers, and insightful, dogged, hardworking, and delightful colleagues. They have collectively spent thousands of hours working on this book; they helped conceive its tone, participated in interviews, did archival research, wrote and edited and redrafted, suggested massive changes in structure, checked details, rechecked hundreds of facts countless times, secured the rights to photographs, reviewed copy edits and page proofs, argued with me when they thought the book should say something other than what I had planned (and were often right), and in all, made it possible for me to write this book. Without them, this volume simply would not have come to be.

Caroline's, Gabi's, and Shira's intellectual, aesthetic, and moral fingerprints can be found on virtually every sentence of this volume; there is simply no way to thank them adequately other than to acknowledge my enormous debt to them and to note that I will always be beyond grateful to them for the wondrous experience of working with them this past year. Each of them is planning additional graduate study, and I am confident that great things lie ahead for each of them in the years to come.

I reached out to experts in the field as I was working on this book, some of them people whom I didn't know at all. They were beyond generous with their time and insight and the immediacy of their willingness to help. To Gordon Wood, professor emeritus of history at Brown University, and Gary Nash, professor emeritus of history at UCLA, and to the Canadian member of Parliament Irwin Cotler, among many others, my deepest thanks.

In addition, I'm grateful to many people who tracked down sources or assisted with research or support for this book in other ways. My thanks to Brian Abrahams, Avishay Ben Sasson-Gordis, Menachem Butler, Leon Gordis, Deena Gottlieb, Aryeh Halivni, Israel Kasnett, Abigail Klionsky, Whitney Lee, Jay Lefkowitz, Yaacov Lozo-wick, Julie Meyer, Josh Nason, Joel Newberger, Asher Ostrin, John Podhoretz, Noah Pollak, and David Wolpe. Amira Stern, director of the archives at the Jabotinsky Institute, was consistently extraordinarily helpful. Eli Spector, a 2012 Shalem summer intern, was gracious with his time and artistry, and took several photographs for this volume.

Numerous people with extensive knowledge of Menachem Begin and the period in which he worked graciously consented to be interviewed for this book. I'm grate-ful to Ambassador Yehuda Avner, Nicky Capelouto, Ariela Cotler, Ralph Goldman, Eric Graus, Ruth Gruber, Nathan Gutman, Yossi Klein Halevi, Hart Hasten, Profes-sor Charles Hill, Freda Hurwitz, Hillel Hurwitz, Hertzel Katz, Avi Katzman, Lenny Kohll, Jay Lefkowitz, Masha Leon, Sheldon Lerman, Peleg Levi, Rafael Medoff, Minis-ter Dan Meridor, Shlomo Nakdimon, Aryeh Naor, Minister Yair Shamir, Shoel Silver, and Morris Strauss. Yechiel Kadishai, Menachem Begin's longtime personal secre-tary, was generous both with his time and with materials from his personal library. Menachem Begin's children, through Benny Begin, declined to be interviewed.

The Menachem Begin Heritage Center is a veritable treasure trove of informa-tion about Menachem Begin, Betar, Herut, and related subjects, and has, in addition, a deeply knowledgeable and helpful staff. Herzl Makov, director of the Menachem Begin Center, made it clear that my staff and I would be welcome as often as we would like, which made all the difference. To Moshe Fuksman Shaal, and Dror Bar Yosef, my thanks for their consistent availability and warmth. Rami Shtivi-Shahar, chief archivist at the Begin Center, consistently went far beyond the call of duty to assist us. Particular thanks go to my friend, and now my teacher, Yisrael Medad, director of information and educational resources at the Begin Center. I have known Yisrael for years, but this project afforded me an opportunity to work with him much more closely than I ever had. He was unflagging in his support, generous with his prodi-gious knowledge about Begin, clear about his perspective but understanding that he and I sometimes simply did not agree, and was kind enough to read a rough draft of this manuscript and to point out mistakes where he saw them. For his extraordinary friendship, I'm deeply grateful; obviously, responsibility for any errors that might remain in the manuscript is mine alone.

For gracious hospitality that enabled me to work on this book for extended periods with no interruption when far from home, special thanks to Suzanne Muchin and David Brown, David and Barbara Messer, and Laura and Howard Roselinsky.

Financial support for the research in this project and its dissemination has come from several generous sources, to which I am very grateful. For several years now, the Koret Foundation has been supporting my research and writing; I am grateful to be the Koret Distinguished Fellow at Shalem College, and honored to be associated with the Koret Foundation and its work. Mark Charendoff and the Maimonides Fund were among the very first to offer support for this project, and enabled me to embark on the process of assembling the superb team of assistants that made completing this work possible. For their generosity, and to Mark, for his warm friendship, I'm deeply grateful. Rabbi Robert Hirt and Virginia Bayer, Harold Grinspoon and the Harold Grinspoon Foundation were also generous benefactors of the project.

To Professor Gerald Steinberg and the Israel Research Fellowship, my thanks for funding Gabriel Mitchell's work with me during the course of the writing of this book.

To George Rohr and his extraordinary family, my deepest thanks for their generosity. I was privileged to know George's father, Mr. Sami Rohr, whom I have included in the dedication of this volume. What George and his family have done to honor their extraordinary father, both during his lifetime and after he passed away, by supporting the world of Jewish writing, will, I hope, be a model for many others to emulate.

To Michael and Polina Liberman, longtime treasured friends, and to Morris Benun, a new friend, my deepest thanks for underwriting the publication of the Russian and Hebrew translations of this volume, respectively. Translations from the Hebrew Bible are taken from *Tanakh: The Holy Scriptures, The New JPS Translation According to the Traditional Hebrew Text*, often with emendations on my part.

I have dedicated this book to my parents, on this, their eightieth year. Just as Menachem Begin's life story is at its core a tale of loyalty and dedication, so, too, my parents continually modeled those values for my brothers and me. The three of us were raised in a home rich in Jewish tradition and learning, passionately committed to the Jewish people and to Israel. We spent years in Israel as children, learned to speak the language and to love the land; the fact that Elisheva, our children, and I all live in Israel is thanks in no small measure to the home in which my parents raised us. That they have now joined us in making Jerusalem their home is a fulfillment of their lifelong devotion to the Jewish people and its state.

As they have grown older, my parents' devotion to each other, apparent all throughout their lives, has grown only more extraordinary. Eighty, the Mishnah says, is the "age of strength." In recent years, my parents have needed that strength, but they have demonstrated time and again that the reservoirs of their fortitude run deeper than we might ever have imagined. This book is dedicated to them with gratitude, with admiration, and with love.

When Elisheva and I were on our honeymoon in Hawaii and read that Begin had attacked Iraq's nuclear reactor, neither of us imagined that I might someday write a book about him; we were far too young to have much of a plan. But even then, Elisheva did have a plan for us to live in Israel, and when we made *aliyah* some eighteen years later, it was primarily thanks to her courage, her vision, and the principles that have always animated her life. Her utterly selfless devotion to my parents these past years has been indescribable; our children, who have always had in her the model of an extraordinary mother, have now been afforded an opportunity to learn from her what true devotion to parents can also be.

Our children—Talia and Avishay, Avi and Micha—are all now older than Elisheva and I were when we had our first chat at the pool at Camp Ramah one quiet Friday afternoon thirty-something years ago. I cannot imagine how radically different my life would have been had she not told me, in no uncertain terms, that she did not care that the pool was closed, and that she was coming in to sit quietly and to read. For having opened the gate that day, I have been rewarded with a friend unlike any I could ever have imagined and with love, infinitely deeper than I knew was possible, that has shaped literally everything.

The Talmud (Sotah 2a) is clearly right when it asserts that making matches is God's work. Whatever the future may hold, I've already been blessed far beyond merit.

Shavu'ot 5773
May 2013
Jerusalem

NOTES

Abbreviations Used

MBC Menachem Begin Heritage Center, Jerusalem

MFA Israel Ministry of Foreign Affairs digital archives, www.mfa.org.il

IZL *Ha-Irgun Ha-Tzav'i Ha-Le'umi B'Eretz Israel: Ossef Mekorot Umismakhim, Vol. 3 and Vol. 4, Jan. 1944–Dec. 1946.* [Heb.] Ed. Yitzhak Alfassi (Tel Aviv: Jabotinsky Institute, 1994).

Introduction

1. Barak Ravid, "Punitive Measures Hurt Israel as Much as the Palestinians," *Haaretz*, December 3, 2012. http://www.haaretz.com/blogs/diplomania/punitive-measures-hurt-israel-as-much-as-the-palestinians.premium-1.481969.

2. Anita Shapira, *Israel: A History*, p. 249.

1. Between the Kaiser and the Czar

1. Seth Lipsky, "The Peacemaker," *Jewish Ideas Daily*, November 26, 2012. http://www.jewishideasdaily.com/5424/features/the-peacemaker.

2. Ned Temko, *To Win or to Die: A Personal Portrait of Menachem Begin* (New York: William Morrow, 1987), p. 19.

3. Eric Silver, *Begin: The Haunted Prophet* (New York: Random House, 1984), p. 5.

4. Menachem Begin, "Horay" [Heb.], MBC digital archives. http://db.begincenter.org.il/he-il.

5. Eric Lohr, "The Russian Army and the Jews: Mass Deportation, Hostages, and Violence During World War I," *Russian Review* 60, no. 3 (July 2001), pp. 404–5.

6. M. Kaplan, "The Jews of Brest in the 19th Century," trans. Dr. Samuel Chani and Jenni Buch. In *Brisk de-Lita: Encyclopedia Shel haGaluyot (Vol. II)*, ed. E. Steinman (Jerusalem: 1958), pp. 93–102. http://www.jewishgen.org/yizkor/brest2/Brest2.html#TOC353.

7. Avi Shilon, *Menachem Begin: A Life*, trans. Danielle Zilberberg and Yoram Sharett (New Haven, Conn.: Yale University Press, 2012), p. 3.

8. Silver, *Begin*, p. 2.

9. Shilon, *Menachem Begin*, p. 7.

10. Menachem Begin, "Horay" [Heb.], MBC digital archives. http://db.begincenter .org.il/he-il.

11. Temko, *To Win or to Die*, p. 31.

12. Ofer Grosbard, *Menachem Begin: The Absent Leader* (Glilot, Israel: Strategic Research and Policy Center, National Defense College, IDF, 2007), p. 33.

13. Mordechai Zalkin, "Brest," trans. I. Michael Aronson. In *Yivo Encyclopedia of Jews in Eastern Europe*, http://www.yivoencyclopedia.org/article.aspx/Brest#author; and Kaplan, "The Jews of Brest," pp. 93–102.

14. Shilon, *Menachem Begin*, pp. 21, 33.

15. Menachem Begin, "Three Things," trans. Dr. Samuel Chani and Jenni Buch. In *Brisk de-Lita: Encyclopedia Shel haGaluyot (Vol. II)*, ed. E. Steinman (Jerusalem: 1958), pp. 291–98.

16. Silver, *Begin*, p. 3.

17. Begin, "Three Things," pp. 291–98.

18. Silver, *Begin*, p. 3.

19. Temko, *To Win or to Die*, p. 29.

20. Silver, *Begin*, p. 6.

21. Rachel Halperin, "Re'ayon Radio Im Rachel Halperin" [Heb.], transcr. Shoshana Margalin. Interview no. 1718, MBC, p. 5.

22. Ibid.

23. Temko, *To Win or to Die*, p. 32, and Shilon, *Menachem Begin*, p. 12.

24. Temko, *To Win or to Die*, p. 32.

25. Ibid., p. 318.

26. Menachem Begin, *The Revolt*, trans. Samuel Katz, 1951 (1951; repr. Bnei Brak, Israel: Steimatzky, 2007), p. 3.

27. Temko, *To Win or to Die*, p. 23.

28. Silver, *Begin*, p. 2.

29. Temko, *To Win or to Die*, pp. 23–24.

30. Ibid., p. 28.

2. A Pit of Decay and Dust

1. Shmuel Katz, *Lone Wolf: A Biography of Vladimir (Ze'ev) Jabotinsky*. 2 vols. (New York: Barricade Books, 1996), p. 21.

2. Ibid., p. 145.

3. Ibid., p. 626.

4. Ibid., p. 920.

5. Ibid., p. 561. The words were repeated by a doctor at his bedside, but their validity remains in doubt.

6. Vladimir (Ze'ev) Jabotinsky, "Ideology," *World Betar Movement*. http://Betar .org.il/en/content/view/10/6/.

7. Ibid.

8. Ibid.

9. Menachem Begin, *White Nights*, trans. Katie Kaplan (1957; repr. Bnei Brak, Israel: Steimatzky, 2008), p. 51.

10. Temko, *To Win or to Die*, p. 37.

11. Ibid., p. 35.

12. Ibid., p. 36.

13. Ibid., pp. 34–37.

14. Katz, *Lone Wolf*, pp. 149, 162, 334.

15. Ibid., pp. 966–87.

16. Shilon, *Menachem Begin*, p. 332.

17. Katz, *Lone Wolf*, p. 1425.

18. Ibid., pp. 1420–27.

19. Shilon, *Menachem Begin*, pp. 38–45.

20. Ibid., pp. 13–16.

21. Temko, *To Win or to Die*, pp. 16, 34.

22. Shilon, *Menachem Begin*, p. 17.

23. Dan Meridor, interview with the author, January 2, 2013.

24. Shilon, *Menachem Begin*, p. 11.

25. Ibid., p. 15.

26. Grosbard, *Menachem Begin: The Absent Leader*, p. 50.

27. Nachum Hyman, ed., *Ba-Or U-Va-Seter: Mishirei Ha-Oz Ve-Ha-Meri* (Israel: Foundation for the Heritage of Hebrew Song, 2010), p. 44.

28. Eran Kaplan, "A Rebel with a Cause: Hillel Kook, Begin, and Jabotinsky's Ideological Legacy," *Legal Studies* 10, no. 3 (Fall 2005), pp. 87–103.

29. Temko, *To Win or to Die*, p. 47.

30. Betar oath. Courtesy of the Jabotinsky Archives.

31. Yehuda Avner, interview with the author, October 24, 2012.

32. Begin, *White Nights*, p. 125.

33. Temko, *To Win or to Die*, p. 53.

3. This Year We Are Slaves

1. Emanuel Melzer, "Betar," trans. David Fachler. In *The Yivo Encyclopedia of Jews in Eastern Europe*. http://www.yivoencyclopedia.org/article.aspx/Betar.

2. Temko, *To Win or to Die*, p. 55.

3. Ibid., p. 57.

4. Ibid., pp. 57–58.

5. Katz, *Lone Wolf*, pp. 1775–76.

6. Begin, *White Nights*, p. 28.

7. Temko, *To Win or to Die*, p. 58.

8. Begin says he took with him a Bible and a biography of Disraeli, but the archives maintain that he had the biography and a German-English dictionary (Begin, *White Nights*, pp. 15, 32).

9. Ibid., p. 53.

10. Ecclesiastes 3:19 and Begin, *White Nights*, p. 65.

11. Begin, *The Revolt*, pp. 2–3.

12. Begin, *White Nights*, p. 94.

13. Ibid., pp. 92–113, and Begin, *The Revolt*, pp. 4–5.

14. Begin, *White Nights*, p. 102.

15. The story about Garin appears also in Begin, *The Revolt*, pp. 16–22.

16. Begin, *White Nights*, p. 223.

17. Ibid., p. 138.

18. Ibid., pp. 65, 186.

19. Ibid., pp. 255–57.

20. That line is not included in the current version of "Hatikvah."

21. Begin, *White Nights*, p. 260.

22. Similarly to his discussion of Kroll, *The Revolt* questions whether Garin has died (Begin, *The Revolt*, p. 25). In *White Nights*, however, Begin leads the reader to believe that the man will die in prison shortly (Begin, *White Nights*, p. 261).

23. Begin, *White Nights*, p. 185.

24. Begin does not give an end date for his time at the labor camp, but it can be estimated to September 1941 (Temko, *To Win or to Die*, p. 64).

25. Begin, *White Nights*, p. 278.

26. Begin, *The Revolt*, p. 24.

27. Ibid., p. 25.

28. Temko, *To Win or to Die*, p. 65.

4. We Fight Therefore We Are

1. There is some disagreement as to when Begin arrived in Palestine. In *The Revolt* he claims he arrived in May, but some evidence shows a mid-April arrival. See Begin, *The Revolt*, p. 65, and Yisrael Medad, "Matei Hegi'a Menachem Begin Artzah?" [Heb.], *Begin Center Diary*. March 7, 2012. http://begincenterhebrew.blogspot.co.il/2012/03/blog-post_07.html.

2. Original document, MBC.

3. Survivors say that Begin's father and brother were drowned in the River Bug in July 1941, although Menachem's sister, Rachel, heard a different account of their deaths, in which Ze'ev Dov was shot by a Nazi soldier. According to records from the Brisk ghetto, Begin's mother was issued a departure visa in December 1941. Begin himself heard from survivors that she was killed by Nazis in a hospital when she had pneumonia; presumably this happened after December 1941 but before the end of 1942, when the entire Jewish population of Brisk had been destroyed. In contrast, Avi Shilon lists her death conclusively as August 1941. See "Zev Dov Begin" and Pesach Novick, "In My Hometown of Brest," trans. Dr. Samuel Chani and Jenni Buch, in *Brisk Edicion Aniversario* (Buenos Aires: La Sociedad de Brest y alredeores, 1953), http://www.jewishgen.org/yizkor/brest/Brest.html#TOC; the Brest Ghetto Passport Archive, available through the United States Holocaust Memorial Museum, http://resources.ushmm.org/hsv/person_view.php?PersonId=4089131; Temko, *To Win or to Die*, p. 336; and Shilon, *Menachem Begin*, p. 5.

4. A reference to the *kinnot*, the Jewish mourning poetry, recited on occasions of religious and national mourning, most notably on the ninth of Av.

5. Menachem Begin, "Horay" [Heb.], MBC digital archives. http://db.begincenter .org.il/he-il.

6. Yehuda Bauer, "From Cooperation to Resistance: The Haganah 1938–1945," *Middle Eastern Studies* 2, no. 3 (April 1966), pp. 182–210.

7. Katz, *Lone Wolf*, pp. 1543–47.

8. Shlomo Nakdimon, "Menachem Begin—Essrim v-Echad Chodashim shel Hamtana So'eret," *Hamordim—Ma'avak Etzel ba-Britim 1944–1948: Diyun Mechudash* [Heb.], ed. Yaakov Markovitzy (Jerusalem: Menachem Begin Heritage Center, 2008), p. 132.

9. Ibid., pp. 127–38.

10. "Report of the Palestine Royal Commission," *Jewish Virtual Library*, http://www.jewishvirtuallibrary.org/jsource/History/peel1.html.

11. "British White Papers of 1939," *The Avalon Project: Documents in Law, History and Diplomacy*, http://avalon.law.yale.edu/20th_century/brwh1939.asp.

12. Anita Shapira, *Israel: A History*, trans. Anthony Berris (Waltham, Mass.: Brandeis University Press, 2012), p. 88.

13. Joseph Heller, *The Stern Gang: Ideology, Politics, and Terror, 1940–1949* (London: Frank Cass, 1995).

14. Yechiel Kadishai, interview with the author, April 18, 2013.

15. Hagai Segal, "Yad Yemino," *Makor Rishon*, October 5, 2012.

16. Nakdimon, "Menachem Begin," p. 128.

17. Begin did not return to the Polish Army because he claimed that by the time the year had elapsed, he was deeply involved in the Zionist struggle against the British Empire and had become a citizen of the "State of Israel" (eighteen months before it was established), and had therefore ceased to be a citizen of the Polish Republic. Ibid., p. 134.

18. Shilon, *Menachem Begin*, p. 51.

19. Begin was alluding to God's rebuke of Cain after his murder of Abel in Genesis 4:10—"the voice of the blood of your brother is crying out to me from the earth!" Begin, *The Revolt*, p. 40.

20. Ibid., p. 41.

21. Ibid., pp. 122–31.

22. A fascinating account of the murder and the trial can be found in Gerold Frank, "The Moyne Case: A Tragic History," *Commentary* 1, issue 2 (December 1945): pp. 64–71.

23. Michael J. Cohen, "The British White Paper on Palestine, May 1939, Part II: The Testing of a Policy, 1942–1945," *The Historical Journal* 19, no. 3 (September 1976): pp. 729–32.

24. Edward Kern, "Storm Centers on the New Map: Israel," *Life*, October 20, 1967.

25. David Ben-Gurion and Moshe Shertok, "To Expel the Instigators of the Terrorist Crimes," *Davar*, November 9, 1944.

26. The Etzel leadership was angry for two reasons: The Lechi had gone behind the Etzel's back and had planned the assassination without notifying the Etzel of the plan, despite the agreement between the Etzel and the Lechi to work together. In addi-

Notes

tion, the Etzel felt that the political assassination had turned the public sentiment of the *yishuv* against the Etzel, since the *yishuv* associated it with the Lechi. Shlomo Lev Ami, a member of the Irgun command under the pseudonym of "Danny," contended: "The weak party needs to always be in the right and only thus can he overcome all the difficulties, but they [the Lechi] now place themselves on the defensive from a moral standpoint, which pulls the ground out from under us in our struggle." *IZL*, pp. 139–42.

27. Shilon, *Menachem Begin*, pp. 69–79.

28. Ibid., pp. 69–79.

29. Begin, *The Revolt*, pp. 149, 152.

30. William R. Louis, *The British Empire in the Middle East: 1945–1951* (New York: Oxford University Press, 1984), p. 394.

31. "Tnu'at HaMeri HaIvri" [Heb.], *Ynet Encyclopedia*. http://www.ynet.co.il/yaan /0,7340,L-20078-MjIwNzhfOTUwMDA3NjZfMTQ4Njg3MjAw-FreeYaan,00 .html.

32. "LeilHaGesharim"[Heb.],*YnetEncyclopedia*.http://www.ynet.co.il/yaan/0,7340,L -15063-MTUwNjNfMTMoNjUzNTY2XzEoODY4NzIwMAeqeq-FreeYaan,00.html.

33. Ibid.

34. Yaakov Marcovitzky, *Hamefaked: Menachem Begin Ke-Manhig shel Irgun Gerilla Ironit* [Heb.] (Jerusalem: Carmel, 2012), p. 159.

35. Yehuda Lapidot, "Black Sabbath," trans. Chaya Galai. Etzel website, http:// www.etzel.org.il/english/ac09.htm.

36. Yehuda Avner, interview with the author, October 24, 2012.

37. *IZL*, p. 260.

38. Yehuda Lapidot, "The King David Hotel" [Heb.], *Da'at*, http://www.daat .ac.il/encyclopedia/value.asp?id1=1709.

39. Shilon, *Menachem Begin*, p. 90.

40. Thurston Clarke, *By Blood and Fire: The Attack on the King David Hotel* (London: Hutchinson, 1981), p. 40.

41. Ibid., p. 86.

42. Ibid., p. 84.

43. Ibid., pp. 86–87, 105.

44. Temko, *To Win or to Die*, pp. 90–91.

45. Clarke, *By Blood and Fire*, p. 93.

46. Ibid., pp. 106, 204.

47. Ibid., pp. 116–35.

48. Ibid., pp. 134–50.

49. Ibid., p. 158.

50. Marcovitzky, *Hamefaked*, pp. 160–61.

51. Temko, *To Win or to Die*, pp. 91–92.

52. Clarke, *By Blood and Fire*, p. 160.

53. "2 Admit '46 Bombing of Hotel in Jerusalem," *The Washington Post*, February 9, 1972.

54. Clarke, *By Blood and Fire*, pp. 160–61.

55. Ibid., p. 180.

56. Ibid., pp. 215, 236.

57. Ibid., pp. 230–52.

58. Shilon, *Menachem Begin*, p. 92.

59. Clarke, *By Blood and Fire*, p. 277.

60. *IZL*, 253.

61. Alex Small, "Bomb Kills High Britons: Round up Jews After Attack in Palestine: Zionists Disavow Terrorist Acts," *Chicago Tribune*, July 23, 1946.

62. Begin, *The Revolt*, pp. 59–60.

5. A Brutal Act

1. Joseph Levy, "Palestine Tense on Hanging Today," *The New York Times*, June 29, 1938.

2. John Bowyer Bell, *Terror out of Zion: The Fight for Israeli Independence* (1977; repr. New Brunswick, N.J.: Transaction, 2009), p. 40.

3. Ibid., p. 40.

4. Ibid., p. 41.

5. Tom Segev, *One Palestine, Complete: Jews and Arabs Under the Mandate*, trans. Haim Watzman (New York: Henry Holt, 2000), p. 385.

6. "2 Palestine Jews to Die: British Court Dooms Them in Raid on Army Camp," *The New York Times*, June 14, 1946.

7. Begin, *The Revolt*, p. 245.

8. Ibid., p. 249.

9. Peleg Levi, interview with the author, September 4, 2012.

10. Clay Gowran, "Terrorists Flog 4 British Soldiers in Palestine," *Chicago Daily Tribune*, December 30, 1946.

11. See Jewish Telegraphic Agency, "Commissioner Stops Flogging Practice," *The Jewish Advocate*, July 26, 1928, and David Killingray, "The 'Rod of Empire': The Debate over Corporal Punishment in the British African Colonial Forces, 1888–1946," *Journal of African Studies* 35, no. 2 (July 1994): pp. 201–16.

12. Peleg Levi, interview with the author, September 4, 2012.

13. *IZL*, 274.

14. "Irgun Reprisal Due in Order for Whipping," *The Washington Post*, December 24, 1946.

15. Peleg Levi, interview with the author, September 4, 2012.

16. "The Flogging of British Soldiers in Palestine: Colonial Secretary's Statement," *The Manchester Guardian*, January 23, 1947, and Gowran, "Terrorists Flog 4 British Soldiers in Palestine."

17. "Gruner, Three More Hanged in Palestine," *Chicago Daily Tribune*, April 16, 1947.

18. *IZL*, 276.

19. Exodus 2:11.

20. House of Commons, "Debate Jan. 31 1947," British Parliament online archives, http://hansard.millbanksystems.com/commons/1947/jan/31/palestine-jewish -terrorism#S5CV0432P0_19470131_HOC_156.

21. Begin, *The Revolt*, p. 236.

22. Jon Kimche, "Agency Condemns Flogging," *The Palestine Post*, December 31, 1946.

23. Gowran, "Terrorists Flog 4 British Soldiers in Palestine."

24. "Synagogue Blaze Linked to Flogging," *The Christian Science Monitor*, January 4, 1947.

25. "Vicious Spiral," *The Palestine Post*, December 31, 1946.

26. Shaul Zadka, "Jewish Armed Struggle in Palestine in the 1940s: Its Impact on British Morale and Public Opinion," *Israel Affairs* 5, no. 4 (1999), pp. 181–97.

27. "Fraternization Is Banned," *The New York Times*, January 4, 1947.

28. Dare Wilson, *With 6th Airborne Division in Palestine, 1945–48* (Yorkshire, U.K.: Pen & Sword Military, 2008), p. 102.

29. Bowyer Bell, *Terror out of Zion*, pp. 176–77.

30. Clay Gowran, "Jew Sentenced to Hang; Joined Raid on Police," *Chicago Daily Tribune*, January 2, 1947.

31. Two appeals were made, both of which were inadequate and therefore not even considered. In British law, only the convicted individual could request an appeal, and since Gruner did not recognize the legitimacy of the court that was judging him, he refused to make such an appeal. One appeal was made on his behalf by the mayor of Tel Aviv, which was summarily rejected because it did not have Gruner's signature, and another appeal was made by Gruner's American uncle that was rejected for the same reasons. Then a lawyer convinced Gruner that the entire Etzel was urging him to appeal the decision, so Gruner signed an appeal, but when he learned that in fact the Etzel supported whatever decision he chose to make, Gruner immediately revoked his signature and the signed appeal did not reach any court. The British therefore did not need to take time to examine the pleas, since they had no legal basis on which to stand (Clifton Daniels, "Gruner Plea Lost by Tel Aviv Mayor," *The New York Times*, April 8, 1947, and Bowyer Bell, *Terror out of Zion*, p. 205).

32. Begin, *The Revolt*, p. 263.

33. Peleg Levi suggested that the men were hanged on a day of the week that was against Mandatory protocol for scheduled hangings (Peleg Levi, interview with the author, September 4, 2012).

34. Begin, *The Revolt*, p. 268.

35. Ibid., pp. 263–64.

36. Ibid., p. 275.

37. "Death Sentences in Palestine," *The Manchester Guardian*, April 18, 1947.

38. Begin, *The Revolt*, p. 273.

39. Some sources say it was two oranges—see Yair Sheleg, "The Good Jailer," *Haaretz*, April 7, 2007. http://www.haaretz.com/weekend/magazine/the-good-jailer-1.217549.

40. Ibid.

41. Marcovitzky, *Hamefaked*, p. 188.

42. Bowyer Bell, *Terror out of Zion*, p. 228.

43. Yehuda Lapidot, "The Acre Prison Break-In," *Da'at*, http://daat.ac.il/encyclopedia/value.asp?id1=1719.

44. Begin, *The Revolt*, p. 286.

45. Lapidot, "The Acre Prison Break-In."

46. Begin, *The Revolt*, pp. 286–88.

47. Ibid., pp. 284–88.

48. Peleg Levi, interview with the author, September 4, 2012.

49. M. Braverman, "Readers' Letters," *The Palestine Post*, July 25, 1947.

50. Begin, *The Revolt*, p. 288.

51. Peleg Levi, interview with the author, September 4, 2012.

52. "Nathanya Siege Lifted," *The Palestine Post*, July 28, 1947.

53. Bowyer Bell, *Terror out of Zion*, p. 243.

54. Linda Grant, "The Real Exodus," *The Guardian*, June 30, 2007, http://www .guardian.co.uk/world/2007/jun/30/israelandthepalestinians.lindagrant.

55. Golda Meir, *My Life* (New York: Dell, 1975), pp. 198–99.

56. House of Commons, "Debate Jan. 31 1947," British Parliament online archives.

57. Marcovitzky, *Hamefaked*, p. 190.

58. "Pleas for 2 Sergeants," *The Palestine Post*, July 30, 1947.

59. Ofer Aderet, "The 'Cruel Revenge' That Helped Drive the British out of Palestine," *Haaretz*, August 7, 2012, http://www.haaretz.com/news/features/the-cruel -revenge-that-helped-drive-the-british-out-of-palestine-1.456440.

60. Marcovitzky, *Hamefaked*, p. 191. Some say that one of the sergeants, who had been kept in those unsanitary conditions for over a fortnight, had in fact already died due to the horrible conditions of the bunker in which they were kept. Even if that were true, Begin may not have known it (Peleg Levi, interview with the author, September 4, 2012).

61. Bowyer Bell, *Terror out of Zion*, p. 253.

62. House of Commons, "Debate Jan. 31 1947," British Parliament online archives.

63. Shai Lavi, "The Sanctity of Death: History of the Death Penalty in Israel," *Law and Society*, Chicago. Oral Presentation, Summer 2004. *Politics Forum*, http://www .politicsforum.org/forum/viewtopic.php?f=65&t=58760.

64. Ian Colquhoun, *Over the Hills and Far Away: The Ordinary Soldier* (Bloomington, Ind.: iUniverse, 2008), p. 74.

65. "British Ignore Irgun's Threat, Plan to Execute Trio Today," *The Washington Post*, July 29, 1947.

66. Marcovitzky, *Hamefaked*, p. 178

67. Nick Kardahji, "A Measure of Restraint: The Palestine Police and the End of the British Mandate," MPhil thesis presented May 4, 2007, pp. 32–33, http://users.ox.ac .uk/~metheses/KardahjiThesis.pdf.

68. House of Lords, "Debate Aug. 05 1947," British Parliament online archives, http://hansard.millbanksystems.com/Lords/1947/aug/05/palestine.

69. Kardahji, "A Measure of Restraint," pp. 32–33.

70. Shilon, *Menachem Begin*, p. 444.

6. Deadly Road to Jerusalem

1. "Official Summary of UNSCOP Report: Between Dan and Beersheba," *The Palestine Post*, September 2, 1947.

2. Bowyer Bell, *Terror out of Zion*, p. 258.

Notes

3. Benny Morris, *1948: The First Arab-Israeli War* (New Haven, Conn.: Yale University Press, 2008), p. 65.

4. Ibid., p. 76.

5. *IZL*, p. 155.

6. Morris, *1948*, p. 85.

7. Ibid., pp. 77–78.

8. Ibid., pp. 111–12.

9. Ibid., p. 114.

10. Ibid., p. 121.

11. Ibid., p. 125.

12. Temko, *To Win or to Die*, p. 367.

13. Shilon, *Menachem Begin*, p. 107.

14. Temko, *To Win or to Die*, p. 112.

15. Yehuda Avner, *The Prime Ministers* (Jerusalem: Toby Press, 2010), pp. 93–94.

16. Morris, *1948*, p. 127; Shilon, *Menachem Begin*, p. 108; and Benny Morris, "The Historiography of Deir Yassin," *Journal of Israeli History: Politics, Society, Culture* 24, issue 1 (August 2006), p. 87. But even Martin Gilbert, in his authoritative history of Israel published in 1998, notes that 245 Arabs, "many of them women and children," were killed (Martin Gilbert, *Israel: A History* [New York: William Morrow, 1998], p. 169).

17. Morris, "The Historiography of Deir Yassin," p. 96.

18. Morris, *1948*, p. 128.

19. Ibid., p. 128.

20. Ruth Gruber, interview with the author, January 14, 2013, based on her own interview with Menachem Begin shortly after he emerged from hiding.

7. A Civil War with the Enemy at Our Gates

1. Begin, *The Revolt*, pp. 166–67.

2. Shilon, *Menachem Begin*, p. 119.

3. Ibid.

4. Silver, *Begin: The Haunted Prophet* (New York: Random House, 1984), p. 99.

5. *Altalena*, dir. by Ilana Tsur (Argo Films and Keshet Broadcasting, 53 minutes, 1994).

6. Silver, *Begin*, p. 100.

7. Ibid., p. 101.

8. Jerold S. Auerbach, *Brothers at War: Israel and the Tragedy of the* Altalena (New Orleans: Quid Pro Books, 2011), p. 43.

9. Ibid., p. 50.

10. Nathan Gutman, interview with the author, July 2012, and personal memoir entitled "*Altalena* Untold," written July 2001.

11. *Altalena*, dir. by Ilana Tsur.

12. Silver, *Begin*, p. 101.

13. Nathan Gutman, interview with the author, July 2012, and "*Altalena* Untold."

14. Yehuda Lapidot, "The *Altalena* Affair," trans. Chaya Galai, Etzel website, http://www.etzel.org.il/english/ac20.htm.

15. Shilon, *Menachem Begin*, p. 123.

16. Temko, *To Win or to Die*, p. 118.

17. Ibid.

18. Ibid.

19. Ibid.

20. Silver, *Begin*, p. 103.

21. Lapidot, "The *Altalena* Affair."

22. Martin Gilbert, *Israel: A History* (New York: William Morrow, 1998), p. 211.

23. Zvi Harry Hurwitz, *Begin: His Life, Words, and Deeds* (Jerusalem: Gefen Publishing, 2004), p. 27.

24. Temko, *To Win or to Die*, pp. 119, 120.

25. Ibid., p. 120.

26. Silver, *Begin*, p. 99.

27. Ibid., p. 105

28. *Altalena*, dir. by Ilana Tsur.

29. Silver, *Begin*, p. 105.

30. *Altalena*, dir. by Ilana Tsur.

31. Temko, *To Win or to Die*, p. 121.

32. Arthur Koestler, *Promise and Fulfillment: Palestine 1917–1949* (New York: Macmillan, 1949), p. 249.

33. Begin, *The Revolt*, p. 172.

34. *Altalena*, dir. by Ilana Tsur.

35. Silver, *Begin*, p. 106.

36. Temko, *To Win or to Die*, p. 121.

37. Auerbach, *Brothers at War*, p. 70.

38. Shilon, *Menachem Begin*, p. 127.

39. Ibid., p. 127.

40. Begin, *The Revolt*, p. 175.

41. Silver, *Begin*, p. 107.

42. *Altalena*, dir. by Ilana Tsur.

43. Auerbach, *Brothers at War*, p. 67.

44. Uri Dromi, "Hillel Daleski, Israel Prize Recipient for Literature, Dies at 84," *Haaretz*, December 24, 2010, http://www.haaretz.com/weekend/anglo-file/hillel-daleski-israel-prize-recipient-for-literature-dies-at-84-1.332633.

45. *Altalena*, dir. by Ilana Tsur.

46. Shilon, *Menachem Begin*, p. 128.

47. Begin, *The Revolt*, p. 176.

48. Silver, *Begin*, p. 107; Lapidot, "The *Altalena* Affair"; and *Altalena*, dir. by Ilana Tsur.

49. Martin Gilbert and Arthur Koestler think that forty people died in total (Gilbert, *Israel*, p. 212; Koestler, *Promise and Fulfillment*, p. 249).

50. Koestler, *Promise and Fulfillment*, p. 265. The Etzel website, on the other hand, estimates the number of Irgun fighters arrested to be two hundred (Lapidot, "The *Altalena* Affair").

51. Auerbach, *Brothers at War*, p. 64.

52. *Altalena*, dir. by Ilana Tsur.

53. Shilon, *Menachem Begin*, p. 128.

54. "Pamphlet from June 22, 1948," *MBC*, p. 14.

55. Temko, *To Win or to Die*, p. 123.

56. "Commands from June 23–24, 1948," courtesy of Jabotinsky Archives.

57. Lapidot, "The *Altalena* Affair."

58. Before Begin was elected prime minister, many English-speaking newspapers spelled his name in a variety of ways, including "Beigin" and "Biegin." Koestler used "Biegin," which I have changed for consistency throughout this book.

59. *"Altalena* Incident," Sitting Five of the Provisional Council, June 23, 1948. *Major Knesset Debates 1948–1981*, ed. Netanel Lorch (Jerusalem: Jerusalem Center for Public Affairs, 2011), http://jcpa.org/wp-content/uploads/2011/09/Altalena.pdf.

60. Shilon, *Menachem Begin*, p. 130.

61. Begin, *The Revolt*, p. 169.

62. Ibid., p. 170.

63. Auerbach, *Brothers at War*, p. 106.

64. *Altalena*, dir. by Ilana Tsur.

65. "Israel Cracks Down on Rebel Elements," *The Washington Post*, June 24, 1948.

66. Joseph J. Ellis, *Founding Brothers* (New York: Alfred A. Knopf, 2000), pp. 39–40.

67. Auerbach, *Brothers at War*, p. 109.

8. Say "No" to Forgiveness

1. "The State of Israel," MFA.

2. Shilon, *Menachem Begin*, p. 161.

3. Naama Barzel, "Dignity, Hatred and Memory—Reparations from Germany: The Debates in the 1950s," *Yad Vashem Studies* 24 (1994), p. 249.

4. M. Rosensaft and J. Rosensaft, "The Early History of German-Jewish Reparations," *Fordham International Law Journal* 25, no. 6 (2001), p. S-7.

5. Ibid., p. S-12.

6. George Lavy, *Germany and Israel: Moral Debt and National Interest* (London: Frank Cass, 1996), p. 6.

7. Rosensaft and Rosensaft, "The Early History of German-Jewish Reparations," p. S-21.

8. Barzel, "Dignity, Hatred and Memory," p. 252.

9. Lavy, *Germany and Israel*, p. 7.

10. *Herut*, December 14, 1951. It is possible that the fury was expressed in more than words. In March 1952, five members of the former Etzel would be blamed for an assassination attempt on Konrad Adenauer, the German chancellor. In a book published in 2006, a former Irgun member implicated Begin in this assassination attempt, insisting that the future prime minister approved the plan and contributed his own money to it, though it is very difficult to know how much stock to put in this very belated claim. The German newspaper *Frankfurter Allgemeine Zeitung* ran an article dramatically and overemphatically entitled "Begin war Drahtzieher des Anschlags auf Adenauer" ("Begin Was Perpetrator of the Attack on Adenauer"), June 12, 2006. See

also Luke Harding's article with an appropriate use of quotation marks, "Menachem Begin 'Plotted to Kill German Chancellor,'" *The Guardian*, June 15, 2006.

11. Shilon, *Menachem Begin*, p. 168.

12. Ibid.

13. Ibid., pp. 168–69.

14. The end of the book of Judges recounts an incident, the concubine on the hill, which led to civil war in ancient Israel. In response to a woman being gang-raped and killed, and the sense that an unprecedented abomination had occurred ("there never was nor was there seen the likes of this since the days of the Israelites' exodus from Egypt until this day" [Judges 19:30]), civil war erupted between the tribe of Benjamin and the rest of the tribes.

15. Menachem Begin, "Devarim Ba-Atzeret Ha-Hamonim Neged Eskem Hashilumim in Germanya," in *Ne'um Lekol Et* [Heb.], ed. Tamar Brosh (Ra'anana, Israel: Yediyot Sefarim, 1993), http://lib.cet.ac.il/pages/item.asp?item=7188.

16. Moshe Sharett, *Pulmus haShilumim: Moshe Sharett beMa'arakhot haMassa veMatan al haShilumim miGermanya* [Heb.], ed. Ya'akov Sharett (Tel Aviv: Ha'amuta LeMoreshet Moshe Sharett, 2007), pp. 323–28.

17. Yonan Roychman, "Hayom shBo Nichbesha haKnesset," September 28, 2006, http://www.ynet.co.il/articles/0,7340,L-3306796,00.html.

18. Sharett, *Pulmus haShilumim*, p. 327.

19. Ibid., p. 328 n. 14.

20. Ibid., pp. 329–32. Small emendations in translation were required for clarity.

21. Hayyim Nahman Bialik, "The City of Slaughter," in *Complete Poetic Works of Hayyim Nahman Bialik*, ed. Israel Efros (New York: The Histadruth Ivrith of America, 1948), vol. 1, pp. 129–43.

22. Bialik. According to Jewish law, Kohanim, men of the priestly class, are not permitted to have sexual relations with their wives if their wives have had sex with anyone else. Bialik's suggestion that these men were more concerned about the question of their wives' permissibility to them than they were about caring for those women was among his most pointed accusations. In large measure, Ben-Gurion shared that disdain for the religious world of Jewish Europe. Begin still revered it.

23. Katz, *Lone Wolf*, p. 111.

24. Wolf Moskovich, "Kishinev," *The Yivo Encyclopedia of Jews in Eastern Europe*, http://www.yivoencyclopedia.org/article.aspx/Kishinev.

25. Shilon, *Menachem Begin*, p. 173.

26. "The State of Israel," MFA.

9. Of Whom Were We Afraid?

1. Mordechai Kremnitzier and Amir Fuchs, "Menachem Begin on Democracy and Constitutional Values" (Jerusalem: Israel Democracy Institute, 2012), pp. 9–10.

2. Ibid., p. 5.

3. Ibid., p. 9.

4. Shilon, *Menachem Begin*, p. 152.

Notes

5. David Anderson, "Soblen Convicted as Spy for Russia: Death Penalty Unlikely for Doctor, Ill with Leukemia," *The New York Times*, July 14, 1961.

6. "Psychiatrist Arrested as Spy for Russians; Brother in Jail," *The Hartford Courant*, November 30, 1960.

7. Lawrence Fellows, "Soblen Flees to Israel and Is Arrested; U.S. Asks Return, Seizes $100,000 Bail," *The New York Times*, June 29, 1962.

8. "Soblen Tries to Kill Self! Spy Cuts Wrist and Abdomen on Flight to U.S.," *Chicago Tribune*, July 2, 1962.

9. "Israel to Investigate Expulsion of Soblen," *The New York Times*, July 23, 1962.

10. Menachem Begin, "Lo BeTachbulot Ta'ase Mishpat" [Heb.], *Herut*, July 13, 1962.

11. Ibid.

12. Psalm 24:4–5: "He who has clean hands and a pure heart, who has not taken a false oath by my life or sworn deceitfully. He shall carry away a blessing from the Lord, a just reward from God, his deliverer."

13. Proverbs 24:6. Author's translation. The Hebrew word *takhbulot* translates as "trickery, deception, cunning."

14. Begin, "Lo BeTachbulot Ta'ase Mishpat."

15. Ibid. Italics added.

16. Beginning with a technical defense of the expulsion, Ben-Gurion claimed that "this state is founded on the supremacy of the law," and therefore "the courts do not have the authority to annul the authority of the state." Since Soblen had entered the country illegally, on a passport that was not his, the minister of the interior was fully within his rights to expel Soblen. Not to be one-upped by Begin's biblical allusion, Ben-Gurion also explained that "the concept of 'justice' [*mishpat*] has numerous definitions in the Hebrew Bible"—the implication being that whatever biblical basis might be found to support the supreme authority of *mishpat*, it did not necessarily mean the supremacy of the judiciary over the legislative branch. David Ben-Gurion, "Yisra'el Miklat leOlim veLo leNochlim," *Davar*, July 24, 1962.

17. Louis R. Rukeyser, "Airline Refuses to Fly Soblen to U.S.: El Al Defies British Directive on Israel Government Orders," *Baltimore Sun*, August 4, 1962.

10. The Style of a Good Jew

1. Shilon, *Menachem Begin*, p. 192.

2. "Remains of Jabotinsky to Be Exhumed Today for Reburial in Israel," Jewish Telegraphic Agency, July 3, 1964, http://archive.jta.org/article/1964/07/03/3077387 /remains-of-jabotinsky-to-be-exhumed-today-for-reburial-in-israel;and"HugeCrowds Participate in Jabotinsky Funeral," Jewish Telegraphic Agency, July 7, 1964, http:// archive.jta.org/article/1964/07/07/3077414/huge-crowds-participate-in-jabotinsky -funeral-procession-in-new-york.

3. Ben-Gurion is not mentioned in the accounts of dignitaries who were present. See "Impressive Ceremony Marks Jabotinsky's Reinterment in Jerusalem," Jewish Telegraphic Agency, July 10, 1964, http://archive.jta.org/article/1964/07/10/3077457 /impressive-ceremony-marks-jabotinskys-reinterment-in-jerusalem.

4. Aryeh Naor, *Begin in Power: A Personal Testimony* [Heb.] (Tel Aviv: Yediot Ahronoth Books, 1993), p. 102.

5. Shilon, *Menachem Begin*, pp. 110, 366.

6. Sandy Tolan, *The Lemon Tree: An Arab, a Jew, and the Heart of the Middle East* (New York: Bloomsbury, 2006), pp. 129, 329.

7. Anita Shapira, *Israel: A History*, 282–84.

8. Sheldon Lerman, interview with Gabriel Mitchell, December 30, 2012.

9. Michael Oren, *Six Days of War* (New York: Oxford University Press, 2002), p. 136.

10. Zvi Yehuda Kook, "Mizmor Yud Tet Le'Eretz Israel," in *Eretz Hatzvi*, ed. Zalman Baruch Melamed, http://www.yeshiva.org.il/midrash/shiur.asp?id=2282.

11. Michael Oren, *Power, Faith, and Fantasy* (New York: W. W. Norton, 2007), p. 525.

12. Naor, *Begin in Power*, p. 103.

13. Minutes from the cabinet meeting of June 6, 1967, Israel National Archives, made available by Yaacov Lozowick; translation by the author.

14. Temko, *To Win or to Die*, p. 185.

15. Avner, *The Prime Ministers*, p. 269.

16. Gil Troy, *Moynihan's Moment: America's Fight Against Zionism as Racism* (Oxford, U.K.: Oxford University Press, 2013), p. 35.

17. Gil Troy, "Happy Birthday, Mr. Kissinger," *Tablet Magazine*, May 23, 2013, http://www.tabletmag.com/jewish-news-and-politics/132819/happy-birthday-mr-kissinger#xCoSwz6BrWoH2hzI.99.

18. Shilon, *Menachem Begin*, p. 235.

19. Ibid., p. 187.

20. Gilbert, *Israel*, pp. 110, 475.

21. Mizrachi Jews, or *Benei Edot Hamizrach*, refers to any Jew from the "Eastern" communities: essentially any Jew in/from Muslim lands can be considered "Mizrachi." Sephardic Jews, on the other hand, technically refers only to Jews originally from Spain, many of whom were expelled in 1492 and settled in North Africa and the Ottoman Empire (joining the local Jews already there), although the terms are now often used interchangeably.

22. Begin, *The Revolt*, p. 78.

23. Shilon, *Menachem Begin*, p. 180.

24. Grosbard, *Menachem Begin: The Absent Leader*, pp. 152–53.

25. Ibid., p. 156.

26. Temko, *To Win or to Die*, p. 146.

27. Avner, *The Prime Ministers*, p. 391.

28. Ibid., p. 349.

29. Daniel Gordis and Rafael Medoff, "Ed Koch and the Jewish Underground," *Jerusalem Post*, February 7, 2013, http://www.jpost.com/Opinion/Columnists/Article.aspx?id=302470.

30. "Herut Ends Boycott of Israel Parliament at Beigin's Request," Jewish Telegraphic Agency, January 28, 1952, http://archive.jta.org/article/1952/01/28/3030339/herut-ends-boycott-of-israel-parliament-at-beigins-request.

31. Hart Hasten, interview with the author, January 27, 2013.

32. Letter from Dan Frenkel to Yisrael Medad, October 29, 2008. Blog of Betarim of North America, http://betarimna.blogspot.co.il/2008_10_01_archive.html.

33. Begin, *The Revolt*, p. 316. Though the quote is from Begin himself, other evidence corroborates his claim that Silver supported Revisionist Zionism and the Etzel, which was an unusual stance for an American Zionist and Reform rabbi. He allegedly remarked during the discussion over Begin's contested visit to America in 1948 that Begin was "one of the great heroes of Israel and the Irgun has written one of its most glorious chapters." Rafael Medoff, *Militant Zionist in America: The Rise and Fall of the Jabotinsky Movement in the United States 1926–1948* (Tuscaloosa: Alabama University Press, 2002), p. 213.

34. Eric Graus, interview with the author, March 6, 2013. See also Graus, "Letter to the Editor," *Jerusalem Post*, March 1, 2013.

35. Lenny Kohll, interview with the author, January 24, 2013.

36. Hertzel Katz, interview with the author, January 24, 2013.

37. "Dump Begin Movement in Likud," Jewish Telegraphic Agency, June 15, 1976, http://archive.jta.org/article/1976/06/15/2975755/dump-begin-movement-in-likud.

38. Shapira, *Israel*, p. 357.

39. Marcus Dysch, "Why 'Hook-Nosed' Begin Was Denied Entry to UK," *The Jewish Chronicle*, June 23, 2011, http://www.thejc.com/news/uk-news/50700/why-hook-nosed-begin-was-denied-entry-uk.

40. Shapira, *Israel*, p. 365.

41. "Kind . . . Honest . . . Dangerous," *Time*, May 30, 1977.

42. Avner, *The Prime Ministers*, p. 347.

43. Naor, *Begin in Power*, pp. 65–66.

44. Israeli Broadcasting Authority (IBA), May 30, 1977. The Hebrew can be translated, equally correctly, as either "in the style of a good Jew" or "in a good Jewish style."

11. Give Those People a Haven

1. Ian Black, "Israel Opens Doors: Boat People in Familiar Plight," *The Observer*, August 27, 1979, http://news.google.com/newspapers?id=RVU_AAAAIBAJ&sjid=mvIMAAAAIBAJ&pg=3554,4219774&dq=vietnamese+boat+people+israel&hl=en.

2. "Vietnamese Refugees Find New Home," *Observer-Reporter*, June 27, 1977, http://news.google.com/newspapers?nid=2519&dat=19770627&id=Y4JiAAAAIBAJ&sjid=hncNAAAAIBAJ&pg=2791,3775570.

3. Menucha Chana Levin, "Vietnamese Boat People in the Promised Land," *Aish*, November 24, 2011, http://www.aish.com/jw/id/Vietnamese_Boat_People_in_the_Promised_Land.html.

4. "Vietnamese Refugees Find New Home."

5. Levin, "Vietnamese Boat People."

6. "Speech by Jimmy Carter on White House Lawn, Washington, D.C., July 19, 1977," MFA.

7. "Speech by Menachem Begin on White House Lawn, Washington, D.C., July 19, 1977," MFA.

8. Hillel Hurwitz, interview with the author, January 24, 2013. I am also grateful to Dr. Rafael Medoff, an expert on this period, for bringing the incident to my attention.

9. Lenny Kohll, interview with the author, January 24, 2013. He recalled that Jabotinsky also refused to ride in a rickshaw when he visited South Africa; Rafael Medoff, "Jabotinsky's Anti-Racist Legacy," JNS.org, July 22, 2012, http://www.jns.org/latest -articles/2012/7/22/jabotinskys-anti-racist-legacy.html.

10. Gad Shimron, *Mossad Exodus: The Daring Undercover Rescue of the Lost Jewish Tribe* (Jerusalem: Gefen Publishing House, 2007), p. 12. There is no "proof" that Begin said those exact words, but they have come to represent his feelings at the time.

11. Their Scripture consisted of the Old Testament, plus many apocryphal books such as the book of Tobit, Jubilees, Enoch, Ben Sira, and Wisdom of Solomon. Their Bible, which appears in the classical Ethiopian language, Ge'ez, is apparently a translation from the Septuagint; it is likely that the Ethiopian Jews had never been exposed to Hebrew or Aramaic before the twentieth century.

12. "Falashas," *Encyclopedia Judaica* (Jerusalem: Keter Publishing House, 1996), p. 1153.

13. "Law of Return 5710-1950," MFA.

14. Howard M. Lenhoff and Jerry L. Weaver, *Black Jews, Jews, and Other Heroes: How Grassroots Activism Led to the Rescue of the Ethiopian Jews* (Jerusalem: Gefen Publishing House, 2007), pp. 42–43.

15. Shimron, p. 15.

16. "Background," Ethiopian National Project, www.enp.org.il.

17. Shimron, *Mossad Exodus*, p. 14.

18. Ibid., p. 21.

19. "Telecast to the Nation, May 1, 1979," MFA.

20. "Statement in the Knesset, January 8, 1985," MFA.

21. Zvi Harry Hurwitz, *Begin: His Life, Words and Deeds* (Jerusalem: Gefen Publishing House, 2004), p. 267.

22. Ibid., p. 266.

23. Gal Beckerman, *When They Come for Us, We'll Be Gone: The Epic Struggle to Save Soviet Jewry* (New York: Houghton Mifflin Harcourt, 2010), p. 103.

24. Albert D. Chernin, "Making Soviet Jews an Issue: A History," in *A Second Exodus: The American Movement to Free Soviet Jews*, ed. Murray Friedman and Albert D. Chernin (Hanover, N.H.: Brandeis University Press, 1999), p. 61.

25. Hurwitz, *Begin*, p. 84, and Tom Shachtman, *I Seek My Brethren: Ralph Goldman and "The Joint"* (New York: Newmarket Press, 2001), p. 120.

26. Yehuda Avner, interview with the author, October 24, 2012.

27. Fred A. Lazin, "Refugee Resettlement and 'Freedom of Choice': The Case of Soviet Jewry," *Backgrounder* (June 2005), http://cis.org/RefugeeResettlement -SovietJewry.

28. Ibid.

29. Shachtman, *I Seek My Brethren*, p. 120.

30. Lazin, "Refugee Resettlement and 'Freedom of Choice.'"

31. David Friedman, "Beigin Calls for 'Interim' Period Before Aid Ends to Soviet Dropouts," Jewish Telegraphic Agency, November 17, 1976, http://archive.jta.org /article/1976/11/17/2976834/beigin-calls-for-interim-period-before-aid-ends-to-soviet

-dropouts. Note that by 1976, English-speaking journalists had not established their version of Begin's name.

32. Lazin, "Refugee Resettlement and 'Freedom of Choice.'"
33. "Telecast to the Nation, May 1, 1979," MFA.
34. Lazin, "Refugee Resettlement and 'Freedom of Choice.'"
35. Grosbard, *Menachem Begin: The Absent Leader*, p. 288.
36. Frederick A. Lazin, *Politics and Policy Implementation: Project Renewal in Israel* (Albany, N.Y.: SUNY Press, 1994), p. 19.
37. "Project Renewal," *Encyclopedia Judaica* (Farmington Hills, Mich.: Gale Group, 2008), http://www.jewishvirtuallibrary.org/jsource/judaica/ejud_0002_0016 _0_16111.html.
38. Naor, *Begin in Power*, pp. 113–14.
39. Hart Hasten, interview with the author, January 13, 2013.

12. A Time for War and a Time for Peace

1. Howard Sachar, *A History of Israel: From the Rise of Zionism to Our Time* (New York: Alfred A. Knopf, 1979), p. 616.
2. Gilbert, *Israel*, p. 310.
3. Anwar El-Sadat, *In Search of Identity: An Autobiography* (New York: Harper and Row, 1978), p. 306.
4. Avner, *The Prime Ministers*, p. 459.
5. Ibid., p. 457.
6. Ibid., p. 458.
7. Harry Hurwitz and Yisrael Medad, eds., *Peace in the Making: The Menachem Begin–Anwar El-Sadat Personal Correspondence* (Jerusalem: Gefen Publishing House, 2011), p. 7.
8. Ibid., p. 8.
9. Avner, *The Prime Ministers*, p. 471.
10. Ibid., p. 460.
11. Gilbert, *Israel*, p. 489.
12. Hurwitz and Medad, eds., *Peace in the Making*, p. 26.
13. Ibid., p. 36.
14. Avner, *The Prime Ministers*, p. 495.
15. "Golda Meir Scorns Soviets," *The Washington Post*, June 16, 1969.
16. Yechiel Kadishai, interview with the author, April 18, 2013.
17. Quoted in Bradley Burston, "Here's to the '67 Borders, the New Middle of the Road," *Haaretz*, December 31, 2007, http://www.haaretz.com/news/here-s-to-the-67 -borders-the-new-middle-of-the-road-1.236269.
18. Gershom Gorenberg, *The Accidental Empire: Israel and the Birth of the Settlements, 1967–1977* (New York: Times Books, 2006), p. 361.
19. Temko, *To Win or to Die*, p. 198.
20. Shilon, *Menachem Begin*, p. 319.
21. "Settlement Activity, 1967–1990," Foundation for Middle East Peace, http://

www.fmep.org/settlement_info/settlement-info-and-tables/stats-data/settlement
-activity-1967-1990.

22. Shilon, *Menachem Begin*, p. 293.

23. Avner, *The Prime Ministers*, p. 473.

24. Temko, *To Win or to Die*, p. 216.

25. Zbigniew Brzezinski, *Power and Principle* (New York: Farrar, Straus and Giroux, 1983), p. 24.

26. Temko, *To Win or to Die*, p. 218.

27. "Anwar Sadat: Architect of a New Mideast," *Time*, January 2, 1978.

28. Ibid.

29. Grosbard, *Menachem Begin: The Absent Leader*, p. 232.

30. Jimmy Carter, *Keeping Faith: Memoirs of a President* (Toronto: Bantam Books, 1982), p. 308.

31. Grosbard, *Menachem Begin*, p. 239.

32. Temko, *To Win or to Die*, p. 219.

33. Avner, *The Prime Ministers*, pp. 480–82.

34. Shilon, *Menachem Begin*, p. 297.

35. Grosbard, *Menachem Begin*, p. 242.

36. Ezer Weizman, *The Battle for Peace* (New York: Bantam Books, 1981), pp. 310–11, and Grosbard, *Menachem Begin*, p. 243.

37. Weizman, *Battle for Peace*.

38. Silver, *Begin*, p. 191. Yechiel Kadishai insisted that Begin would never have said "concentration camp deluxe," but instead had said "detention camp deluxe." Yechiel Kadishai, interview with the author, April 18, 2013.

39. Carter, *Keeping Faith*, p. 313.

40. "Menachem Begin Television Address, September 2, 1978," in Grosbard, *Menachem Begin*, p. 250.

41. Vladimir Ze'ev Jabotinsky, "The Iron Wall" [Heb.], Jabotinsky Institute in Israel, http://www.jabotinsky.org/multimedia/upl_doc/doc_241007_29453.pdf.

13. It Belongs to My People

1. Ofer Grosbard, *Menachem Begin: The Absent Leader* (Glilot, Israel: Strategic Research and Policy Center National Defense College, IDF, 2007), p. 252.

2. Carter, *Keeping Faith*, p. 351.

3. Grosbard, *Menachem Begin*, pp. 264–65.

4. Brzezinski, *Power and Principle*, p. 262.

5. Aryeh Naor, interview with the author, April 29, 2013.

6. Grosbard, *Menachem Begin*, p. 255.

7. Brzezinski, *Power and Principle*, p. 263.

8. Yechiel Kadishai, interview with the author, April 18, 2013.

9. Hurwitz and Medad, eds., *Peace in the Making*, p. 82.

10. Carter, *Keeping Faith*, p. 407.

11. Shilon, *Menachem Begin*, p. 310.

12. "Presentation Speech Delivered by Aase Lionaes," Official Website of the Nobel Prize, http://www.nobelprize.org/nobel_prizes/peace/laureates/1978/press.html.

13. Grosbard, *Menachem Begin*, p. 271.

14. Hurwitz and Medad, eds., *Peace in the Making*, p. 109.

15. Ibid., pp. 110–11.

16. Ibid., p. 113.

17. "Now or Never: Jimmy Carter's Fateful Visit to Israel in March 1979—On the Way to Peace Between Israel and Egypt" [Heb.], Israel State Archives, http://www .archives.gov.il/ArchiveGov/pirsumyginzach/HistoricalPublications/CarterVisit/.

18. Avner, *The Prime Ministers*, p. 491.

19. "A Tale of Two Anthems: Hatikvah and Psalm 126," Hillel: The Foundation for Jewish Campus Life, http://www.hillel.org/jewish/textstudies/special/anthems.htm.

20. *Koren Rosh Hashana Mahzor*, trans. Rabbi Jonathan Sacks (Jerusalem: Koren Publishers, 2011), p. 112.

21. Avner, *The Prime Ministers*, p. 499. Transliterations have been slightly altered.

22. *Biography: Anwar Sadat*, prod. by Michael Joseloff (CBS News Productions for A&E Network, 45 minutes, 2004).

23. Avner, *The Prime Ministers*, p. 574.

24. Ibid., p. 591.

25. Ironically, most were not residents of the town.

26. "Address by Menachem Begin Broadcast on Israeli Television, April 27, 1982," MFA.

14. Crazy Like a Fox

1. Moshe Fuksman-Sha'al, ed., *Israel's Strike Against the Iraqi Nuclear Reactor 7 June 1981*, trans. Ruchie Avital (Jerusalem: Menachem Begin Heritage Center, September 2003), p. 31.

2. The name Osirak originates from the word *Osiris* (the name of the French plant that inspired its Iraqi counterpart) combined with the French spelling of the country, "Irak." Apparently it was popular among Israeli circles to refer to it as "Oh-Chiraq," mocking Jacques Chirac, French prime minister, 1974–76.

3. Hal Brands and David Palkki, "Saddam, Israel, and the Bomb: Nuclear Alarmism Justified?" *International Security* 36, issue 1 (Summer 2011), p. 133.

4. "On the Dangers of Non-Conventional Weapons in the Hands of Arab States: Menachem Begin Address During Knesset Deliberations on June 24, 1963," in *Israel's Strike Against the Iraqi Nuclear Reactor 7 June 1981* [Heb.], ed. Moshe Fuksman-Sha'al (Jerusalem: Menachem Begin Heritage Center, March 2003).

5. Brands and Palkki, "Saddam, Israel, and the Bomb," p. 155.

6. Shlomo Nakdimon, *First Strike: The Exclusive Story of How Israel Foiled Iraq's Attempt to Get the Bomb* (New York: Summit Books, 1987), p. 209.

7. Shilon, *Menachem Begin*, p. 340.

8. "Possible Role of Mideast Agents in Toulon Reactor Blast Studied," *The New York Times*, April 14, 1979.

9. Grosbard, *Menachem Begin: The Absent Leader*, p. 300.

10. Yitzhak Shamir, "The Failure of Diplomacy," in *Israel's Strike Against the Iraqi Nuclear Reactor 7 June 1981* [Heb.], ed. Moshe Fuksman-Sha'al, trans. Ruchie Avital (Jerusalem: Menachem Begin Heritage Center, September 2003), p. 14.

11. Brands and Palkki, "Saddam, Israel, and the Bomb," p. 146.

12. *Tammuz*, dir. by Nir Toib (Gan Tikshoret, 92 minutes, 2007).

13. Avner, *The Prime Ministers*, p. 553.

14. Ibid., p. 558.

15. Yair Shamir, interview with the author, October 25, 2012.

16. Avner, *The Prime Ministers*, p. 556.

17. Shamir, "The Failure of Diplomacy," p. 16.

18. Gary D. Solis, *The Law of Armed Conflict: International Humanitarian Law in War* (New York: Cambridge University Press, 2010), p. 182.

19. Shlomo Nakdimon, interview with the author, April 28, 2013.

20. Avner, *The Prime Ministers*, p. 559.

21. "Israel's Illusion," *The New York Times*, June 9, 1981.

22. Ibid.

23. Joseph Kraft, "For Begin, the End? He Should Be Voted Out for Raid That Further Isolates Israel," *Los Angeles Times*, June 11, 1981.

24. "United Nations Security Council Resolution 487 (1981)," United Nations official site (2013), http://domino.un.org/UNISPAL.NSF/0/6c57312cc8bd93ca852560df00653995?OpenDocument.

25. Ronald Reagan, *An American Life* (New York: Simon and Schuster, 1990), p. 413.

26. "Dick Cheney Letter to Menachem Begin," in *Israel's Strike Against the Iraqi Nuclear Reactor 7 June 1981* [Heb.], ed. Moshe Fuksman-Sha'al, trans. Ruchie Avital (Jerusalem: Menachem Begin Heritage Center, September 2003), p. 77.

27. Translated from http://www.youtube.com/watch?v=zbDqj3LE26M&feature=related (Video archives of June 1981 election campaign, address by Shimon Peres).

28. Translated from http://www.youtube.com/watch?v=zbDqj3LE26M&feature=related (Video archives of the June 1981 election campaign, address by Menachem Begin in Petach Tikvah).

29. "Excerpt from Begin Speech in Malchai Yisrael Square, Tel Aviv, June 26, 1981," in *Israel's Strike Against the Iraqi Nuclear Reactor 7 June 1981*.

30. Dan Raviv and Yossi Melman, *Spies Against Armageddon: The Mossad and the Intelligence Community* (Israel: Yediot Ahronoth Books, 2012), p. 334.

31. Richard Nixon, *Leaders* (New York: Warner Books, 1982), p. 296.

15. Nobody's Cowering Jew

1. Gil Troy, *Moynihan's Moment: America's Fight Against Zionism as Racism* (Oxford, U.K.: Oxford University Press, 2013), p. 73.

2. "Statement in the Knesset by Prime Minister Begin on Security Council Resolution 465-1980—March 6, 1980," MFA.

3. Gadi Bloom and Nir Hefez, *Ariel Sharon: A Life* (New York: Random House, 2006), p. 213.

4. Zeev Schiff, "The Green Light," *Foreign Policy*, no. 50 (Spring 1983), pp. 73–85.

5. Shilon, *Menachem Begin*, p. 369.

6. "Middle East: A Sabbath of Terror," *Time*, March 20, 1978.

7. Grosbard, *Menachem Begin: The Absent Leader*, p. 239.

8. Zvi Harry Hurwitz, *Begin: His Life, Words, and Deeds*, p. 211.

9. Avner, *The Prime Ministers*, pp. 555–56, 606.

10. Ibid., p. 607.

11. Temko, *To Win or to Die*, p. 278.

12. Ibid., p. 435.

13. Avner, *The Prime Ministers*, p. 606.

14. Bloom and Hefez, *Ariel Sharon*, pp. 205–6.

15. Temko, *To Win or to Die*, p. 270.

16. Ibid., p. 264.

17. Yechiel Kadishai, interview with the author, April 18, 2013.

18. Temko, *To Win or to Die*, p. 264.

19. Shilon, *Menachem Begin*, p. 387.

20. Yechiel Kadishai, interview with the author, April 18, 2013.

21. Aryeh Naor, interview with the author, April 28, 2013.

22. Avner, *The Prime Ministers*, p. 496.

23. Ibid., p. 264.

24. Temko, *To Win or to Die*, p. 440.

25. Ibid., p. 275.

26. Howard Sachar, *A History of Israel: From the Rise of Zionism to Our Time* (New York: Alfred A. Knopf, 1979), p. 916.

27. Ibid.

28. Avner, *The Prime Ministers*, p. 643.

29. Ibid., p. 625.

30. Ibid., p. 616.

31. Bloom and Hefez, *Ariel Sharon*, p. 232.

32. Ibid., p. 235.

33. Yechiel Kadishai, interview with the author, April 18, 2013.

34. Temko, *To Win or to Die*, pp. 283–84.

35. Thomas Friedman, *From Beirut to Jerusalem* (New York: Farrar, Straus and Giroux, 1989), p. 162.

36. Michael Oren, *Power, Faith and Fantasy: America in the Middle East, 1776 to the Present* (New York: W. W. Norton, 2007), p. 554.

37. Ariel Sharon, *Warrior* (New York: Simon and Schuster, 2001), p. 505.

38. Avner, *The Prime Ministers*, pp. 641–42.

39. Ibid., p. 645.

40. Shilon, *Menachem Begin*, p. 404.

41. Temko, *To Win or to Die*, p. 284.

42. Sharon, *Warrior*, p. 510.

43. Temko, *To Win or to Die*, p. 285.

44. Begin, *White Nights*, p. 125.

45. Temko, *To Win or to Die*, p. 285.

46. Shilon, *Menachem Begin*, p. 409.

47. Hurwitz, *Begin*, p. 225.

48. Hart Hasten, *I Shall Not Die!* (Jerusalem: Gefen Publishing, 2003), pp. 228–29.

49. Temko, *To Win or to Die*, p. 286.

50. Shilon, *Menachem Begin*, p. 409.

51. Temko, *To Win or to Die*, p. 286.

52. Ibid., p. 286.

53. Bloom and Hefez, *Ariel Sharon*, pp. 246–47.

54. Ibid., pp. 249–50.

55. Temko, *To Win or to Die*, p. 288.

56. Avner, *The Prime Ministers*, p. 643.

57. Elliot Jager, "Power and Politics: Breaking Begin," *Jerusalem Post*, March 6, 2007, http://www.jpost.com/Opinion/Columnists/Article.aspx?id=53718.

58. Yaacov Lozowick, "Secret Documents from Israel's Archives," *Tablet*, February 21, 2013, http://www.tabletmag.com/jewish-news-and-politics/124809/secrets-from-israels-archives?all=1.

59. Avner, *The Prime Ministers*, pp. 647–48.

60. The reference is to the "broken heifer" discussed in Deuteronomy 21:7.

61. The allusion is to a biblical passage (Deut. 21:7), which states that when an unidentified corpse is found in a given town, the elders of that town must perform a ritual that involves declaring "our hands have not spilt this blood." Deaths that take place under a town's jurisdiction, even if not directly caused by the town, are its responsibility. For the biblical expression linking speech to shame, see Ezekiel 16:63, 29:21. "Minutes of the 124th Meeting of the 10th Knesset (February 14, 1983 04:16)," Official Website of the Knesset, http://knesset.gov.il/tql/knesset_new/knesset10/HTML_27_03_2012_05-50-30-PM/19830214@19830214004@004.html.

62. Aryeh Naor, interview with the author, April 29, 2013.

16. I Cannot Go On

1. The literal translation of the verse is "I can no longer go out and come in." The language used here is taken from the NIV translation of the Bible.

2. Shilon, *Menachem Begin*, p. 412.

3. Temko, *To Win or to Die*, pp. 289–90.

4. Shilon, *Menachem Begin*, pp. 411–15.

5. Ibid., pp. 416–18, 434.

6. Ibid., p. 418.

7. Avi Shilon, *Begin: 1913–1992* [Heb.] (Tel Aviv: Am Oved, 2007), p. 418; and Shlomo Nakdimon, "Begin's Legacy/'Yehiel, It Ends Today,'" *Haaretz*, February 22, 2012, http://www.haaretz.com/weekend/magazine/begin-s-legacy-yehiel-it-ends-today-1.414173. Begin, it should be noted, had already entered into a political relationship with Germany. In addition, he had met the former chancellor and shook his hand at Sadat's funeral (though he also called him a Nazi sympathizer. See "Begin Again Attacks Schmidt on Role under Hitler," *The New York Times*, May 7, 1981, http://www.nytimes.com/1981/05/07/world/begin-again-attacks-schmidt-on-role-under-hitler.html).

8. Shilon, *Menachem Begin*, p. 420.

9. Temko, *To Win or to Die*, 290.

10. Shilon, *Menachem Begin*, p. 421.

11. Ibid., p. 421.

12. Ibid., p. 425.

13. Shilon, *Begin: 1913–1992*, p. 419.

14. Shilon, *Menachem Begin*, p. 427.

15. Ibid., p. 433.

16. Yechiel Kadishai, interview with the author, April 18, 2013.

17. Anita Shapira, "On Silence," *Jewish Ideas Daily*, April 15, 2013, http://www .jewishideasdaily.com/6313/features/on-silence/.

18. Zvi Harry Hurwitz, *Begin: His Life, Words, and Deeds*, p. 233.

19. Glenn Frankel, "The Prisoner of Zemach Street," *The Washington Post*, December 1, 1987.

20. Thomas Friedman, *From Beirut to Jerusalem*, p. 178.

21. Gil Sedan, "52 Years After Arlosoroff Murder Panel Clears 3 Revisionist Suspects," Jewish Telegraphic Agency, June 17, 1985, http://archive.jta.org /article/1985/06/17/3001714/52-years-after-arlosoroff-murder-panel-clears-3-revisionist -suspects.

22. Shilon, *Menachem Begin*, p. 430.

23. Hurwitz, *Begin*, p. 232.

24. Frankel, "The Prisoner of Zemach Street."

25. Shilon, *Menachem Begin*, p. 430.

26. Charles Hill, interview with the author, December 12, 2012.

27. Shilon, *Menachem Begin*, p. 434.

28. Thomas Friedman, "Sharon, Replying to Critics, Opens Lebanon War Scars," *The New York Times*, August 13, 1987, http://www.nytimes.com/1987/08/13/world /sharon-replying-to-critics-opens-lebanon-war-scars.html.

29. Shilon, *Menachem Begin*, p. 441.

30. Ibid., p. 442.

31. Ibid., p. 444.

32. Ibid., p. 445–46.

33. Display, MBC.

34. Hurwitz, *Begin*, p. 239.

35. Yoram Bilu and André Levy, "The Elusive Sanctification of Menachem Begin," *International Journal of Politics, Culture, and Society* 7, no. 2 (Winter 1993), p. 304.

Epilogue

1. "Speech in Mughrabi Square, July 6, 1958," MBC digital archives, http:// db.begincenter.org.il/he-il.

2. Menachem Begin, "What We Learned from Ze'ev Jabotinsky," *Ma'ariv*, July 30, 1976. MBC digital archives, http://db.begincenter.org.il/he-il. For the original Jefferson quotes, see his "Letter to James Madison of January 30, 1787," Thomas Jefferson Papers, Library of Congress, http://memory.loc.gov/cgi-bin/ampage?collId=mtj1&

fileName=mtjɪpageoo6.db&recNum=ɪɪɪo; and "Letter to William Stephens Smith of November 13, 1787," Thomas Jefferson Papers, Library of Congress, http://memory .loc.gov/cgi-bin/ampage?collId=mtjɪ&fileName=mtjɪpageoo8.db&recNum=5ɪ4.

3. Joseph J. Ellis, *Founding Brothers: The Revolutionary Generation* (New York: Alfred A. Knopf, 2000), p. 15.

4. Ibid., pp. 39–40.

5. Rafael Medoff, "Menachem Begin as George Washington," *American Jewish Archives* 46, no. 2 (1994), p. 18.

6. Ibid., p. 189.

7. Yair Shamir, e-mail to author, February 28, 2013, and conversations with author in summer 2013.

8. In the fifth Knesset, Begin advocated for the gradual lifting of military law over areas with large Arab populations. It was, in his mind, an extension of the law that breaches individual liberties and freedoms and was a mark of Israel's character. "One of the founding principles of a free country," he posited, "is that military commanders should monitor soldiers and civilians [should monitor] civilians." (Shilon, *Menachem Begin*, p. 191).

9. See, for example, Simon Rabinowich, ed., *Jewish and Diaspora Nationalism: Jewish Peoplehood in Europe & the United States* (Waltham, Mass.: Brandeis University Press, 2012), particularly the Introductory Essay, and especially pp. xxxii–xxxvi.

10. Begin, *White Nights*, 271.

11. Thomas Friedman, *From Beirut to Jerusalem*, p. 144.

12. Begin, *The Revolt*, p. 316. It is an extraordinary assertion, but backed up by the evidence. (Though the quote is from Begin himself, other evidence corroborates his claim that Silver supported Revisionist Zionism and the Etzel, which was an unusual stance for an American Zionist and Reform rabbi. He allegedly remarked during the discussion over Begin's contested visit to America in 1948 that Begin was "one of the great heroes of Israel and the Irgun has written one of its most glorious chapters." (Rafael Medoff, *Militant Zionist in America: The Rise and Fall of the Jabotinsky Movement in the United States 1926–1948* [Tuscaloosa: Alabama University Press, 2002], p. 213.) Begin's rendition was clearly correct. Indeed, when the NKVD archives were opened up and were shown to dovetail perfectly with what his father had written in *White Nights*, Benny Begin famously remarked that the similarity was proof not of his father's accuracy, but of that of the archives. Of his father's punctiliousness, he'd never had any doubt.

13. Deuteronomy 29:13–14.

14. Dan Meridor, interview with the author, January 2, 2013.

INDEX

Index

Index

Index

Index

Index